Mr. Lee's
Publicity Book

A Citizen's Guide to Public Relations

UNPUBLISHED WRITINGS OF IVY LEE, 1928

Ivy Lee

with Burton St. John III, Ph.D.

Mr. Lee's Publicity Book: A Citizen's Guide to Public Relations

Unpublished Writings of Ivy Lee, 1928

By IVY LEDBETTER LEE
With BURTON ST. JOHN III, Ph.D., APR

© 2017 PRMuseum Press, LLC
All rights reserved. Printed in the U.S.A.
First edition, 2017
Library of Congress Control Number: 2017951706
ISBN 978-0-9990245-2-2

PRMuseumPress

PUBLISHED BY PRMUSEUM PRESS, LLC, NEW YORK, NEW YORK

The Expanded Words of Ivy Lee

[Ivy Lee] was rarely able to explain his work
adequately or to gain understanding for the
underlying principles by which he operated. He often
admitted that he did not know what to call himself,
and that what he did was an art that he could not
explain.

— Ray Eldon Hiebert
Courtier to the Crowd, 1966

I have never been able to find a satisfactory phrase
to describe what I try to do.

— Ivy Lee
N.Y. Transit Commission Hearings, 1927

IN 1928, IVY LEDBETTER LEE, considered one of
the dominant forces in the new field of public
relations, had made the decision to put into one book
his views of how this new field was shaping. That
summer, he parceled out portions of the drafting
process to six of his staff at his firm, Ivy L. Lee and
Associates. In an undated memo that appears to be
from later that year—one that is apparently directed
to these staffers—Lee said that the text, though typed
and organized into chapters, was not a finished
project and that he needed more feedback. He then

pointed out three main items the book was intended to do: 1) reveal the "methods and objects of publicity," 2) help the reader to be able to discern what is "disguised publicity," and 3) point out how a democracy acquires information through publicity so as to "arrive at social justice."[1] From this effort, he and his staff accumulated in a binder, called *Mr. Lee's Publicity Book*, 300 pages of typed drafts that spanned 23 chapters.[2]

Then, nothing.

Well, not exactly nothing. As Meg Lamme and Tom Watson point out in the commentary section of this book, by the mid-1920s Lee was particularly interested in international affairs. He traveled regularly overseas and also spoke and wrote about the need for better foreign relations—especially when such improved relations benefited his clients. His increasing interest in the international affairs arena, coupled with the onset of the Great Depression in 1929, would appear to be contributing factors in

---

[1] Untitled memo. Box 7, Folder 12. Ivy Ledbetter Lee Papers, Princeton University Library, Department of Rare Books and Special Collections, Seeley G. Mudd Manuscript Library, Public Policy Papers. All subsequent references to boxes and folders are from this collection.

[2] In Box 7, Folder 12, there are 86 pages that are labeled as being part of this effort to compile a publicity book. The vast majority of the content on these pages did not make it into the binder. As such, these pages from the Lee Papers collection are not included in this book.

holding off on publishing a book. The massive
downturn in the domestic and worldwide economy
would not be an auspicious time for releasing a book
that offers several examples and justifications for how
the business world can use public relations to help
direct people toward ends that suit corporations.
Then, in the early 1930s, Lee was being
investigated by Congress concerning potential
business ties to the Nazis.[3] By October 1934, emerging
to some degree from the perceptions of scandal, he
had been devoting more energies to encouraging his
firm to recalibrate how it conceptualized public
relations; he saw a need for the field to move beyond
publicity into counseling clients on more innovative
ways to anticipate client concerns and engage their
audiences.[4] Lee, however, had been in failing health
for some time—he died, at 57, in November 1934. The
thoughts he may have had about building on such a
new vision for his firm, and whether such a new
journey would have led to the eventual release of this
volume in some form, went with him.

---

[3] No conclusive evidence has even been found that Lee knowingly
worked for the Nazis. See Hainsworth, B.E. (1987). "Retrospective:
Ivy Lee and the German Dye Trust," *Public Relations Review 13*, pp.
35–44

[4] "Ivy Lee and T. J. Ross Partner's Dinner, The Cloud Club, New
York, Thursday, October 4, 1934," Box 27, Folder 13.

However, with the publication of this 1928 draft—*Mr. Lee's Publicity Book: A Citizen's Guide to Public Relations*—practitioners and scholars have some more information on how Lee was attempting to articulate where public relations fit within the spectrum of society. In that sense, it covers a wide horizon. The book opens with how public relations likely influences how individuals are given frames of references throughout their daily activities—it ends with more diffuse claims on how public relations uses publicity to help promote justice in society, primarily by interpreting the public's concerns to corporations so as to promote ethical action by business.

These, and other observations throughout this book, are important to consider. They reflect the views of a man who—despite a claim of inarticulateness about the subject—sought understanding about the power of public relations in the modern world. These words are significant because of Lee's stature within the profession. In its obituary for Lee, the *Literary Digest* said that he "was the number 1 publicity man for big business," noting that the already well-published Bernays was the "runner-up to Lee in the art of selling industry to the people."[5] Others in the decades since his death have also pointed to Lee's primary role in codifying what

---

[5] *Literary Digest* (1934, November 17). Quoted in Tye, L. (1998). *The Father of Spin*. New York: Henry Holt, p. 231.

was becoming the professional field of public relations. In 1963, John Hill, the co-founder of public relations powerhouse Hill & Knowlton, said that Lee "was unquestionably the father of the modern practice of public relations counseling."[6] Tye's book on Bernays notes that "many chroniclers...regard Lee as the closest thing public relations has to a patriarch."[7] Numerous public relations textbooks over the decades have pointed to Lee as having a notable influence in establishing what would become the public relations profession. One prominent textbook, now in its 11th edition, said that Lee's "practice, writings, and preachments helped make public relations an occupation."[8]

Meanwhile, although published scholarly work on Lee is sparse, it tends to similarly situate Lee's role as distinctively prominent in the rise of the public relations field. This is because researchers find Lee to have a notable part in 1) situating public relations as a practice that emphasizes a *public information role* (i.e., transparency about information and intentions in the public arena), 2) developing *public relations strategies that focused on humanizing organizations and influencing*

---

[6] Hill, J.W. (1963). *The Makings of a Public Relations Man*. New York: David McKay Co., Inc., p. 16.

[7] Tye, L. (1998), p. 231.

[8] Broom, G. & Sha B-L (2013). Cutlip & Center's *Effective Public Relations* (11th ed.). Upper Saddle River, New Jersey: Pearson, p. 88

opinion leaders, especially through offering concrete examples that appealed to both reason and emotion, 3) *moving public relations from publicity toward consulting*, and 4) asserting that *public relations could have an impact in fostering positive international relations*.[9]

Each one of these four areas appears to varying degrees in this book. For example, the public information role is clearly visible across the chapters, whether Lee discusses the posturing of nations and powers during World War I, or dissects how public

---

[9] The first two points are broadly covered in the scholarly literature. See, for example, Hiebert R.E. (1966). *Courtier to the Crowd: The Story of Ivy Lee and the Development of Public Relations*, Ames, IA: Iowa State University Press; Cutlip S.M. (1994). *The Unseen Power. Public Relations: A History*, Hillsdale, New Jersey: Lawrence Erlbaum Associates Harrison, S. & Moloney, K. (2004). Comparing two public relations pioneers: American Ivy Lee and British John Elliot, *Public Relations Review 30*, pp. 205–215; Lamme, M.O. (2014), *Public Relations and Religion in American History: Evangelism, Temperance, and Business*. New York: Routledge; Russell, K.M. &. Bishop, C.O. (2009). Understanding Ivy Lee's declaration of principles: U.S. newspaper and magazine coverage of publicity and press agentry, 1865–1904," *Public Relations Review 35*, pp. 91–101; St. John III. B. (2006). "The case for ethical propaganda within a democracy: Ivy Lee's successful 1913–1914 railroad rate campaign," *Public Relations Review 32*, pp. 221–228, and Marlin, R. (2003). *Propaganda and the Ethics of Persuasion*. Peterborough, Canada: Broadview Press. As regards Lee attempting to move publicity toward consulting, see Hallahan, K. (2002). Ivy Lee and the Rockefellers' response to the 1913–1914 Colorado coal strike. *Journal of Public Relations Research 14*, pp. 265–313 and Ewen, S. (1996) *PR! A Social History of Spin*. New York: Basic Books. For research on Lee's thoughts about public relations and international relations, see Hainsworth (1987).

utilities, in the wake of the National Electrical Light
Association investigations of 1928, can better
advocate for themselves in straightforward ways.
These thoughts are in keeping with Lee's history of
speaking and writing about how corporations need to
be communicative, both internally and externally,
about their policies, procedures, and needs.
Lee also writes here extensively about how
organizations can develop better strategies to sway
the public—but this volume, significantly, is thin on
notions of approaching opinion leaders (with the
exception of some descriptions of war scenarios) or
humanizing the corporation. Instead, he offers more
observations on the power of the crowd; chapter 18
presents a survey of authors (Le Bon, Tarde, Trotter,
etc.) who had written on the difficulty the crowd plays
in allowing for informed decision making. While
fascinated with such observations, the book tends to
avoid establishing Lee's take on how to wrestle with
the crowd. Chapter 19 offers that the public relations
person will need to consider how to appeal to both
reason and emotion; the first operates out of an
accretion of experience, the second operates often in
the moment, as a product of desires. While Lee
finishes this chapter acknowledging that "the tides of
emotion are...acted upon by whatever is near..." he
maintains that experience/reason determines how
people make decisions. However, there is little in the

volume about pursuing strategies that cut through the amorphous crowd, and its emotions, in order to attempt to influence others purely through reason. For example, the book mostly elides how crowds can be segmented or how an organization can pursue rhetorical strategies that seek to build a sense of human-like consonance between it and the individual. None of this is a surprise, as concepts of audience segmentation were still evolving during this time period. However, as regards rhetorical appeals, it is important to note that Lee pointed out, on page 153, that department store John Wanamaker offered advertisements that signaled that "you and the store, as fellow human beings, can afford to chat a moment about...things"; chapter eight discusses how Alabama Power Company successfully used public relations to show it was a relatable entity to the communities it served.

This volume is also light on Lee's thoughts on public relations moving more fully into the consulting role. Such discussions are apparent as an undercurrent, particularly in repeated references to publicity as most effective when it is truthful. While these comments may not appear to be a momentous revelation of effective consulting by today's standards, Lee was well aware of then complicating factors that included: 1) public cynicism about how persuasive messaging, often deceptive, had led to support for entering into World War I, 2) the tendency for press agents and other hucksters to proclaim themselves as bonafide publicity and public relations operatives, and 3) continuing strains of reluctance exhibited by corporations to embark on this relatively new straight talk approach toward the public. Most notable, however, is Lee's final chapter, called "The Advisor in Public Relations," where, perhaps tentatively, he puts forth that, beyond sharing information, the public relations counsel has a vital role in "representing the public side when any policy is in question" (p. 354). This concept had already been discussed, at least preliminarily, by Bernays five years earlier when he wrote that the public relations counsel "...interprets the client to the public, which he is enabled to do in part because he interprets the public to the client."[10] Still, Lee gamely attempts to detail some of his own vision, claiming that public relations offers a route toward upholding justice in society—an argument that Bernays paralleled to some degree by asserting, in his 1928 book *Propaganda*, that the activities of the public relations counsel could, ideally, contribute to the advancement of pro-social causes.[11] However, in a

---

[10] Bernays, E.L. (1923). *Crystallizing Public Opinion*. New York: Horace Liveright Publishing Company, p. 14.

[11] For more on Bernays' contemporaneous messages about the pro-social capacity of public relations, see St. John III, B. (2010). *Press Professionalization and Propaganda: The Rise of Journalistic Double-mindedness*, 1917–1941. Amherst, New York: Cambria Press, pp. 80–

notable contrast, while Bernays' rhetoric about public relations in 1928 tended toward hyperbole and the aspirational, Lee finishes his final chapter of this book acknowledging that observers criticize the power of the publicist; they do this, he says, because the publicity man has too often relied on his power and "has only begun to use justice" (p. 357). Here, Lee is referring to his comments in the previous chapter, where he points out that publicity can serve "as a deterrent to anti-social practice" (p. 349). In this sense, Lee again writes in a way that parallels Bernays' comments through the mid-to-late 1920s that public relations/propaganda can act as a pro-social force. Still, by emphasizing the negative—that publicity is a preventative—Lee avoids the Bernaysean hyperbolic tone. There are indications here that Lee, though aware of Bernays' claims, attempted in this brief chapter to strike a middle ground; still, one staffer, upon reading the very last paragraph of the book, hand wrote below it, "I don't like this section."

As regards international relations, there is little doubt that, throughout this book, Lee has, at a minimum, attempted to contextualize how public relations and publicity has been well apparent, especially in relations regarding Europe. This is

---

90 and St. John III, B. & Lamme, M.O. (2011). The evolution of an idea: Charting the early public relations ideology of Edward L. Bernays. *Journal of Communication Management 15*, pp. 223–233

particularly notable in the numerous areas within Part
I and Part II where Lee discusses how various
combatants in World War I (and some earlier
warfare) used publicity operations to bolster their
home front while attempting to destabilize the
enemy. However, it is interesting that some of the
more analytical segments that involve international
relations tend toward describing how powerful actors
portrayed an image, rather than offering insights
about how nations developed public relations
strategies. Woodrow Wilson, though halting at times,
pursued rhetorical approaches that conditioned the
public to gradually approve of entering the war, said
Lee. Still, said Lee, while Wilson's largely abstract
speech—which portrayed him as a crusader for
democracy in the world—was largely effective during
the war, he came across as an ineffective abstruse
sloganeer when making similar arguments for America
to adopt the League of Nations. In contrast, he
pointed out elsewhere in the volume that Mussolini,
while a dictator, offered an image of an efficient
authoritarian who "places himself on the side of the
emperors of Rome," and, through braggadocio,
appealed to Italians as one who embodied their
aspirations (p. 200). Curiously, there is little in the
volume that discusses public relations' role in
amplifying discussions about tense international
affairs concerns like, for example, Germany's war

reparations or pursuing engagement with the Soviet Union, something that Lee had been writing and talking about for years contemporaneous with this book.[12]

In sum, there is a mixed bag here when it comes to how extensively *Mr. Lee's Publicity Book: A Citizen's Guide to Public Relations* reveals new takes on existing scholarly research on Lee. First, although Lee talked often of "publicity," it is apparent that, in this book, he is more often working through how to articulate the emerging field of public relations (hence, the words "public relations" in this title). This work clearly offers more on Lee's take on public relations' important role in informing (and not simply selling) the public. In contrast to Bernays, in totality it offers a more measured perspective on how public relations wields a degree of power that attempts to lead the crowd in a manner that is conscious about concepts of reason and justice. Indeed, Lee points out that the public relations person's ability to understand this power and consult the client on how to use it appropriately, is the mark of becoming a public relations advisor. In contrast, there is less here about two areas Lee has been associated with—strategic

---

[12] On war reparations and other concerns from World War I, see Lee, I. (1929, May). "The Black Legend." *Atlantic Monthly*, pp. 577–588. On the Soviet Union, see Lee, I. (1928). *Present-Day Russia*. New York: Macmillan.

outreach to audience groups and public relations' role as an adjunct to international policy. Readers may find that other themes appear in the book that have not been widely researched about Lee, yet have resonance for today. Discussions about publicity, lying, and ethics appear at different points; Lee offers, at times, a mix of ethics and pragmatism that, in 2017, may be insufficient to address increasing concerns about "fake news." The book also offers what appears to be a very early discussion of the importance of identity construction and branding—this is apparent in chapter seven's examination of Napoleon III and his pursuit of multiple approaches to build a persona so as to garner public support. Considering how public relations has tended to too often cede notions of branding to marketing, public relations practitioners and scholars may find interesting this persona-focused (rather than product/service-focused) description of a successful branding campaign.

Finally, though parts of this volume reveal thoughts and words that Lee had shared previously in pamphlets, articles, and speeches, *Mr. Lee's Publicity Book: A Citizen's Guide to Public Relations* offers the best compilation of what Lee thought were priorities in articulating what public relations meant in society. Considering what was happening regarding post-war disillusions with propaganda and Bernays' widespread and contemporaneous attempts to valorize propaganda (while conflating it with public relations), Lee's attempt, while patchy, was substantial. Then, with the pressures of other events and interests, the project ceased. Clearly, it was a struggle for him to place it all in one volume. Although the product here is uneven, it is instrumental for revealing how a pioneer in the profession of public relations saw that his experiences in the field, and his interests in world affairs and corporate initiatives, afforded him a chance to define a new occupation. While others before and since have tended to discuss public relations in the service of products, services, and causes, Lee notably, if tentatively, struck a different route—grappling with public relations as a vehicle to address the conflicting reasons, emotions, and agendas that make up humans.

A few notes about the editing process. The manuscript in the binder was fully typed, with Lee's hand edits appearing intermittently. As the Lee archives reveal several iterations of early book drafts in the 1920s,[13] the number of edits (hand and otherwise) in the original text were minimal. As such, no additional information was added to the original

---

[13] The Lee archives hold folders for several undated but apparently earlier 1920s drafts of proposed books that go by such titles as *The Meaning of Publicity, Constructive Publicity, Publicity: The Profession of Persuading the Public,* and *An Intelligent Citizen's Guide to Propaganda.*

binder material. Great care was taken to make edits that, in this editor's estimation, allowed the book to clarify Lee's thoughts and offer continuity. Footnotes were added to explicate information (e.g., names, events, and locations) that may not reasonably be common knowledge in 2017.

Lastly, thanks to Lee biographer Ray Eldon Hiebert for preserving the original complete book draft so that it can now be available for all to see.

July 2017

BURTON ST. JOHN III, PH.D., APR, is Professor and Interim Chair of the Communication and Theatre Arts Department at Old Dominion University, Norfolk, VA. In 2017, he published the co-written book *Crisis Communication and Crisis Management: An Ethical Approach* (SAGE) and the sole author book *Public Relations and the Corporate Persona: The Rise of the Affinitive Organization* (Routledge). He was also lead editor of the 2014 volume *Pathways to Public Relations: Histories of Practice and Profession* (Routledge), which was a first-ever public relations volume to be a finalist for the AEJMC Tankard Book Award. Prior to his academic career, he worked in the public relations field for 15 years.

IVY LEDBETTER LEE, (July 16, 1877–November 9,
1934), was born in Cedartown, Georgia to Methodist
Minister Dr. James Wideman Lee. After graduating
from Princeton in 1898, he worked as a journalist for
several New York City newspapers, including *The
New York Times*. With George Parker, he established
in 1905 the public relations firm Parker & Lee, one of
the first PR firms in the United States. During the
pre-World War I years, Lee served in prominent
public relations positions for coal mine operators, the
Pennsylvania Railroad, and Standard Oil. During
WWI, he served in a publicity capacity for the
American Red Cross. After the war, Lee became more
interested in international relations, notably
promoting relations between the U.S. and the Soviet
Union and the U.S. and Germany. He died of a brain
tumor at the age of 57.

Contents

IV. SPECIAL APPLICATIONS AND CASES

V. PUBLICITY AND THE CROWD, JUSTICE, AND THE PUBLIC RELATIONS ADVISOR

VI. COMMENTARIES

Introduction

PART I: Publicity in Daily Life

PART II: Propaganda, Truth, Facts, & Responsibility,

PART III: The Forms of Publicity—Short-Term and Long-Term

PART IV: Special Applications and Cases

PART V: Publicity and the Crowd, Justice, and the Public Relations Advisor

Part One begins with the incidence of publicity in daily life; it proceeds to the analysis of President Woodrow Wilson's technique in preparing the country for war and with these two chapters as a background showing the importance of publicity (and its non-technical aspects), sketches the range of publicity, both in time and in variety of applications.

Part Two discusses propaganda, its relation to the truth, and proceeds to question the possibility of arriving at impartiality in selection of facts; countering this possibly pessimistic view with a review of the theme of responsibility in fuller length.

The third part deals with the known forms of publicity, using advertising as a chief example. It dismisses the stunt briefly and takes up long-run publicity, creation of indirect motivations, etc. This section is closely related to the psychology of attention, behaviorism, etc.

The fourth section deals with special cases: corporations, finance, etc.

The final section parallels the third, except that it is related to social ethics, rather than to psychology.[14]

---

[14] Section V, contrary to this statement, contains several items related to psychology—particularly crowd psychology and its relationship to publicity.

Part I

Publicity in Daily Life

Chapter 1.
The Dilemma of Mr. Jones

ALTHOUGH HIS FATHER AND GRANDFATHER
were Republicans and he himself had always been
loyal to the party, Mr. Jones once felt compelled to
vote the Democratic ticket. At first he was frightened
at the audacity, but looking back on it, he felt that
vote was his declaration of independence. Thereafter
he voted the Republican ticket faithfully, but he no
longer considered himself a slave to any party, or to
influence of any kind.

To himself, Jones appeared as the perfect
embodiment of Robert Burns' ideal—"the man of
independent mind."[1] He rather looked down on
people whose minds were continually being made up
for them.

In order to get to his office on time, Jones had to
get up at 7:45 a.m., but he rose regularly at 7:30 a.m.
and spent a quarter of an hour doing deep breathing
and calisthenics by an open window. As part of his
breakfast he insisted upon an orange from a certain
state, although he never examined the comparative

---

[1] Robert Burns (1759–796) was a Scottish Poet. "The man of an
independent mind" comes from his poem "A Man's a Man for A'
That."

food values of oranges from other states and could not tell the difference in taste between them.

Every day as he went downtown, Jones complained about the transit system of his city. On Mondays, Wednesdays, and Fridays his complaint was directed against the transit company. Jones had not examined the company's books, but he was convinced that the stockholders were getting enormous returns, that the stock was watered, the financial reports fraudulent, and the company generally a menace to the city. On Tuesdays, Thursdays, and Saturdays, Jones still complained, but the object of his attack was the public service commission which was hamstringing the transit company, refusing it permission to charge an adequate fare, and standing in the way of the creation of new subway lines. Jones was far too busy to attend the public hearings of the commission, but he was pretty sure that all its members were political appointees without any adequate knowledge of the city's needs and no public spirit.

Swaying from a strap, Jones read his newspaper and when he got to his office he frequently remarked to his partner, Mr. Smith, that "that was a great speech the governor (or the president) made last night." Sometimes, if his mail was light, he took time to tell Smith what was on his mind in regard to farm relief and the situation in China. Jones had never been on a farm, and his acquaintance with Chinese matters

was limited to a pronounced distaste for chop suey
(which he believed to be a native Chinese dish); but
he had pretty definite opinions on these subjects
whenever Smith ventured to hold a hostile view. Jones
remarked that Smith was getting all his ideas out of
the peculiarly untrustworthy paper he read, and wasn't
thinking for himself at all.

Jones's office was up to date. It was furnished
with the proper number of push-buttons, filing
cabinets, trays, and under the glass top of his desk
there lay two cards: a list of his insurance policies with
the dates premiums were due, and the motto "Do It
Now." Jones had once been in the office of a great
American executive and saw his insurance list under a
desk top, and, although Jones' own insurance was all
in one company, which always sent him notices of
premiums due a month in advance, he thought the
executive's idea a good one. As for "Do It Now,"
everyone had that card.

It had been Jones' habit to eat some meat at
lunch, but one day a friend had argued the
immeasurable benefits of crackers and milk and, from
that time, Jones, although he occasionally felt a bit
faint at four o'clock, ate lightly at mid-day. At 4 p.m.,
he fell into the habit of chewing a chocolate bar. It
was his own idea and he wondered why more people
didn't do the same; one day he saw chocolate
advertised for this very purpose and pointed out the

ad to a friend. He was rather annoyed to later discover that the advertisement had been displayed in the same place (which Jones passed every day on his way to work) for several years.

Jones had grown a beard when he started in business for himself, because he thought it made him look older and more dependable, but as he grew older and his business prospered, he decided that he could afford to be clean-shaven. It was entirely his own idea and he was pleased to see that other people followed his lead. His wife, who kept up with Charles Dana Gibson's[2] heroes seemed particularly pleased, and Jones was convinced that a man of initiative need never fear the consequences if he acts boldly. Many years later, when his wife bobbed her hair, he discovered to his amazement that he did not dislike the effect (although he had originally protested loudly against the change). He was glad to find that he was liberal-minded, and the fact that millions of imitators of Irene Castle[3] had made bobbed hair as familiar to him as bread and butter never occurred to him.

In dress, Jones was never swayed by fashion. Advertisements of sport shirts and baggy trousers, pronouncements from English tailors, the snappy

---

[2] Charles Dana Gibson (1867–1944) was a popular magazine illustrator, especially prior to WWI.

[3] Irene Castle (1893–1969) was a ballroom dancer, famous both on Broadway and in silent films.

appearance of young men home from college, did not affect him. Jones chose his own clothes, to suit his own personality. The result was that Jones was dressed as a good conservative business man should be dressed, his clothes rich not gaudy, and not expressed in fancy. He never wore a soft collar or a bow tie to the office; his suits were dark and woolen; his handkerchief was never in his sleeve. Jones did not know it, but he dressed exactly as he had been told to dress—told by his observation of other conservative business men, by his friends, by his reading of advertisements, by listening to sarcastic remarks about novelties, by an ingrown fear of being eccentric. This complication of forces Jones was not aware of, and he called his taste in clothes an expression of his own personality.

Although he disliked walking, Jones walked halfway home from his office and kissed his wife whenever she happened to meet him in the hallway of their home. There was nothing freakish about the furnishings of the house, but each room was just what Mr. and Mrs. Jones wanted it to be. The twin beds which had replaced their original four-poster were of the same kind as those used by a duchess and a New York society leader. Jones had a reclining chair that had a trick button that pushed out a foot-rest. Every month the Joneses received and read a book which was the best book of the month. They had recently switched from auction to contract bridge[4] and their Mahjongg tiles had all disappeared into odd corners of the children's playroom. They never slapped their children.

Jones' beliefs were almost all of the result of his own thinking. He went to the church into which his father and mother had brought him, but he was not bigoted. In politics, he once voted against his party, and in local elections he put character above party, voting always for the best man and being gratified to discover how often his party managed to select a more competent and more honest man than their opponents. He was a liberal in international affairs, believing that the European nations ought to pay their debts, but that they ought not to spend money on armaments and that the United States ought not to be too harsh in its terms. He disapproved of Soviet Russia and thought that nationalization of women[5] was a crime against human decency. He never got over the fact that during the war the Germans were disrespectful to their own dead, and when he heard

---

[4] Auction bridge had evolved from straight bridge in 1904. Subsequent changes to auction bridge were called "contract bridge."

[5] After WWI, several critics pointed to Russian decrees that allegedly claimed that women were property of the state. Other observers pointed out that such decrees were facetious, indicative of political infighting within Russia.

that the cadaver-melting factory[6] was a fake, he was much relieved, but he maintained that Germany, under the Kaiser, had nevertheless set itself outside the bounds of international honor. He thought Mussolini a great man, but wished that Italy had freedom of the press.

Jones had been in the habit of going to his Rotary Club luncheon, because he considered the fellow members the salt of the earth, but one day he discovered he did not care for them so much. It was an entirely independent decision and it was out of his own personal experience that he decided the Rotarians were "a bunch of Babbitts."[7] Instead he went to lunch at a restaurant picked out at random as he walked down the street and was surprised to find half a dozen of his friends there.

"Joining the crowd, eh?" one of them called to him. "Everybody's lunching here nowadays."

Jones took a vacant seat and presently was discussing prohibition. He said that it had reduced crime. Pressed for proof, he confessed that the figures escaped him, but he was sure he was right. While his

---

[6] During WWI, unproven claims circulated widely about the Germans having a cadaver-melting factory for the purposes of making soap from human corpses.

[7] This term comes from the 1922 novel *Babbitt* by Sinclair Lewis. It refers to a businessperson who adheres to prevailing middle-class norms.

neighbor was talking to him, Jones overheard another man say that Mammoth Motors was about to go into the airplane business.

"I'm in a position to deny that," he cut in.

"Oh, really? I didn't know you were on the inside."

"I'm not," replied Jones, "But they issued a statement to their stockholders today and specifically denied it."

There was some discussion, but in the end, Jones felt he had carried his point. Cheered by the impression he had made on his friends, he decided that he would take his wife to the theater that night. "What's a good show?" he inquired.

"They say *The Black Hat* is selling out weeks in advance," someone told him.

His wife, over the phone, was delighted at the thought of going to *The Black Hat*. "Everybody's seen it," she said.

Jones, having selected the play by the use of his independent judgment, was well pleased.

One day, Jones was staring at a "Safety First" sign and smiling at the thought of people who needed to be warned to take care of themselves. In his amusement he stepped off the curb and was promptly run down by a motor car.

In the delirium which followed, a terrible thing happened to Jones. He saw himself as he really was.

He discovered that his clothes, his habits of living, his thoughts, everything he considered part of his individual personality, were all the results of outside influence. He looked around for a name for this influence and decided that the best one was "propaganda" because it had a suggestion of impropriety. He realized that even when he went against the current, he only did so because some outside force had suggested that idea to him. He became sadly aware of his ignorance about Congress and China and of the street-car situation. He had a flash of insight during which he decided that he loved his wife, but that the perfunctory kiss he gave her when he came home was not due to his affection but to reading little sermons on happy marriage in his evening paper. He knew that he did not slap his children because a great fuss had been made in public about new ideals for child education. He discovered a suppressed desire for loud socks.

During his convalescence, Jones determined that when he got out of the hospital he would really live independently. He would armor himself against propaganda of every sort. He would read only the facts in the newspapers and would reject all propaganda whether it was in the form of editorials, electric signs, or word-of-mouth.

On his first day after he was released from the hospital, Jones waited for the streetcar at his usual place, but the car whizzed by him and he noticed the laughter of a few people in the car. After two more cars had refused to stop, Jones noticed that the motorman was waving him toward the next corner. He went there and got on the next car, learning from the conductor that a skip-stop plan[8] had been instituted.

"You might let people know," Jones said angrily.

The conductor, making change for someone else, muttered something about Jones needing to read the newspaper.

At his office, Jones had nothing to say to his partner after his accident had been exhausted as a topic, and when his partner asked him what he thought of the situation in Nicaragua,[9] Jones had to confess that he hadn't had time to study the subject. Nor was Jones able to understand Smith's reference to a new coastwise shipping line to which he wanted to throw some business, and when a client came in and began to discuss the presidential campaign, all Jones could say was that, until a man studied the whole situation, he ought not to make up his mind.

---

[8] A "skip-stop" plan is an approach used by streetcar operators to save power consumption. It centers on reducing the number of streetcar stops along a route.

[9] In 1926 and 1927, Nicaragua was engaged in a civil war.

That evening he started to study the whole situation. A methodical man, he summarized his investigation under headings: domestic affairs, farm relief, corporations, tariffs, financial policies, electric power and the Boulder Dam, foreign affairs, European debts, The League of Nations, treaties for outlawing war, Latin America, and so on. What he wanted was impartial statements of the facts—no propaganda. On the third night of his studies, he began to be aware of a difficulty. He discovered that each of his subjects was a special field of study on which experts had worked for years, and that the experts often did not agree.

He found that facts were pretty slippery things unless you knew exactly how to handle them.

Gradually, he was snowed under. He could not understand the statistics on which he had pinned his hopes. Reparations and payments of war debts began to create a chaos of meaningless figures in his brain. In connection with the League of Nations he discovered that there were no facts, only arguments, and he rejected all argument because it was propaganda. He kept his mind clean of prejudice—but his mind refused to make any decisions of any kind.

He dined at a neighbor's house and was called on to admire the new refrigerator. Instantly he was aflame with envy, because he wanted to be the first in his gang to introduce the new system. "How did you get onto this?" he asked, and was told that there were ads in all the papers about it.

On the streetcar that night, Jones had stopped reading the paper after he had got "the facts alone" and had plenty of time to listen to his neighbors.

"Johnson's breaking up," said one, mentioning the name of a prominent city official.

"So I hear," said the other. "Wife's divorcing him, hey?"

"Not only that. They've got him for using municipal bonds for security—he speculated in the market and lost."

"Too bad."

Jones was shocked. After dinner he was talking to his host, while their wives chatted about schools for the children, and he said, "Too bad about Johnson."

"It sure was," said his host. "A coincidence like that—."

"I mean about speculating and getting divorced," Jones said, not quite understanding what his friend meant.

"Yes. Of course it's all straightened out. "

"I get the idea he'd resign rather than be brought into court."

"What the dickens would he resign for?"

"Well, they say—."

"Good Lord man, don't you read the papers?"

Jones muttered something about propaganda and his host went on.

"You don't mean to tell me you're still under the impression that was really Johnson? Why everybody knows it was a distant cousin of his with the same name. Of course a rumor like that hurts a man—but thank God the facts came out promptly."

Jones said he was glad to hear it.

A few days later he heard that Complicated Petroleum was due for a slump and sold all his shares. It went up eight points, and Jones belatedly looked up the financial report of the company to learn why.

Another matter that annoyed Jones was connected with electricity. He had been receiving letters from the utility company, but, with his new resolve not to pay attention to publicity, he had thrown then into the waste basket unread. When Wilkins, who occupied the adjoining apartment, spoke of taking advantage of the new contract offered by the utility company, Jones laughed vaguely, until Wilkins explained that the new contract saved him $40 a year.[10]

When Jones had to invite some friends to the theater, he found himself unable to choose a play. Since he would not be influenced by publicity, nor by the propagandized minds of his friends, the only way

---

[10] Forty dollars in 1928 is the equivalent of $558.00 in 2017.

he could evaluate them was to go to all the plays himself and to judge their merits unaided. He could not afford this and the situation baffled him.

He was being baffled, in fact, by a great many things. He seemed to be living in a void. He read the news items in the papers, but he could not quite understand what the significance of the items were, hardly knowing whether the election in France meant a victory for sound finance or for socialism, and remaining utterly at a loss about the qualifications of the several candidates for alderman in his own ward. From the conversation of his friends he realized that new things were going on in the world—new inventions, new ideas, new motor cars—but Jones had no opinions on them whatever. Somehow the materials for making up his own mind were lacking.

In his discomfort, Jones became fanatical. He decided that he was against everything advertised, everything publicized. He began to dream of a society in which these things did not exist, and gradually he eliminated everything he hated, not from his daily life, because his wife saw to that, but from his imagined, ideal city. There were no streetcars and no motors, no telephones and no newspapers, no electric light, no running water, no elections.

Jones came to with a start. In his mind he was becoming a savage. The things that had made life desirable were all products of advertising, publicity, and information. So long as he lived as a respectable father, husband, and citizen, he was part of a group created by the forces of public opinion. And he wanted to be in the group. He wanted to be among those who went to the movies, and among those who use the best razor, and among those who voted for the best man.

So long as he rejected all publicity, he isolated himself. He took on the impossible burden of solving all problems of the universe unaided and alone. He had to do the work of a 100,000 experts before he could make the simplest decision. On the other hand was the plight of Jones before his accident—when everything was decided for him by outside forces. It was a dilemma.

It remains a dilemma for every intelligent citizen. The solution is not to be found in running away from publicity, in condemning it, or trying to forbid it by law. Nor is it found in an abdication of all intelligence, in supinely accepting whatever publicity and propaganda put forth.

The solution, as in most other human affairs, can be discovered only when the facts are known. It lies in an analysis of publicity, in a critical examination and an informed judgment of all its works. The exaggerated success of some forms of publicity and the exaggerated fear of publicity in all its forms, both stem from the same source: ignorance of the methods and purposes of publicity itself. This book, in no sense an exposé, is intended as an exposition on the technique of publicity—not the trivial technique of getting paragraphs into newspapers, but the technique by which, in manifold ways, human beings exert influence on others, change their minds, and redirect their activities.

The more the people know of this technique, the more rapidly they recognize it in action, the better prepared they will be to accept and reject publicity on its own merits or demerits. As soon as they know the methods by which they are victimized, they will cease to be victims. And, so far as they recognize publicity based on a reasonable conception of public decency, they will be able to accept the good in it without danger of falling into the evils of publicity that is anti-social and harmful.

Chapter 2.
A Classic oExample

PUBLICITY IS THE ART OF INFLUENCING men's minds. It is not advertising, although advertising is a part of publicity, nor is it the knack of getting desirable notices into the press; it is neither ballyhoo nor scandalous revelation.[1] Properly conceived, publicity is the sum of all the arts used to influence public opinion and move it in a desired direction.

All the common terms used in connection with these arts are a little under suspicion: press agent, propagandist, and the various phrases based on the term "public relations." It is not the purpose of this book to defend these names or the professions they represent. The purpose is to provide a measuring rod for publicity, to show what it is, how it affects the common man, and how the common man may learn to discriminate between publicity which is to his advantage and publicity which is not.

The essential thing is the knowledge that publicity is not merely the work of those professional men who have specific titles. Publicity is the work—any work from writing a song to signing a labor

---

[1] "Ballyhoo" was a common early 20th century term for extravagant publicity.

agreement—of any man who attempts to influence the public. The United States Steel Corporation had a staff of experts for handling its press matters, but its true publicity man, until the day of his death, was Judge Elbert Gary, the president of the company.[2] His position and his character both made him the connecting link between U.S. Steel and the public. It was not that he got his name in the papers; instead, it was his ability to act as the focal point, concentrating the interest of the public in the plans and policies of the corporation. The function, not the functionary, is important.

Just how far publicity affects the lives and fortunes of men can be judged by examining in some detail the manipulation of American opinion between the outbreak of the war and our own entrance into the struggle.[3] It seemed to most people at the time that American opinion was being influenced entirely by those foreign agents to whom the name of propagandist was applied. With the perspective of time, the great influence, counteracting all other propaganda, is seen to have been that of President Wilson himself.

---

[2] County judge Elbert Henry Gary (1846–1927) brought together several influential partners to found U.S. Steel in 1901.

[3] All references in this work to "the war" or the "Great War" refer to World War I.

The first admonition of the president was specifically a warning against the exercise of judgment. After his formal proclamation of neutrality to the warring nations, Wilson turned to his own countrymen and urged them to be neutral in thought as well as in action, saying that the United States was not a country sitting in judgment on other countries. As an attempt to anesthetize the American mind in relation to the war, the proclamation failed. A great public event was taking place and publicity was needed. Before the war ended, hundreds of millions were spent for the purpose. In the 20 months before we entered the war, Germany alone spent $80 million in this country.

The president proved himself a master of the principles of influencing others as soon as the American situation became serious. The sinking of the *Lusitania*, although hinted at in advance by publicity from the German Embassy, found the American people wholly unprepared.[4] The only suggestion of policy which the president had made public was in his warning to Germany that she would be held to "strict accountability"; but the application of the phrase was uncertain, and for three days after the sinking there was chaos in the minds of the American people.

---

[4] A German submarine sank the British ocean liner *Lusitania* on May 7, 1915. It went down 11 miles off the shores of Ireland.

Into that chaos the president threw the bombshell of his Philadelphia speech with the unhappy phrase "too proud to fight." It was the president's single serious mistake in publicity until the peace conference went into secret session[5] and desperate efforts were made to explain it away. The president himself repudiated the idea that the phrase had anything to do with his intentions toward Germany, saying that a public address to newly-accepted citizens was not the proper place to declare international policy[6]; strong supporters of the president insisted that Mexico had been on his mind, not Germany.[7] If "too proud to fight" expressed a policy, it was too abruptly announced. In the future, when Wilson had something decisive to say or to do, he led up to it by the most gradual approaches, studying the ground and putting forth feelers until the public mind was prepared.

In the *Lusitania* affair, the reaction was prompt and unfavorable. There was something sanctimonious in Wilson's phrase as it fell on the ears of the

---

[5] Wilson had sent his chief policy advisor, Colonel Edward House, to Europe in both early 1915 and early 1916 to attempt to broker peace talks with German, British, and French representatives.

[6] Wilson's speech was an address to 4,000 newly-naturalized citizens gathered at Convention Hall in Philadelphia on May 10, 1915.

[7] Relations with Mexico were strained, due to several recent U.S. interventions in that country. Wilson had ordered a military invasion of Veracruz in April 1914.

belligerents, and, to the American spirit, something
faintly suggesting a coward's defense. The net result of
the reaction against the president's phrase was that
nothing like it appeared in the stern note which the
president dispatched to Germany—a note reflecting
public opinion in America and received with universal
approval.[8]

In the following weeks the ground was prepared
for the reception of the German reply. It was
humanly impossible to expect a complete
capitulation, but rumors floated out of Washington
assuring the American people that Germany would
not be obstinate. A contrary rumor, that Germany
would reject the American claims outright, was
promptly denied by German ambassador to the
United States Heinrich von Bernstorff, and the public
mind was appeased by the announcement that
Bernhard Dernburg, a man unpleasantly associated
with German propaganda, was leaving America.[9] Time
also played into the president's hands; in the three
weeks which elapsed between the sinking of the

---

[8] On May 13, 1915, Wilson sent a note to Germany that ended with
the warning that the United States would not "omit any word or
any act necessary to the performance of its sacred duty of
maintaining the rights of the United States and its citizens and of
safeguarding their free exercise and enjoyment."

[9] Bernhard Dernburg (1865–1937) was propaganda chief of a
clandestine German organization that started in 1914 in New York
City called the Secret War Council.

Lusitania and of publication of Germany's defense, the first horror of the news had been dissipated.

Throughout the negotiations, publicity was assumed as a necessary factor. Notes and replies were made public at the earliest moment and confidence was thereby established. The first German reply was, naturally, a defense and an attempt to shift the blame to Great Britain. On the eve of Wilson's second note to Germany, William Jennings Bryan resigned as Secretary of State and the president instantly gave to the press the letter of resignation in which Bryan indicated that the new note to Germany would be so severe that he himself refused to sign it.[10]

Psychologically, the publication of this letter was of tremendous value to the president. It kept alive the main issue between Germany and America. For the moment, however, it focused attention on a subsidiary struggle between Wilson and Bryan where the issue could not be for a moment in doubt—the president could count on national approval in relation to a Secretary who seemed to be insubordinate. And the victory over Bryan linked itself unconsciously with a feeling of victory over Germany. A necessary element of variety had been introduced into the business and the public did not weary of the series of notes until much later.

---

[10] William Jennings Bryan (1860–1925) was the Democratic Party's presidential nominee in 1896, 1900 and 1908.

The negotiations dragged on for two and a half months and the president's hold on the American people was so marked at the end of that time that, when the British ship *Arabic*[11] was sunk, von Bernstorff hurried to give an oral pledge to the United States that thereafter the rights of Americans would be safeguarded.

The presidential campaign of 1916 was fought around the slogan, "he kept us out of war." Six months after his reelection, Wilson had brought the country to complete approval of the declaration of war against Germany. How was this complete reversal of opinion effected? "He kept us out of war" signified, fundamentally, confidence in the president. The essential thing in publicity is that the people should have confidence in those responsible for publicity—and this the president had. It exceeded the natural authority of the presidential office and was highly personal. Translated into the negative, "he kept us out of war" meant "if he cannot keep us out in the future, no one can, because he has done his utmost." The publicity campaign preparing the American mind for all eventualities was based not on the inevitability of war, but on the desirability of peace. The United States considers itself a traditionally pacific nation; in the Russo-Japanese war, Theodore Roosevelt had

---

[11] The *Arabic* was sunk by a German submarine off the coast of Ireland on August 19, 1915.

represented America as the peace-maker.[12] President Wilson appealed to this tradition.

The Germans had proposed negotiations to their enemies on December 12, 1916, in a tone which made refusal inevitable. Undeterred, the president addressed all the belligerents in a note, saying that each of them explained the war in identical terms to its own nationals and to neutrals, and asking them to give specifically the terms upon which they would be ready to make peace. The day Wilson's note was published, counselor for the department of state Robert Lansing said to the press that the United States was drawing nearer the verge of war and therefore felt itself entitled to know the peace objectives of the belligerents "in order that we may negotiate our conduct in the future."[13] If this was a slip, it was precisely in keeping with the president's technique of mentally preparing the country for war by concentrating attention on the objects of the war—i.e., the terms of peace. "Neither the president nor myself," said Lansing, "regards this note as a peace note." Later in the day—such was the effect of the note and his comment—Lansing had to remind the press that the United States was still neutral. He did

---

[12] In 1904–1905, Russia and Japan fought over contested territories in Manchuria (today's northeast China) and Korea.

[13] After serving as counselor of the U.S. Department of State, Robert Lansing (1864–1928) became Secretary of State from 1915–1920.

not mention the fact that, through publicity, the United States was a nation sitting in judgment.[14]

The bitter-enders in all the warring countries cried out that Wilson had assimilated their war aims to those of their enemies; they urged the governments not to reply. But replies were made by the Allies and, after he had set their war aims before the people, Wilson took the next necessary step. He described the kind of peace which the American people would like to see. He called it a peace without victory (which offended the nations at war), but was peculiarly appropriate to a nation which had made no sacrifices and whose passions were not excited so as to need the satisfaction of victory as well as the benefits of peace. More than that, he concentrated his earlier propaganda on a new-world arrangement by declaring for a League of Nations. It was a peace speech; but it was a warlike measure of the first order. Underneath it lay the assumption that this was the kind of peace for which America might be willing to fight—and the definite certainty that if America did have to go to war, it would be for this kind of peace.[15]

---

[14] This is a reference to a term that Lansing used, for example, in a note sent to Austria in August 1915. Lansing's note asserted that, if America refused to ship its arms to the Allies, it would be abandoning its neutral status by favoring Austria and Germany.

[15] Wilson gave a speech to the Senate on January 22, 1917 under the theme of "Peace without Victory." In this speech, he pointed out the need for a "League for Peace."

In advance of the war, Wilson's propaganda had supplied the American people with an ideal for which to fight. When the pressure of circumstances forced the declaration of war, the American people were not in the dark as to the reasons or the motives. The work of publicity over two years had been done with thoroughness and skill. The American mind was ready.

Considering the issues involved, this work of publicity may be called the most far-reaching the world has ever seen. There were other factors in the business of bridging America into the war—publicity cannot operate in a void. But publicity had definitely re-created the American mind and aided the operation of all the other forces. Without it, the whole history of humanity would have been changed. This was publicity separated from its usual trappings of paid agents, news stories, commercial objectives, and the like. It was purely the art of influencing men's minds.

Chapter 3.
The Range of Publicity

IF PUBLICITY IS CONCEIVED AS a special function, exercised by a specific individual at a specific time, the ways and means of meeting it (favorably or unfavorably) are simple enough. The YMCA announces a campaign for a new building and everyone knows that nearly everything appearing in the daily press for the next three months is publicity, and that the billboards, electric signs, sermons, leaflets, broadcasting, and movies dealing with the YMCA are parts of this campaign. The individual need only make up his mind whether he approves of the purposes of the YMCA or would rather give his allotment for charity to some other organization, and let the matter go.

A strike is impending in the Pennsylvania coal mines. The newspapers are filled with contradictory statements, the miners claiming that the conditions of labor are unsatisfactory and that wages are too low, the operators claiming that they are losing money and that conditions are better in their mines than those in Virginia. Pictures appear of starving miners' families and of happy, bright-faced children and buxom miners' wives. It's publicity, says the neutral citizen, from both sides—designed to enlist sympathy in case the strike comes off.

A war breaks out and it is reported that the armies of Zenda[1] are poisoning wells and murdering children. It's propaganda, says the citizen, because they want our sympathy and a loan.

We are much better acquainted with the ways of publicity now then we were in 1914. At the beginning of the war, the news items we now recognize as propaganda were widely accepted as fact. But we are still susceptible to publicity of this obvious kind, and will continue to be so long as the emotional and non-rational parts of our being exist. Even if we were able calmly to criticize and judge each item of specific publicity, knowing its purpose and its source, we should only have made a beginning. For publicity is not a special thing, the work of an easily accessible individual, done at a given time for a definite end. It is something that goes on all the time. It includes every effort made by every human being to influence the mind and ultimately the conduct of any other human being. It is often done unconsciously at the instigation of interested individuals who remain in the background. The contagion of ideas, the spread of a fad, the dropping of one fashion and the acceptance of another, the slow growth of a prejudice, the slow

---

[1] *The Prisoner of Zenda* was a popular novel by Anthony Hope, first published in 1894.

turning away from a once popular restaurant, the
creation of popular heroes—all of these are the work
of the constant internal publicity which affects every
department of daily life.

Nothing in American life seems more a natural
growth than the popularity of baseball. Yet
professional baseball existed for decades on a scale
which today seems pitifully small, and received from
the newspapers a few lines each day, generally only the
box scores. Almost by accident a brilliant Chicago
reporter was once allowed to write a description of a
game. It was a fine, amusing piece of writing and
other newspapers followed that lead. Presently the
star reporters of all the Chicago papers were at the
games, generally writing them up not for the fans but
for those who were not especially interested in the
game—i.e., as good newspaper stories. And step-by-
step with the newspaper discovery and exploitation of
baseball has gone the development of baseball as a
sport and a business. As late as 1903, sports writer
Bozeman Bulger, reminds us, it was hard to get the
city fathers to take any interest in a World Series; in
1924 the President of the United States threw out the
first ball in the World Series contest between the
Giants and the Senators. The president throwing the
ball is dramatized publicity—it differs in no essential
respect from the columns of sport news which now

are more numerous than those devoted to any other single class of news.

The first Long Island duckling was bred in the 1880s. Until 1921 the demand was small and the breeders formed an association which undertook a publicity campaign, largely through direct advertising. In 1922, at the beginning of the campaign, the total sale of ducklings in January and February amounted to 2,000. In 1926, in the same months, 75,000 ducks were sold for the orthodox Jewish market alone and the consumption of branded ducks rose to 3.5 million a year.

Between the 1890s and the 1920s the American people were transformed from a bearded to a clean-shaven nation. Ninety-nine out of 100 men who shaved their beards probably felt that they were doing so of their own volition. But, as a well-known psychologist has said:

> There can be little doubt that the vanishing of a facial adornment was much hastened by the type of pictures to which the American people were brought to attend in the early years of the century. The "Gibson man" was clean-shaven.... Other artists followed; until a type of square-jawed, broad-shouldered, clean-shaven man became the accepted ideal of young American manhood.[2]

---

[2] This quote comes from popular psychology author Harry Overstreet's 1925 book *Influencing Human Behavior*.

The controversy in advertising between the safety razor and the old-fashioned razor, and the recriminations between manufacturers of shaving soap who claimed that their lather did not dry on the face, helped. The net result is that while a young man in the 1890s looked forward to the first stubble on lip and chin in order to let it grow, the youth of the 1920s looks forward to it in order to shave it off.

The climate of Florida and its natural advantages did not change between 1910 and 1920. Yet, in the 1920s, Florida became a boom state overflowing with tin-can tourists, real estate men, and multi-millionaires. Publicity for Florida was partly in reading matter and advertisements, and partly in word-of-mouth descriptions of experience there. Most effective was the exploitation of the law which abolished state income taxes, the importation of William Jennings Bryan to become a citizen of the state (and eventually a speaker at real estate auctions), and the creation of vast cities, like Coral Gables. The swamps of Florida disappeared from the public eye and the heat of its summers was reduced to figures of Fahrenheit which proved that Florida was eminently a livable place. The fact that a rich man's playground offered itself to the poor man as well made of Florida the complete symbol of a desirable escape from ugly winters, from disagreeable work, and from routine. Unconsciously, the trek to Florida made a large portion of the American people, hitherto fixed in their homes, into a race of nomads.

The evil associations with the word propaganda, due to the excesses of the war, have made people forget that propaganda of the same sort has been used to prevent wars and to cement friendship between peoples. It is well-known that German Chancellor Otto von Bismarck was disappointed at the quick recovery of the French after the War of 1870 and felt that Germany would not be secure unless France was "bled white."[3] In 1875, the French minister in Berlin notified Paris that Germany was on the verge of attacking France. Henri Blowitz, the famous correspondent of the *London Times*, informed John Delane, the editor, and insisted that publicity would break down the German plan. Delane sent a special investigator to make sure that the facts were as stated and, as soon as he was convinced, put the whole weight of the *Times* behind the exposure. "The effect produced by the revelation of the German plot was instantaneous, universal and profound," noted journalist Edward Tyas Cook, and Delane wrote to

---

[3] Otto von Bismarck (1815–1898) was the chancellor of Germany from 1871–1890.

Blowitz that, "No greater honor than to have averted war is within the reach of the journalist."[4]

Publicity not only acts on the citizen. It is often the citizen's weapon. A short time ago the relations between Mexico and the United States were at breaking point, and it seemed to the public that the administration intended to push forward to a break. There was an instant flare-up of public protest; the State Department's attitude grew more friendly; the scare died away and businessman Dwight Morrow was sent as ambassador to Mexico, creating (with the approval of the American people and the assistance of Charles Lindbergh[5]) a situation so amicable that even the publication of incendiary (and certainly forged) documents had no effect.

It is recorded that emissaries of Boss Tweed offered Thomas Nast, the cartoonist, $200,000 if he would go to Paris and study art. Week after week, Nast's vicious pictures of the corruption of Tammany

---

[4] This quote comes from Edward Tyas Cook's 1915 book *Delane of the Times*.

[5] Charles Lindbergh (1902–1974) gained notoriety for achieving the first non-stop transcontinental flight from Long Island, New York to Paris in 1927. Lindberg, at Morrow's invitation, did a tour of Mexico in 1927. Lindberg eventually married Morrow's daughter, Anne Morrow.

Hall continued to appear—and eventually William Tweed and his ring were destroyed.[6]

It is the illusion of many Americans that the Declaration of Independence and the Constitution were both spontaneously accepted by the American people. Scholar Moses Coit Tyler corrected this impression in his 1897 book *The Literary History of the American Revolution, 1763–1783*. He said:

> The doctrine of Independence was not taken up and advocated by responsible statesmen in America until many months after it had found more or less open championship among the songwriters and newspaper humorists who, protected by their obscurity, thus flung up into the air a dangerous thought which was already slowly fermenting in the minds of the people.

It took a year and a half to persuade a sufficient number of states to ratify the Constitution. In *The Federalist* and elsewhere, Alexander Hamilton, James Madison, and John Jay defended that instrument, pointed out its merits, and urged its acceptance.[7] At the same time, the promise of the first ten

---

[6] Tweed was described as the "boss" of Tammany Hall in New York City, a powerful Democratic Party operation that influenced elections in both the city and the state of New York in the 19th century.

[7] *The Federalist* is a compilation of pro-Constitution essays published in 1788.

amendments (the Bill of Rights) acted on the people—it was a combination of policy and publicity. In Europe today nothing is more familiar than the statement that "Americans are always in a hurry." In America it was common knowledge before the war that the French "are a frivolous people devoted to dancing and light wine." The British are strong and silent, the Germans efficient, the Italians volatile, the Turk is a gallant fighting man. These international myths color the picture which the traveler sees abroad, they have an effect on international relations. The Briton, for generations, thought of America as a colony which had somehow split off; the European today is being taught by cartoonists, ministers of the gospel and of the state, editorial writers, movies, and every other form of publicity to think of America as a Shylock.[8]

Yet, to take one example, the idea that Americans are always in a hurry is entirely misleading. It may be that the pace of life in the United States is more rapid than it is in Europe, but this does not prove that the American businessman who spends three afternoons a week on the golf links is in a hurry. Actually the phrase "*les Americains toujours pressés*" has

---

[8] Shylock is the principle antagonist in the William Shakespeare play *The Merchant of Venice*. Scholars have long debated if the play is anti-Semitic. The slur "Shylock," according the Anti-Defamation league, refers to unscrupulous Jewish money lenders.

been traced back as far as 1834 and probably occurred earlier. It has been repeated because foreigners always see what they expect to see. And Americans, meeting hundreds of talkative Englishmen, still think of the Briton as reticent, because they have been taught to think so.

Characters in fiction often come to represent whole nations. The Americans created by Charles Dickens in the 1844 novel *The Life and Adventures of Martin Chuzzlewit*—the loudmouthed shysters, chewing tobacco and twisting the lion's tail while they sell swamp lots to the innocent—still remain typical Americans to many Englishmen. Europeans see Babbitt as the typical American real estate man. In America, the pictures of Mr. Pickwick gradually merge into the figure of John Bull and stand for the Englishman.[9] Americans, influenced by the tales of Guy de Maupassant, see the Frenchman as frivolous and adulterous.[10]

Publicity touches everything. It gives, in 1928, a sort of social respectability to a marriage system which, in 1900, would have been universally

---

[9] Dickens' 1836 novel *The Pickwick Papers* featured Samuel Pickwith as the protagonist. John Bull is a characterization of the Englishman—stout and portly—that became visible in British literature and illustrations by the late 18th century.

[10] Maupassant published numerous works in the late 19th century and is considered one of the originators of the modern short story.

condemned as free-love. Give it a new name—
companionate marriage—and comes a flurry in the
newspapers, a barrage of jokes and puns, the authority
of a well-known name, and the thing comes into
being.[11]

It has been said that the test for the influence of
the press is in politics. During the first year of the
Great War, the Northcliffe press in England rose to
an unparalleled position of influence by imperiling its
existence in the exposé of the munitions situation.[12]
After the *Daily Mail* had been burned on the stock
exchange, and the circulation of *The Times* gone to a
low ebb, it was discovered that Northcliffe had been
right.[13] Thereafter his authority was tremendous. He
exercised this authority in an unprecedented way. In
the midst of war, he forced out of office a Prime

---

[11] "Companionate marriage" is a term for a couple that has entered
into marriage for the purpose of companionship rather than raising
children, or for one to seek financial support from the other.
Scholars observed that, in the U.S., this was a conception of
marriage that arose in the 1920s.

[12] The Northcliffe press consisted of several newspapers, including
The Times and the *Daily Mail*. The name comes from the position
carried by these papers' owner, Alfred Harmsworth, who had the
title of Baron Northcliffe in 1905, and then Viscount Northcliffe
in 1918. Northcliffe's press reported, as early as 1914, that British
troops had insufficient ammunition.

[13] In the spring of 1915, approximately 1,500 London stock exchange
members burned copies of the *Daily Mail* and *The Times* in protest
of the Northcliffe press reporting on the munitions shortage.

Minister—Henry Asquith, who was enjoying a parliamentary majority—and put his own nominee in.[14]

That the press of Europe had an important part in creating the situation leading to the Great War has been shown by Jonathan French Scott who, in a 1927 book called *Five Weeks*, has analyzed the newspapers of every country involved in 1914 and shown how the publication *and the omission* of news prepared the public for war. In the past century, according to Bismarck, who was an expert manipulator of public opinion through the press, three wars were brought on by the newspapers. "The Danish press," he said, "forced the King and the Government to annex Schleswig; the Austrian and the south German press agitated against us; and the French press contributed to the prolongation of the campaign in France. The press was the cause of the last three wars."[15]

---

[14] Henry Asquith (1852–1928) was replaced by David Lloyd George (1863–1945) in 1916.

[15] This quote is found in the book *Bismarck: Some Secret Pages of His History*, published in 1898 by Julian Hermann Moritz Busch (1821–1900), a German publicist and close confident of Chancellor Bismarck. This quote came from an October 21, 1877 entry in that book. Scholars assert that Bismarck provoked those three wars against Denmark, Austria, and France. The reference to Schleswig concerns a battle with Denmark over disputed territory that Germany ultimately re-took through Prussian and Austrian forces in 1864.

According to the well-known story reported by James Creelman, the *New York Journal* sent Frederic Remington[16] as a war correspondent to Cuba in 1897 and, when he cabled that everything was quiet there, his employer, publisher William Randolph Hearst replied, "You furnish the pictures and I'll furnish the war."[17] And the press is credited with an overwhelming influence in ending the grave scandals of the Credit Mobilier, the whiskey ring, the star route graft, the Tweed ring, the insurance business, and most recently, the Teapot Dome and allied enterprises.[18]

The examples of the uses of publicity given above are not exhaustive. They are intended to give the

---

[16] Frederic Remington (1861–1909) was primarily known as an illustrator and sculptor well-known for providing images of the American west.

[17] Hearst denied that he ever cabled such a message. No evidence of that telegram exists and scholars express doubt about this claim.

[18] The Credit Mobilier scandal, which arose in 1872, involved a construction company for the U.S. Transcontinental Railroad giving stock shares to congressmen as bribes. The Whiskey Ring scandal was exposed in 1875; it involved federal officials pocketing millions of dollars in federal liquor taxes. The Tweed Ring centered on William Marcy Tweed's efforts to exert vast control over New York City government through his control of political patronage in that city in the late 19th century. The insurance industry scandal in 1905 featured the bribery of officials, particularly in New York State. The Teapot Dome scandal, which arose in 1921 and 1922, concerned oil company bribery of the Secretary of the Interior to garner low rates for oil leases.

range, not to mark down all the targets. Coal strikers, wars, baseball, beards, real estate, ships, shoes, sealing wax, cabbage, and kings—especially kings—are affected by publicity. In some of the instances the news itself is sufficiently important. When the French government declared war in 1870, it was ill-prepared and misled the people into expecting an instant victory.[19] The *news* of defeat caused the overthrow of the French government.[20] But in most cases it is not the news itself, but the *use* to which the news has been put, that has caused changes in governments, parties, national and international policies, and in the daily habits of the ordinary man. It is this use which is called publicity.

---

[19] France declared war on Prussia on July 16, 1870 because of French fears of increasing Prussian ambitions.

[20] A new government was established on September 4, 1870 after French Emperor Napoleon III was captured by Prussian forces.

Part II

Propaganda, Truth, Facts, & Responsibility

Chapter 4.
Publicity and Propaganda

MOST OF THE RECENT WRITERS on propaganda have confessed their inability to frame a satisfactory definition of their subject and to mark definitely the line separating propaganda from publicity. This is largely a theoretical difficulty. In practice everyone knows, or at least says, since one never admits to using propaganda, that "My publicity is education; the enemy's publicity is propaganda." On the other hand, the man who reads both "my publicity" and that of the enemy makes another distinction. Roughly, he thinks that propaganda is all lies. Yet the statement, made a thousand times during the war, that the German people were loyal to their government was not a lie, and it was definitely propaganda.

One extremely useful standard has been suggested. Propaganda is, according to this definition, an attempt to influence opinion by issuing statements the truth or falsehood of which cannot be checked because the propagandist himself controls and censors the sources of information. It is at least partially a workable definition. For example, the loyalty of the Germans may be accepted as truth. The announcement of their loyalty was, none the less, propaganda because virtually no outsider could have disproved the statement. Had there been riots in

every city in Germany, censorship would have
suppressed the news, as in fact censorship did
suppress all news of internal disaffection for several
years.

Similarly, a falsehood may be difficult to check.
During the first days of the war, the absence of
official news lead the French to believe that the
Germans were being driven back, and that the French
armies were, in fact, advancing rapidly into Germany.
At the same time, exaggerated reports led the
Germans to believe, even after the battle of Marne,
that their armies were proceeding to the siege of
Paris.[1] Neither the French nor the German private
citizen had any means of checking the exact situation
since the military and political authorities exercised
the strictest censorship. In these cases the French
negatively and the Germans positively were using
propaganda among their own citizens.

There are, in addition, cases in which the truth is
not disputed and censorship does not operate, but
which the average man feels to be propaganda. The
execution of Edith Cavell offers an example. The
German authorities admitted that they had put the
nurse to death and claimed justification under military
law. The British condemned the execution as brutal
and inhuman and managed to crowd out of the minds

---

[1] The Battle of the Marne was held from September 7–12, 1914,
resulting in an Allied victory.

of neutrals the purely technical justification of the Germans.[2] Harold D. Lasswell, in his 1927 book *Propaganda Technique in the World War*, quotes a conversation between an American newspaperman and the Prussian officer in charge of propaganda for the general staff. The newspaperman asked why the Germans did nothing to counteract the British propaganda about the Cavell case in America. When the Germans expressed bewilderment at the idea, the newspaperman suggested that the Germans "raise the devil about those nurses the French shot the other day"—that is, protest that German nurses were executed substantially for the same reason as Cavell. The German replied, "What? Protest? The French had a perfect right to shoot them!" The British did not mention the execution of the two German nurses and did their best to prevent knowledge of their deaths from coming to neutrals; by constant pressure they made the Cavell case seem unique and terrible. Psychologically, they were using something like censorship, occupying neutral minds so exclusively with one item that there was no place for a counteracting influence. But of actual censorship there was none.

---

[2] Edith Cavell (1865–1915), a British nurse, assisted approximately 200 Allied troops and civilians to escape from German-held Belgium. Germany arrested her, found her guilty of treason, and executed her via firing squad.

Changes in government and changes in military
operations have made it necessary for modern nations
to be sure of their own citizens in time of war. With
professional and hired armies King George III and his
ministers could afford to be almost indifferent to
public opinion, a fact attested to by the open and
unpunished declarations made in London against the
war with the American Colonies. However, when
armies begin to count in the millions, to take soldiers
from every family, and when civilians themselves bear
part of the burden of warfare, the mobilization of
public opinion becomes imperative. Labor, for
example, becomes the key to military operations
because labor controls the output of munition. As
labor in most European countries tends to be socialist
or at least socialistic, it needs to be persuaded from
the very beginning of a war that the war is inevitable,
just, and fought with the loftiest aims. In the first
shock of battle, with the first reports of killed and
wounded, the average man responds in two ways: with
anger or with regret. If regret is dominant, he may fall
under the sway of the pacifist, and it therefore
becomes necessary to persuade the most anti-
militaristic that the present war is fought not for the
usual purposes of war, but to end all wars. The fact of
war itself solidifies national spirit. It revives the
tradition of glory, the desire to avenge old wrongs, the

danger of invasion, the exaltation of facing death. The
business of propaganda is to undermine the enemies
of this solidity and to create a perfect unity of
opinion. In England it was liberal publicists, in France
it was socialists, in Germany it was men of the highest
distinction in the professions, who summoned all
citizens, especially those who hesitated, to the duty of
believing that all the guilt was on the side of the
enemy. The various governments supplied the
ammunition of propaganda by issuing black, red,
white, and blue books dealing with the diplomatic
interchanges preceding the war—not one of which
would now be considered accurate since all of them
omitted essential material and some of them offered
falsified material. War guilt was succeeded, as the
most effective propaganda, by atrocities, and
atrocities by war aims; but the impetus given to this
first endeavor was so great that it went on after the
war and, fortified by a new propaganda against "the
myth of a guilty nation," continues to exercise
scholars and historians ten years after the war is
ended.

The statement of war aims is in itself an instance
of the growing force of public opinion. Wars have
frequently been justified to the citizens called upon to
pay or to suffer, and in this justification the aims of a
war might be mentioned. But the manipulation of
idealistic war aims as a means of preserving the war

spirit has never been so consistently done as in the last war and the entrance of America. That America's entrance was accomplished virtually on the basis of such aims alone is a unique phenomenon. War aims are particularly effective in corralling those individuals whose tendency is to separate from the mass of citizens. To win is a sufficient aim for the majority; to conquer, to gain territory and indemnities are objects worthy in themselves. In the moment of defeat, however, when these objects seem unattainable, the danger of defeatist propaganda is great. That is why complete unity of feeling is necessary (and, incidentally, explains the bitterness against conscientious objectors). The aims may change from month to month, but it is desirable that no open conflict between the various objects announced should be visible.

In his famous "we shall not sheathe our sword" speech, British Prime Minister Henry Asquith[3] announced that country's war aims in general terms, specifically mentioning only the restitution of Belgium and the destruction of German militarism. Before the war was properly begun, liberals, desiring to support the country, suggested that a new orientation of European statesmanship for after the war would alone make the sacrifices bearable. Other

---

[3] Asquith gave this speech on November 10, 1914 at London's Guildhall.

Britons desired nothing so much as the destruction of the German fleet. Others wanted the reduction of Germany to a secondary position as a commercial competitor; statesmen wanted to break up the real or supposed influence of Germany in the Near East; the imperially-minded wished to protect India. Liberals who believed in the war to end war looked forward to an era of reconciliation, whereas the responsible ministry of information spread propaganda during the war against German commercial travelers who might come to Britain after the war. The disparity between British, French, Russian, and Italian interests was even more marked. War aims were therefore stated in broad general terms, and whenever a specific item was made public it was done with the definite purpose of bringing a wavering body of opinion into line.

At the end of 1916, when President Wilson asked for a clear statement of war aims, of the terms upon which peace could be concluded, the objections raised in each country were grave. One reason was that, in the minds of some people, any discussion of aims before victory in the field is assured tends to weaken the war spirit. This seems to have been the dominant mood in Germany, which always evaded statements of terms outside of generalities. Another reason for withholding terms was that if a nation bound itself to a determined list of objectives and made these public they might cause dissension at home just when unity was most needed. The same argument applied to the Stockholm Conference—the proposed 1917 meeting of socialists of the belligerent countries. The dominant parties naturally resented the suggestion that such a minor party could, in a sense, meet the enemy and make terms. The fear of the directors of propaganda was that either the radical or the conservative groups would split off from the body of public opinion which the war and propaganda had created.

The prospect of enlisting America on the side of the Entente was, however, decisive.[4] It coincided with a let-down in civilian morale in Great Britain and France. It became most hopeful during the winter when the chances of a great military triumph to re-establish hope and confidence were small. For these reasons, among others, the Entente made a statement of war aims which was more specific, and more authoritative, than any made before.[5] These aims, idealistic enough for the moralist and self-protective enough for the patriot, won the approval of neutrals, and this approval, in turn, was also used to bolster the fighting spirit.

---

[4] "Entente" refers to the alliance between England, France, and Russia that was formalized through the signing of the Anglo-Russian Entente in 1907.

[5] The Entente powers made a statement of war aims in December 1916 that referred to the rights of nationalities.

Analysts of crowd psychology have noted that the crowd is not affected by reason. It imagines that it has reasons for what it does, but actually these imaginary reasons are only rationalizations (i.e., apparently rational defenses of emotional states and actions based on the emotions entirely). Thus, to the German, the Entente's claim to be fighting for the rights of small nations was wholly illogical. To the German, it was a rationalization of the Entente's desire to prevent Germany from exercising its natural influence over Belgium, Turkey, Bulgaria, and other nations. The real emotion, according to Germany, was fear and jealousy. But, in England, the idealistic phrase touched the moral sense of the British particularly and concealed the truth. The nation, in wartime, is susceptible to mob appeal.

To the Allies, the German claims seemed equally false. One of them was that Germany was fighting on behalf of all other countries against the naval tyranny of Great Britain—obviously a rationalization of Germany's desire to defeat Great Britain and take her place as mistress of the seas. The German instance upon Kultur,[6] the French stand as defender of Latin civilization against Germanic barbarity, the Italian claim that Trieste[7] was really Italian in race and spirit,

---

[6] "Kultur" is a term for German civilization and culture.

[7] Trieste is a city in northeastern Italy, near Croatia. It was annexed into Italy after WWI.

all seemed, to the enemy, false fronts behind which entirely selfish desires were hidden.

The extent to which these rationalizations can go was marked by the *London Times* when, in the spring of 1915, it published an epoch-making editorial declaring that Great Britain did *not* go to war because the neutrality of Belgium was violated, but because her own safety and security were imperiled. In August 1914, the violation of Belgian neutrality had put into the hands of Prime Minister Asquith and Secretary of State for Foreign Affairs Edward Grey the most effective lever for moving the people of Great Britain. Liberals, pacifists, conservatives, and jingoes all coalesced to fight against this violation of international law. But as the war went on, the reality of the struggle overshadowed the idealism of its purpose. The *Times* believed that, so long as the British felt that they were fighting for an abstract right which affected not them but Belgium, they would not put their heart into the war (this was during the time of volunteering, with all its difficulties). The purpose of the editorial, with all the prestige of the *Times* behind it, was to make every Briton feel that the war was his war, that success would give him something he wanted, and failure rob him of his possessions, his liberty, and possibly his life.

This was an appeal to the basic human instinct of self-preservation—an appeal automatically made in France the moment the first German soldier set foot on her soil. In England, this appeal could not be made at the beginning because the English had never conceived the possibility of invasion and defeat, and because the temper of the people, just before the war broke out, was generally pacifist. Generations of living in "splendid isolation" from the quarrels of Europe, had produced a frame of mind unsusceptible to threats of disaster.[8] The public mind was changed by the success of Germany in the field, and the propaganda which the *Times* editorial started sharpened the point of the argument.

Bringing war aims home to every individual is the business of propaganda. Thus business men were assured that, after the war, they would capture Germany's (or Britain's) trade. The war became a racial struggle, a conflict between systems of philosophy or of morals, and a war between schools of painting and of music. German dancing, theatre craft, science, and habits of eating were marked as hostile to French and Anglo-Saxon civilization. Whatever one did or thought or felt was put in peril by what the enemy did or thought or felt. Short of panic, the

---

[8] "Splendid isolation" was a term coined in 1896 by Canadian politician George Eulas Foster. It referred to England's decades-long policy of avoiding alliances with other countries.

propagandist desired every citizen to remain in mortal terror of the enemy. Official war aims could not recognize these personal conflicts. Toward the end of the war, in fact, it was made clear to the Germans that if they abandoned their militarist principles (and the ruling family) they might hope to be received into the family of nations and no punitive indemnities were threatened against them. The governments which announced these terms were aware in advance that they would irritate the bitter-enders who desired a march on Berlin. But this group could be counted on for loyalty in any event, whereas the enthusiasts for a negotiated peace could only be kept in line by concessions. Propaganda, which had been directed at the beginning of the war to creating a solid mass of opinion, now considered the main body as safe and directed itself to those portions which gave signs of falling away.

In America, the situation differed because, as has been noted, the country came into the war virtually as a demonstration in favor of specific terms of peace and of a new world arrangement thereafter. The practical situation differed also. The government had no subsidized press, no recognized organ by which to reach the people, and there was no tradition of censorship. The first move in European countries when war broke out was to establish censorship and

to direct the activities of the press. The first move in
America was to establish a bureau of publicity.
Patriotism and partisanship may declare that the
Committee of Public Information educated and
informed and publicized the world, but never, except
through inadvertence, used propaganda. The facts are
not favorable to this view. Except that the Committee
did not deliberately tell lies, its work was as much
propaganda as that of the Germans or the French or
the British. In connection with the president's
speeches and the Fourteen Points in particular, the
Committee broadcast promises which Germans insist
were not kept in the terms of the Peace Treaty.[9] The
Committee put the most favorable interpretation on
news; it dropped over the German lines pictures
illustrating the growth of the American army which
the Germans could in no way verify. It issued the
German-Bolshevik documents and reports of Edgar
Sisson, although their authenticity was always under
fire.[10] Its Four Minute Men spoke of atrocities of

---

[9] President Wilson articulated 14 points related to war aims and
peace terms in a speech given on January 8, 1918.

[10] In October 1918, the Committee released a pamphlet called "The
German-Bolshevik Conspiracy" that claimed communications
between Germany and Russia revealed that the heads of the
Bolshevik government were German agents. Edgar Sisson, who was
a Committee liaison in Russia, obtained the documents that
informed this pamphlet. The authenticity of these documents has
still not been established.

which no certain knowledge was at hand.[11] In short, the Committee was a propagandist. The novelty about the Committee was, however, that its major field of work was making public every fact and every bit of news concerning America's involvement in the war (with the small exception of items of military and naval information which might be of service to the enemy).

It hardly matters by what name such a work is called, and to call it propaganda does not belittle it. The fact remains that, for the first time, a government took its people almost completely into its confidence, realizing that there was no other way in which a people's war could be waged while recognizing at the same time the legitimate desire of the people to have authoritative information. Everything sent out by the Committee of Public Information was vouched for, not only by that Committee directly, but by the three branches of the government which it served: the Army, the Navy, and the State Department. In a special way it was also the channel of communication of the Executive. It helped to create as near to perfect unanimity of opinion as has ever existed in a modern nation. This meant not only that the people approved

---

[11] Four Minute Men were volunteers who went to public places (e.g., theatres) to present short speeches on subjects provided to them by the Committee.

of the war, but, to an extent unimaginable in foreign countries, were aware of the purposes of the war and accepted them as their own.

Publicity, as it was managed in the United States, put an end to rumor. Stories were circulated, but information out sped them. The American people as a whole were never depressed by false stories of disaster and were never cast down from an exalted state by hearing that rumored victories were actually defeats. The contrast with the European countries of the first months of the war is striking. The typical incident in England, true or not true, was the ejection of a newspaper man from the prime minister's residence on the day war broke out. Trained in a tradition which despised the press, Prime Minister Asquith never came to terms with it, never used it properly, was ineffective in stopping its abuses, and eventually succumbed to it. It took months before British General Headquarters would receive accredited correspondents and longer before the official eyewitness was supplemented by more independent observers. Rumor lived on this suppression of news. The coming of the Russians and of the angels at Mons were only the more notorious stories.[12] Returning wounded soldiers dropped hints of disaster. Secrecy about munition plants gave rise to stories of

---

[12] The angels of Mons is a legend that a group of angels protected British troops at the Battle of Mons in late August 1914.

explosions. The desire to have a weapon as deadly as poison gas was reflected in a rumor that workers in a chemical factory were incurring hundreds of deaths in horrible tortures. There were stories of disagreement between France and Great Britain and of rebellion in the troops, especially at the Etaples encampment.[13] Even as late as the summer of 1915 the habit of looking to rumor, rather than to official news, was so strong that the failure of the offensive brought exaggerated fears to the people.[14]

In France nearly an entire month elapsed without official news bearing on the position of the armies. This was during the retreat to the Marne, and the wisdom of withholding bad news has been defended on the ground that the civilian populace could not master the strategy of retreating in order to attack on favorable ground.[15] During the month of anxiety, Paris was fed with rumors. Under the ever-present fear of a repetition of 1870,[16] there rose the expectation of complete victory and the end of the

---

[13] Etaples was a French fishing port where British Empire soldiers mutinied in September 1917.

[14] An August 1915 British offensive at Gallipoli, a peninsula in Turkey, was repelled by the Turks.

[15] British and French troops retreated to the River Marne in France from August through September 1914.

[16] France lost territory to Germany at the end of the Franco-Prussian war, commonly referred to in France as the War of 1870.

war by Christmas. It was thought that the armies of the right front had crossed into Germany and that the armies under French general Joseph Joffre were still near the Belgian frontier. On a particularly black day, when no official communiqué of any sort was issued, the people of Paris were informed that the Czar would soon dictate conditions to Germany! When the French Government departed for Bordeaux and the taxicab army dashed through Paris to the nearby front, the true position of the armies, within sound of Paris, was revealed and the city was in panic.[17]

The same military events, not withheld from the public but offered in exaggerated form, led the Germans to believe that the march on Paris was virtually over. For four years, official Germany did not admit that there had been a battle on the Marne. Regimented and docile as the Germans may have been, they could not help seeing, after the winter of 1914, that the capture of Paris had not come off. The willingness to believe in 1918 that their leaders had betrayed them was partially due to the long disappointment extending from the earliest days of the war.

The Americans from the beginning, and the British after brief experience, determined to make public the news of disaster immediately. One of the

---

[17] French taxicabs transported approximately 5,000 French reinforcements to the Battle of the Marne on September 6, 1914.

famous occasions on which the British failed to make
public a loss was that of the sinking of the British
battleship *Audacious*. It occurred October 27, 1914 and
was announced on November 13, 1918, two days after
the armistice. The late Sir Edward Cook, in his sound
and entertaining 1920 book *The Press in War-time*, tells
why. The fact that the ship had sunk was first
rumored and then accepted as absolute truth. Several
British newspapers alluded to it and certain magazines
mentioned it directly. Worse, the disaster was seen by
American passengers on the *Olympic*, and an
American newspaper had published a picture of the
Audacious just as it was sinking.[18] This newspaper had
circulated in both England and Germany. There
seemed no reason in the world for the Admiralty to
continue to conceal the fact. Yet British Admiral
John Jellicoe particularly insisted, and the reason was
that until the British officially conceded the loss,
there was a chance that Germany would not be sure
about what had happened. The American newspapers
had published two accounts of the mining of the
Audacious——one said that the vessel had sunk,
another that it had been towed into harbor. The
second might have suggested to Germany that the
Audacious could be repaired and sent to join the fleet.

---

[18] The *Olympic* was a cruise liner that was on the scene shortly after
the *Audacious* struck a German mine and began to sink. Crew
members escaped to the *Olympic* via lifeboats.

As the Admiral did not wish Germany to know just how far mines and submarines had depleted the fleet, he preferred to keep the whole matter secret.

Secrecy about important events becomes more and more difficult to attain. It is said that every American in Paris knew of the secret preparations for the Meuse-Argonne offensive of our armies ten days before the attack began.[19] A substantially correct version of the murder of Grigori Rasputin, coupled with an accurate forecast of the first Russian revolution, was current in London six weeks before that revolution started.[20] Yet the introduction of the tanks in the war was managed as a surprise, and the anti-submarine device known as the paravene worked successfully for months before the public even knew of its existence.[21] Technicalities and troop movements can be kept secret; but battles cannot.

Admiral Sir Cyprian Bridge represented the attitude of the fighting forces perfectly when he said, "as long as a war lasts there is no limit to the length of time that ought to elapse before a full report of naval

---

[19] The Meuse-Argonne offensive was the final Allied offensive of WWI, lasting from September 26, 1918 until November 11, 1918, when the Armistice was signed.

[20] Rasputin was a confidant to the family of Nicholas II, the last tsar of Russia. He was murdered on December 30, 1916.

[21] The paravene, introduced in WWI, was an underwater glider designed to swoop up mines so that they could be destroyed.

and military operations can be safely published."[22] The reason for this is that no matter when a report is published, it tells something to the enemy—it enables him to check up false information and gives him an insight into the temperament of the man he is fighting. Taken at full value, this view would demand total suppression of all news relating to battles until after the war was over.

British Lieutenant General Sir Douglas Brownrigg took the opposite view. He tells how Winston Churchill juggled the news, holding back a disagreeable item a few days in the hope of getting a bit of good news to send out at the same time, and then tells how his own plea for immediate publication of news of disasters finally was allowed. Yet it took a long time for the British public to accustom itself to believing official reports and no others. The handling of the news of the Battle of Jutland illustrates all the difficulties publicity met with in a country unused to it.[23] The first announcement of the battle was the German claim of a great naval victory. The German Fleet, nearer its base than the British, supplied the news. The British Admiralty was compelled to make an announcement on insufficient information. It

---

[22] This quote comes from Cook's book *The Press in War-Time*.

[23] The Battle of Jutland was the only full-scale clash of battleships during WWI. It occurred in the North Sea from May 1, 1916– June 1, 1916.

followed the new principle of making public all losses of ships and men, but it was not able to give a complete account of the German losses. The two items, Germany's claim of victory and the Admiralty's admission of losses, were put together and almost the whole of the British press confessed defeat and disaster. Some of the papers tried to belittle Jutland and to call it an incident. Others noted that Germany had defeated England on the seas, and opponents of Prime Minister Grey, of First Lord of the Admiralty Arthur Balfour, and of the general direction of the war, used the defeat to further their own ends. There was a break in the stock market. For a day, the whole of The British Isles believed that a disaster of irreparable magnitude had fallen on the navy. This was due to the fact that the German announcement came in first and that no one believed the Admiralty had willingly made public its losses. The habit of complete confidence in publicity from the government was not established. Slowly the reports of German losses drifted in—from the British, from admissions by the German Admiralty, and from neutrals. The public despair was mitigated to a degree; naval experts pointed out that the decisive factor in a naval engagement was not comparative losses, but control of the sea (which remained in British hands— the Germans, of course, insisted that losses were the measure of victory). The best the Germans could

claim during the war was that it was not a defeat—a
negative totally incapable of firing the enthusiasm of a
country.

One little-known aspect of the Jutland story is
revealed by Sir Edward Cook in his book *The Press in
War-Time*. He said:

> The Empire owes a debt of gratitude to the
> General Secretary of the Navy League, who, lest the
> pessimistic tone of the British Press should be carried
> overseas, took it on himself without a moment's delay
> to cable every one of the League's branches that "the
> greatest victory since Trafalgar had been achieved."[24]

The student of propaganda is advised to study
this sentence in all its implications. Did the man who
sent that cable believe it? Months later, when the full
account of comparative losses could be tabulated,
enthusiasts might claim that Jutland was a British
victory. That it was as great a victory as Trafalgar,
where Admiral Lord Nelson drove the enemy's ships
to the bottom of the sea or to ports in which they
were helpless, no one ever maintained. The wording
of the cable suggests that Jutland somehow equaled
Trafalgar, and the fact that no tremendous British
victory had been won between Trafalgar and Jutland is
lost sight of. The cable set up an association in the
mind of the reader—Trafalgar-Victory-Jutland. Was

---

[24] The Battle of Trafalgar was the British Navy's victory over French
and Spanish fleets on October 21, 1805.

it a false association? Was the message a lie? Was it merely an exaggeration? Was it legitimate? Was it effective?

On the final point the critic of propaganda notes only that the message was sent by an official of the Navy League—i.e., by one pledged in advance to make the best possible case for the navy. If the message was printed as official, or semi-official, it must have done much to counteract the German announcement of victory.

The United States helped the Allies with more than men, munitions, and capital. It provided a new set of symbols to captivate the minds of the public. The sufferings of Belgium had grown stale to a public which had had difficulties with too many refugees. "Our glorious Allies" had proved themselves a little less than invincible in the field. The fact that the Germans cut down fruit trees in 1916 and 1917 was not as effective in stirring emotions as the rumor that they cut off baby's fingers. In fact, the whole early system of war emotions was exhausted. The United States stepped in with new fervor and new phrases. The rights of small nations was reaffirmed, the distraction of militarism was desired, many of the old ideals were re-established—but over them all was the idea of a society of nations, and the new tone of a struggle for the rights of mankind summed up in the phrase "to make the world safe for democracy."[25] The president's phrases, backed by the American people, supplied an apparently fresh motivation to the war. Among the other forms of home propaganda was that of calling the enemy names. Perhaps the most effective single word in war propaganda was the name "Hun" applied to the Germans. It had definite associations in the mind. To call the Germans murderers, rapists, and destroyers would not have been half as effective, because these words lack picturesqueness—i.e., they do not instantly create a picture in the mind. Hun does, not because any modern man has ever seen a Hun, but because the word sums up all the pictures of barbarism he has ever seen. Historically, as many writers noted, the Germans were not, as a race, descendants of the Huns, but the average mind is chaotic about history and this criticism was ineffective. The word "Hun" summed up Alaric, the Goths and Visigoths, and barbarians generally.[26] It appealed not to logic, but to some primitive memory. Further, it was presented to the world in the effective rhythm of Rudyard

---

[25] On April 2, 1917, Wilson asked for Congress to approve a declaration of war because, in part, "the world must be made safe for democracy."

[26] Alaric was the first king of the Visigoths from 395–410. The Visigoths were one of several nomadic tribes of western Germanic people. The Goths were a different tribe of eastern Germanic people.

Kipling's 1914 poem "For All We Have and Are."
That poem's line, "the Hun is at the Gate," stirs not
the present mind of the city dweller with a key to an
apartment, but the racial memory of iron gates
defended against invaders.

Without these racial memories, name calling is
often ineffective. The Germans defended the conduct
of their soldiers in Belgium by offering proof that
Belgian civilians were sniping.[27] In America the
tendency was to defend the Belgians by saying, "Why
shouldn't they?" A nation familiar with warfare
attaches not only sanctity to the uniform of the
soldier, but allows it privileges. A soldier may fire
from ambush because he is uniformed and, therefore,
runs the risk of being shot in return; but a civilian
must not receive such treatment. In the United
States, sniping done by Belgian civilians seemed
heroic because America, without a large standing
army and with a tradition of farmers leaping to their
rifles in defense of their country, does not share the
German memory.

The notorious cadaver-transforming-factory hoax
began in a similar effort to adapt propaganda to the
intended victims. British Brigadier General John
Charteris has told how he found a picture which

---

[27] German soldiers, fearful of Belgium guerilla fighters, killed civilians
and destroyed communities. This was called the "Rape of
Belgium."

might appear to indicate that the Germans were using dead horses in the creation of fat. He knew that ancestor worship among the Chinese made any violation of the human dead abhorrent and proposed to send out the picture to China with a slightly ambiguous title which would lead the Chinese to believe that the Germans were using human corpses for the creation of war material. Somehow the picture was shifted and appeared at first in the British press and later in the neutral press.[28] There were a hundred reasons for disbelieving the whole story and none for accepting it as truth. General Charteris, after corroborating this account of the hoax in America, is said to have repudiated it in England.[29]

Atrocities, especially sexual atrocities, are prime instruments in the hands of the propagandist. The whole sexual life of a nation is affected by a war, and the two surpassing interests of everyday life—sex and conflict—both are transferred to a dizzying level where nothing is reasoned or balanced. The propagandist, always adapting himself to the psychological state of his audience, works on this. He

---

[28] John Charteris (1877–1946), who was chief of intelligence for the British Expeditionary Force from 1915–1918, claimed that he had taken a caption that was originally used for a photo of German soldiers killed in battle and placed it beneath a different photo that showed horses being delivered to a German processing factory.

[29] One prominent scholar of propaganda, Randal Marlin, has asserted that there is no evidence that Charteris invented the hoax.

denies immorality among his own soldiers, encourages hasty marriages (before a soldier goes out to the front or in the few brief days of his leave) and even war babies. On the soldiers of the enemy he casts every shame he can find using textbooks on the psychopathology of sex. The fact that the soldier, like the civilian, leads an unusual life, especially in the early days of a war when armies are mobile, gives the propagandist sufficient material.

The total effect of home propaganda during the war was to keep the public confident of victory, loyal to their leaders, friendly to their allies, and implacable toward their enemies. War being what it is, what else could propaganda have done? The enemies of propaganda assert that propaganda fed hate which would otherwise have died down, that it set loose base emotions in men, that it consistently favored the jingo, and was deliberately turned against the apostle of conciliation. They claim that the public was forcibly fed, chiefly on lies, and that the result was a spiritual degeneration.

The dividing line between propaganda and policy is not easy to find. The volunteer propagandists supporting President Wilson were pleading the cause of peace without victory at one time and were asking for force without stint or limit at another; they were disseminating policies, not creating them. The distinction between the German people and their

rulers was not an easy one for the common American
to make; propagandists helped him, so that he might
be prepared for peace with Germany, yet ready for
war with the Kaiser and the military oligarchy—again,
this was letting light shine on a policy. In France,
atrocity stories and, in Germany, historical proof that
the French were a degenerate race did inflame
passions—but it was the will of the various
governments that these passions be inflamed.

Through the union of democratic control and
other agencies, an active pacifist propaganda was
carried on in England during the war. This
propaganda denied atrocity stories directed against
the enemy and implied or openly published
disgraceful rumors concerning the Allies. It ascribed
base motives to all those who wanted to carry the war
on to a smashing conclusion and derided the idealistic
aims set forth by the Allied governments. It accused
government propagandists of publishing baseless
rumors about the enemy, and proceeded itself to
circulate faceless rumors which favored the enemy. It
worked on crowd emotions, on fear and on hysteria.
Its range was limited, but its methods were similar in
every respect to that of the propaganda it attacked. In
the minds of patriots, this propaganda set loose the
lowest desires—cowardice and treachery—and
debased all it touched. However, it is only the man
who has given up all efforts to influence others who

can declaim against propaganda. And even while he does so, he will be engaged in propaganda for the distraction of propaganda.

What exactly were the fruits of war propaganda? The usual answer is "hate," but it is a very partial answer, for violent hatred against the enemy was matched buy equally violent, and unreasoning, love and enthusiasm for allied nations. The results differed in different countries. According to German Generals Erich Ludendorff and Paul von Hindenburg, propaganda was the prime cause of Germany's defeat (this statement may itself be considered propaganda in defense of the military organization and the Kaiser; it is an attack on the German civilian population for deserting their leaders). According to many British observers, propaganda was largely responsible for the disaffection of Austria's subject states and for the creation of Czechoslovakia and Yugoslavia in 1918. Propaganda, according to others, made possible conscription in England—and in this propaganda was included not only the usual forms of publicity, but the creation of the semi-voluntary system of recruiting known as the Derby scheme.[30] Propaganda by

---

[30] The Derby Scheme, introduced in the fall of 1915, required men between the ages of 18–41 to make a public declaration that they wanted to be available for conscription by England's military if needed. Because the plan excluded men who worked in exempted positions (e.g., munitions), it was considered a failure.

suppressing bad news prevented the wholesale desertion of Paris in 1914 and, according to the French, kept public confidence in French Commander-in-Chief Joseph Joffre (long after military men had begun to distrust his judgment) thus keeping alive the spirit of victory. Lack of propaganda is considered partially responsible for the breakdown in Russia and the ultimate refusal of the Soviets to continue the war on the side of the Allies.[31]

These are results on the grand scale. If propaganda accomplished even a tenth of what is ascribed to it, it must have surpassed in value most of the armies, commanders, and diplomats of the war. At certain moments this is not an excessive claim. In relation to Czechoslovakia, the diplomats were divided, the armies remote, and it was largely the force of British propaganda (which advised and often led British policy) that brought about the desired effect. Elsewhere, propaganda was a cooperating force, giving support to armies and a weapon to statesmen.

Propaganda proceeded Xerxes in his march against the Greeks, magnifying the strength of his arms; it affected Caesar's legionnaires in Gaul; it enlisted Milton in the struggle between Cromwell and

---

[31] After the Bolsheviks took control of Russia in October 1917, they signed a treaty with Germany and the Central Powers in March 1918.

the Cavaliers.[32] The special feature in the recent war was not propaganda itself, but the organization of propaganda, and its recognition as a vital arm of offense and defense.

---

[32] Xerxes the Great ruled Persia, invading Greek lands in the late 5th century. Roman ruler Julius Caesar invaded Gaul (what is France and nearby European lands in the modern age) during 58–50 BC. John Milton was a 17th century civil servant under the Lord Protector of the Commonwealth Oliver Cromwell.

Chapter 5.
The Naked Truth

I WAS TALKING WITH THE NEWSPAPER MAN the other day who seemed to think that the fact that Mrs. Carlyle threw a teacup at Mr. Carlyle should be given to the public merely as a fact.

But a fact presented to the people without the proper—or even, if necessary, without the improper—human being to go with it does not mean anything, and does not really become alive or caper about in people's minds.

But what I want, and what I believe most people want when a fact is being presented, is one or two touches that will make natural and human questions rise...about like this:

"Did a servant see Mrs. Carlyle throw the teacup? Was the servant an English servant with an English imagination or an Irish servant with an Irish imagination? What would the fact have been like if Mr. Browning had been listening at the key hole? Or Oscar Wilde, or *Punch*, or the *Missionary Herald*, or the *New York Sun*, or the *Christian Science Monitor*?"

— Gerald Stanley Lee[1]

---

[1] Gerald Stanley Lee (1862–1944)—a second cousin to Ivy Lee—was a clergyman who wrote numerous essays and books. This quote is from an undated essay in the *Saturday Evening Post*.

In the second year of the war, when the
apologists for Germany were beginning to encounter
the emissaries of the Allies in America and every
newspaper office had waste baskets full of war
publicity, the *New York Evening Sun* remarked
sardonically that there was no mystery about
propaganda—"it is as easy as lying."

As easy as lying—yet Lee, in the passage above,
indicates that lying itself may be difficult. Did Mrs.
Carlyle throw the tea cup in anger or in fun? Did she
throw it with the intent to harm or was it a gesture of
self-defense against a poker in Mr. Carlyle's hand? For
a good effective lie, credible details are needed, and to
make a lie stick, against denial or disproof, is hard. In
fact it is as complicated and difficult as propaganda.

Imagine the position of a man who had to base a
publicity campaign on a lie. The Kingdom of Sweden,
for example, desires to borrow $100 million dollars in
America and their advisor in publicity can think of no
other way of producing favorable opinion than
announcing the existence of a great diamond field in
Sweden, greater than Kimberley and in itself ample
security for the loan.[2] Getting this lie in print is
simple. On a sheet of paper bearing the Swedish coat
of arms and giving every indication of being official,
the press agent copies out a statement signed by three

---

[2] Kimberly is a city in the northern part of South Africa known for it
store of diamonds.

geologists to the effect that the Swedish diamond
fields are the richest in the world. Trusting the press
agent and the Swedish government, every newspaper
prints that statement, especially if it is accompanied
by an interesting story about the discovery of the
diamonds, the wealth gained by some poor men, or
something of the sort.

From that moment, the press agent has to
contrive to keep silent every man and woman in the
United States who has ever been in Sweden. Even if
he could, somehow, circulate an appeal to every
Swedish-born American and to their descendants—
without letting that appeal get into the hands of
anyone else—and even if they all agreed to
countenance the lie, there would still be thousands of
people who could testify that the diamond fields did
not exist. The press agent (and in some degree every
representative of Sweden in this country) would be
continually at the mercy of blackmailers who would
come to them and threaten to expose them. The cost
of buying silence would not be small. There would be,
in addition, all the geologists, jealous of the honor of
their profession, suspicious of the men on whose
testimony the original claim was made. Professional
jealousy of the opposite type might lead any geologist
to declare these men fakers. The press agent would
have to see to it that none of these hostile scientists
got their views into print.

To keep a lie alive, and to influence human minds effectively, something more than a single statement is needed. The press agent would have to furnish pictures; he might even try to fake some movies. He would have to give names of men and places. The bankers handling the loan would have to be either deluded or, if they were all dishonest, squared. If they sent their own engineers to Sweden, these would have to be bribed or intimidated or otherwise persuaded.

Not only will the press agent have to keep all facts about Swedish diamond fields out of the papers, he would also have to prevent the law from investigating. And behind all these difficulties, both the individual agent and the responsible Swedish officials would have the menace that if their lie was ever exposed, public confidence in them would be gone forever.

George Creel, chairman of the Committee on Public Information during the war, was accused of trying to keep a lie alive—the story of the submarine attack on American transports which was issued as a Fourth of July gift to the American people.[3] Creel, a newspaperman with an active conscience, devotes some 16 pages of his 1920 book, *How We Advertised America*, to a discussion of this story. He tells how the

---

[3] George Creel's (1876–1953) account concerned the press coverage of the first U.S Navy transports to arrive in Europe in late June 1917.

original cable came from U.S. Admiral Albert Gleaves, telling of submarines being beaten off; how the Secretary of the Navy refused to issue the dispatch verbatim (owing to fear that, by doing so, the Germans might break the American cypher), and how the elaborated dispatch was finally issued to the public. He then notes that the story was not questioned until an entirely anonymous group of American naval officers were reported as denying any submarine attack. The story was, at once, attacked as a hoax and Creel confesses that, in his defense, he used the word "cryptic" in regard to the original cable and the word "elaboration" in connection with the story as issued. These two words were made much of, and the impression spread that if anything at all occurred to the transports, it was something utterly trivial—perhaps the U.S. Navy fired at a piece of wreckage because it looked like a periscope—and that the Navy and the Committee had spun out the story.

Addressing these anonymous denials, Creel then quotes the long and detailed statement of the submarine attack (more elaborate than the first press story) as sent by Admiral Gleaves on the 12th of July, 1917. He quotes corroboration from the very newspapers which attacked the elaborate "hoax." And he confesses that "although disproved fully, the falsehood (i.e., the accusation against Creel of having sent out an untrue story) persisted to our hurt and discredit, and even to this day there are people honestly of the opinion that the initial troopships had a 'safe and uneventful voyage.'"

Creel was not trying to keep alive a lie. He was trying to make people believe an item of publicity which had *merely been questioned*. After three years of war news, the American people had become so suspicious of propaganda that even the faintest doubt cast on a piece of news served to turn them against it and *against its authors*. It was to the Committee's "hurt and discredit," said Creel, indicating how newspapers and readers looked askance at the Committee after the accusation of falsehood was made. Had the story been a lie—had there been no possibility of proving that submarines actually attacked—what would the position of the Committee and of Creel have been? If an unproved and anonymous denial caused so much trouble, what would an authoritative nailing of a lie have done?

In commerce, the difficulty of lying becomes enormous. The publisher of a famous work of reference guarantees that it is a new work, everything in it being especially written, and that the work is purely original, not founded or based upon any other similar work. A competing publishing house thereupon sends out a pamphlet of over 100 pages of parallel columns, indicating the identity of the work of reference with one published 60 years ago. If the original claim is a lie, keeping it effective will take an amount of ingenuity. These difficulties in the practice of lying are noted here because they indicate precisely the difficulties of telling the truth. Except in the fourth dimension, parallel lines do not meet, and twice five is always ten. The facts which can be expressed in an algebraic formula are absolutely true— but few of the facts of human relations are reducible to formula. Where is the truth to be found?

The Young Men's Christian Association (YMCA) in a large city was once preparing a campaign for funds and came for advice to a man professionally engaged in handling the relations of a great industrial concern with its public. The representatives of the YMCA said that they wished to set before the people "only the facts." There was not, in fact, any necessity for lying or for exaggeration; there was nothing to conceal. But the professional had to ask the amateurs what portion of the facts they proposed to make public. Certain statistics might be interesting to the average reader, but the complete catalogue of books in the library would make dull reading, and so would the detailed expenses of the club house. If the Y's tennis courts were superior to others and the rate charged per hour was correspondingly higher, the circumstances would take far too much explanation to make that fact good publicity. The members of the YMCA were finally persuaded that they really meant to make the public aware of those portions of the whole body of facts which were interesting to the average man and favorable to themselves.

In the complication of modern life, the average intelligent man is completely incapable of judging the truth of 95 percent of the information he receives. He has neither the equipment or knowledge necessary nor the time to investigate. The plausible and the incredible mingle with facts colored for special purposes and with accurate information, and there is no internal evidence for discrimination between them.

There is, however, an external measuring rod by which publicity can be judged: responsibility.

Chapter 6.
On Whose Authority?

IN TWO OF THE BLACKEST MOMENTS of the war, the people of England heard news of a great army rushing to their aid. The first occasion of this news was in 1914, after the retreat from Mons, when it seemed certain that the British Expeditionary Force would be annihilated and Paris be taken. The army of which the English heard comprised one million Russian soldiers who had sailed from a Baltic port, had disembarked in Scotland, and had been transported behind curtained railway carriage windows to Dover. These soldiers had been observed late at night at provincial railway stations, their strange language had been heard, and their exotic faces had been seen. At any moment they were due on the western front.

The second occasion was when the submarine warfare threatened to starve Great Britain, when tonnage and cargoes were lost in a terrifying rate, and Germany was commissioning new submarines faster than England could sink the old. At that moment announcement was made of the transports carrying American soldiers to France. Within the limits imposed by military necessity, the actual size of the American Expeditionary Force was made public, and precise figures on the rate of increase were given to the exhausted British on the home front.

The Russians in England constituted one of the great rumors of the war. Their existence was semi-officially denied; they never appeared at the Front. Yet in 1917 and 1918 there were still people who believed that the Russians had been in England. Perhaps the Russians had been sent back, perhaps they had rebelled at the Front, perhaps they had been annihilated—everything was possible, but many believed they had been there. The alleged appearance of Russians in England occurred at a time when publicity was totally neglected. A minimum of official news was issued, but communiqués were barren and unsatisfying. No responsible correspondents were given free rein to tell the public what was happening. Any rumor, consequently, was believed. A writer composed a fantasy in which Saint George appeared to a soldier at Mons and, when this was published, hundreds of thousands of people took it to be a statement of fact. Nurses wrote to the author assuring him that wounded soldiers had told them the story, and the basest motives were computed to the author, Arthur Machen, for insisting that, so far as he knew, his story was purely imaginative.[1] The public preferred

---

[1] Welsh author Arthur Machen published a short story called "The Bowmen" in the September 29, 1914 *London Evening News*. The piece, which offers a fictional first-hand perspective of Allied

to cling to a hallucination rather than be left without any information.

The British authorities knew perfectly well that the story of the Russians would have a disastrous effect on public morale, but they were helpless. They knew that as soon as the rumor exploded, the plight of the small British force would seem a hundred times worse, since no vast army of Russians on which the public was beginning to depend had come to its aid. Denial was laughed at; governments always deny anything during a war, and disproof was impossible.

The crux of the matter was that no one could tell how the rumor started. No single responsible person could be found to take the blame for the story, to withdraw it, and to dispel the illusion it had created.

The story of the American army was exact and official. Behind it stood the good faith of the American government and the personal reputations of the men over whose signatures the facts were made known. There could be no disappointment. Still, among the other announcements of the Committee on Public Information was a misleading story of American airplanes being shipped to France. This story was connected in the public mind with a correspondent's story that Secretary of War Newton Baker had seen "a thousand American airplanes in

---

forces calling on St. George to destroy the Germans, was not labeled as fiction.

France." In the midst of the war, when public confidence had to be kept up, the whole matter was aired in the papers, and the unhappy truth was brought out to check the enthusiastic lie.

Where responsibility exists, a lie in publicity can be checked, countered, and discredited.

Responsible publicity is the enemy of rumor. The individual or institution having relations with the public needs to establish a sense of responsibility more even than a reputation for accuracy. An error in a statement may be corrected without impugning good faith, but irresponsibility is fatal.

There are cases of the responsible publication of inaccuracies. A New York theatrical producer employed a witty press agent whose whole duty seemed to be the spreading of comic inaccuracies about his employer. The style was quickly recognized and it made the producer a special figure among his rivals. One read that he was going to London and to Chicago on the same day. Another read that he was going to produce Shakespeare in the manner of a bedroom farce. A complete, and completely false, personality was deliberately created. The public was in no way misled because the articles were signed by the name of the press agent who became responsible for their fantastic inaccuracies.

Responsibility in serious publicity is essential because it creates an authority which automatically commands attention. The name of the responsible person becomes a center around which favorable impressions crystallize. The General Electric Company, for example, has hundreds of diverse contacts with the public. In one year, according to Roger William Riis and Charles Bonner in their 1926 book *Publicity: A Study of the Development of Industrial News*, 76 items relating to that company appeared in the *New York Times*. The reader, learning from an official announcement that the price of incandescent lamps would be reduced, and finding them subsequently reduced in the shops, establishes two associations with the General Electric name. First, that its news is important to himself. Second, that it is trustworthy. Perhaps the next item he reads is that the company has been working on a new device to test heartbeats. This does not affect his pocket, but he finds it interesting, and he adds human interest to his associations with this concern and, vaguely, he adds the idea of scientific research. This last association is fortified by the next item: that chlorine gas has been tested for curing colds. Here his personal interest is intense, and an entirely new element is added to his complex: the company is interested in things outside of electricity. When he reads that employees are subscribing to the company's stock, he is ready to believe it (because he already associates truth with all announcements coming from the company), and it adds the impression of an industry which is fair to its workers.

In the end the reader, subconsciously, will at least have no prejudice against reading anything in which the name of the General Electric Company appears. This is all the more so because he will have no fear of insidious propaganda. Let him read that soap is bad for the complexion and he will say, "That was put out by a manufacturer of toilet articles for women." Let him read that scientists claim soap is best for the skin and he will suspect soap manufacturers. It is natural that the producers should spread favorable publicity, and natural that the citizen should be on guard. But that suspicion cuts under and destroys the very effect the publicity is supposed to create; it establishes a half-negative attitude with the resentment every man feels when he suspects that something is being "put over" on him. Against this resistance nothing is more potent than a frank avowal. Once the reader has found General Electric publicity interesting and accurate, his attitude toward an (imaginary) article in which the Company points out the superior merits of electric light, will be, "They say this because they make electric light bulbs. But they are honest about it—they put their name to it. And they have always told the truth before so there's at least a fifty-fifty chance that they're telling the truth now."

Publicity assails the average man on every side, and gradually he comes to distinguish two great classes: one is openly offered as publicity, bearing the name and authority of its source, and the other is anonymous, vague, and unsupported. And his experience in other fields inevitably leads the average man to the conviction that avowed publicity carries the presumption of truth, whereas hidden publicity carries the presumption of a weak case bolstered by unverifiable assertions, if not by downright falsehood. Unavowed publicity is an anonymous letter, an unsigned check. A man puts his name to things he is sure of and proud of. He omits it when he feels himself in danger. There is another daily more pressing danger, however, for the unattributed publicist who offers false information—the means of verification are becoming more numerous.

A century ago, a London newspaper, arriving in New York three weeks after publication, could announce that a monarch had been received with jubilation in the streets of his capital. Were a denial to be made, it would tarry three weeks behind the original story. By the time the denial came to New York the whole thing would be forgotten. Today, the moving picture record of events is spread before the public almost as rapidly as the newspaper account. The fanciful accounts of public enthusiasm in Havana, when the Pan-American conference met there in early

1928, were made to appear foolish by the newsreels of a calm and rather bored populace. A prize fighter's manager can no longer claim a foul with impunity, because the pictures can be analyzed. The newspaper which publishes a false account runs the risk of having the truth not only published in rival papers, but broadcast by radio. If Benjamin Franklin had been assaulted in the streets of Paris and the news come to America, the two countries might have been at war before any adequate check on the report had been found. If hoodlums throw stones at American sightseers today, the report flashes quickly to America, but counteracting reports come as quickly— not only the news, but the comparative significance of the news is verified. Tens of thousands of returning travelers report courteous treatment; moving pictures show that, in Paris, the American Legion cheered at the Place de L'Etoile[2] and Lindberg mobbed by admirers. These verifications strike at the heart of false publicity because it is impossible to repeat a lie after the truth is known. Publicity, which lives on repetition, is compelled to stick to statements which can be verified.

---

[2] The Place de L'Etoile is a large road junction in Paris, France, that involves 12 straight avenues and the Champs-Élysées. This is now called the Place Charles de Gaulle.

During Grover Cleveland's first candidacy for president in 1884, a whispering campaign concerning his morals was started. The exact details were, of course, not known, but the whispers continued and became so circumstantial that Cleveland's managers finally wired him asking what to say about the scandal. His reply was, "Tell the truth."[3] Before the 1928 presidential conventions, Senator James Thomas Heflin[4] made a number of unsubstantiated accusations about several candidates for the presidential nomination. The *New York World's* editorial comment was extremely hostile to Heflin, but even in his anger, the writer of it confesses the whole case for publicity of the most partisan and even dishonest type in opposition to rumor:

> There are some advantages in having Heflin talk. Every campaign is carried on in part by public speeches and, in part, by malignant whispers. No public man of our time has escaped the whispers. Citizens recall how among recent public men the charges have been whispered about that they were drunkards, that they were unfaithful, that they were of the dubious parentage, and so forth. Until the rise

---

[3] Cleveland was dogged by rumors that he had fathered an illegitimate boy. He admitted paternity of the child.

[4] James Thomas Heflin (1869–1951), a Democratic senator from Alabama, was a proponent of white supremacy. An anti-Catholic, he spoke openly against Al Smith, the Democratic Party's 1928 presidential nominee, and a Catholic.

of Senator Heflin, a public man was the helpless victim of such whispering campaigns. It took years for Roosevelt to catch an obscure editor and have him up on a charge of libel. Wilson never got a chance to deal with his traducers. But, with Heflin in the field, we have the satisfaction of knowing that the most poisonous insinuation of the lowest slanderers will be publicly expounded at $250 a lecture. There won't be anything to whisper about in this campaign if only Heflin can be induced to keep on. He will bellow it to the heavens, and that is a good thing in a campaign which, without him, might be unusually rich in whispered slander.

A peculiarly involved method of spreading rumors, under the appearance of the utmost frankness, occurred in the case of the 1926 novel *Revelry* by Samuel Hopkins Adams. It was—and it was meant to be—common knowledge that the central figure of this book was the late President Warren G. Harding. The book dealt with scandals during Harding's term and was populated by easily identifiable figures of his cabinet and among his intimate acquaintances. About the taste and tact of the writer of any scandalous chronicle there will always be discussion. In this case, these questions are not as important as that of the right to give the impression of fact without giving facts themselves, when these pseudo-facts are not subject to refutation.

It is not only that iconoclasm[5] concerning the presidential office is a disservice to the American people. At whatever point the author deviated from the exact facts he was entitled to plead the privilege of the writer of fiction. Yet the average reader to whom this book was addressed would be totally incapable of making the distinction between fact and fiction, and recognizing fact in one place would, by assimilation, give the authority of fact to what was, in essence, false.

There was published at about the same time another book about the dead president purporting to be the entirely true story of his relation to a woman who bore him a child.[6] Here also questions of ethics arise for, even if the entire story were slander excepting a single dubious episode, it was still unlikely that the relatives of a dead president would bring the subject to the publicity of the courts. Yet the writer of this second book was ethically on higher ground than the author of *Revelry* because the entire book was told as fact and was subject in every detail to attack and refutation.

---

[5] "Iconoclasm" is a term normally applied to the destruction of religious icons (e.g., images, monuments), or images of colonization, for religious or political motives.

[6] *The President's Daughter* was published by Nan Britton in 1927. She alleged that her affair with Harding resulted in the birth of a daughter. Although this claim was long disputed, DNA tests in 2015 revealed that Harding was, indeed, the child's father.

In this connection it may be noted that one of
the most common tricks among blackmailers is to
threaten suit. Since newspapers are privileged to
publish whatever transpires in a court of law, and
since shoddy lawyers manage to bring up irrelevant
matters, and to insinuate what they cannot prove,
honest men in the public eye do their utmost to avoid
suits of this sort. In many cases, blackmailers threaten
to go to newspapers with their rumors and, if that
fails, say they will sue. The most effective reply, as
always, is to acquaint the newspapers with the facts in
the case and to warn them that they are being used as
tools by blackmailers. Newspapers of any standing
reject the ruse as they always reject rumor.

The Pennsylvania Railroad several years ago
made itself responsible for complete and accurate
reports of wrecks. Rare as they have become, railroad
wrecks are—perhaps because of their rarity—given
enormous news space; they are of universal human
interest. If they no longer act as a deterrent to travel,
they still serve to warn the public against a careless
road if a road with a clean record competes in the
same territory. Naturally one would assume that
railroads would be anxious to keep the news of wrecks
down to a minimum, and to belittle the tale of deaths
and injuries. Yet the Pennsylvania has adopted the
policy of complete publicity. This policy was, in a
sense, a matter of self-defense. A few years ago, the

Associated Press (AP) circulated a dispatch from
Pittsburgh about a wreck on the Pennsylvania in
which 11 persons were reported injured. Their names
were given. The narrative had every appearance of
accuracy. The publicity man on the staff of the
president of the Pennsylvania telephoned to
Pittsburgh for the facts. He found that one car had
jumped the track, had been quickly put back on the
rails, and the train had gone on. The claim agent off
the road had come to the car and interviewed every
passenger, inquiring especially whether any one
wished to make a claim for damages. Not a single
claim was made—a rare thing after any accident, no
matter how trivial. The publicity man thereupon
informed the AP that their report had been incorrect
and gave the facts. The AP, responsible to its
members, instantly investigated and reported back
that the report of the wreck had come from a member
newspaper in Pittsburgh, a responsible and regular
source of news. The story had been written by a
reporter on that paper, and the AP felt bound to
circulate the story as it came to them.

This was, apparently, a deadlock. The
Pennsylvania's publicity man seemed to drop the
matter, only requesting AP General Manager Melville
Stone to remember the incident. A searching inquiry
now was made and it transpired that, when the car
jumped the tracks, a passing suburban train stopped

and a reporter ran from it to the derailed car. Excited at being present at the making of an exclusive story, he assumed that all the passengers on the car must have been somewhat injured—by shock if in no other way. He took the names and addresses and hurried to get the story into print, sending it to the AP with the names of the eleven "injured." Responsibility in this case was fixed, and authority found wanting. The Pennsylvania Railroad naturally wished to prevent a recurrence and the AP, jealous of its reputation for accuracy, was sympathetic. But Stone initially demurred when the following proposal was made:

> Whenever there is an accident on the Pennsylvania Railroad, the company's representative will gather all the facts and give them to you. If you ever find that the company is not candid, you are asked to disregard this agreement. But, until then, you are asked to accept no report as authentic unless the company corroborates it.

The publicity man was able to assure Stone that the whole good faith of the Pennsylvania Railroad was behind his proposal, and it was reluctantly accepted. More than fifteen years have passed and the plan is still in operation. The newspapers served by it have found that the railroad, sticking to its bargain, has consistently given them fuller and more accurate accounts than their own men have been able to gather at random. The good faith of the company has never been in the slightest question, and its responsibility for news by nature unfavorable to itself has proved absolutely dependable.

In an autocracy, or in a highly centralized paternalistic government, it may be possible to use the law to protect the public from publicity. In a democracy based on freedom for the individual, responsibility remains the governor and check-rein for publicity. It is the citizen's business to recognize and use the safeguard which is put into his hands.

Chapter 7.
Conditioning the Public

IF A GONG IS SOUNDED EVERY TIME food is placed before a dog, at the end of a few days the dog will respond to the gong when no food is offered precisely as he does to food. His mouth will water and he will show all the outward symptoms of lively hunger. If, several weeks later, an angry tomcat displaces the food when the gong rings, at the end of several days the dog will show symptoms of fear and rage, instead of hungry anticipation, whenever the gong sounds. This process of conditioning and re-conditioning works as effectively for human beings. With babies it works rapidly, with children more slowly, with grown men and women it is a long and laborious operation. It is one of the fundamentals of effective publicity.

In the 1830s, the French people were suffering the aftermath of the Napoleonic era. The oppressive terms of the Congress of Vienna were reflected in the hard lives of the middle class.[1] The country still suffered from the loss of blood due to Napoleon I's

---

[1] The Congress of Vienna was held from late 1814 until the summer of 1815 to determine peace terms in the aftermath of the Napoleonic Wars. France lost all territories that came from its military victories.

wars and from the loss of prestige due to his failure.
The country wanted peace (which it could have only
by repudiating all Napoleonic schemes) and prosperity
(which it could have only through a stable
government). The name of Napoleon I symbolized
warfare, disaster, and disruption.

One man who bore that name remained in the
public eye: Emperor Louis Napoleon III who, after an
abortive uprising in his favor, was banished from
France. Without the benefit of press agents and
public relations counsels, he promptly set to work to
re-condition the mind of all France, to associate with
the name of Napoleon everything desirable to the
French people, and to dissociate from it everything
undesirable. He was exiled, and sometimes a prisoner,
but his propaganda was so successful he became, in
turn, deputy, president, and finally Emperor of
France.[2] It is precisely as if the ex-Crown Prince of
Germany were today at work transforming the spirit
of the German people, making them forget the
disasters of the Great War, and preparing them for
the restoration of the Hohenzollern dynasty with
himself as Kaiser.[3]

---

[2] Napoleon Bonaparte III (1808–1873) was in exile from 1836–1848,
the result of his failed coup attempts in France. He became the
first president of France in 1848.

[3] The House of Hohenzollern traces itself back to princes, kings and
emperors in the German Empire and other principalities like
Prussia and Romania.

Napoleon III was both nephew and step-grandson of Napoleon I. His first business was to persuade the French people that he was, in some mysterious way, the true inheritor of the Napoleonic ideal (although the emperor's son, Napoleon II, still lived at the beginning of this propaganda). Napoleon III allowed the emperor's son to be associated with the disasters of the Napoleonic era, since the consumptive young man lived at the Austrian court. For himself, Napoleon III stood for the purely French side of Napoleon, for glory and for democracy. After the death of Napoleon II, the propaganda took another turn. Napoleon III became openly the pretender to the throne of France and, at the same time, declared himself a republican in spirit. He worried about the slightest detail which could impress the French public. As Philip Guedalla said in his 1922 book *The Second Empire*, "with the assistance of his barber...a mustache was retained as an indication to the world that he was a soldier...but the beard vanished...and in his uniform he looked like any slim young officer of the French army..." This was keeping alive the tradition of glory.

At the same time, Napoleon III was making himself the spokesman for those liberal ideas which were becoming popular with all the dissatisfied elements of society. He did not openly attack King

Louis Philippe.[4] Instead he wrote a book about
Switzerland into which he studiously insinuated an
entirely new portrait of Napoleon I, who appeared as
"the plebeian emperor" and the friend of suppressed
nations. There were enough of these suppressed
nationalities to make European diplomacy difficult in
1833, and the young man explained that, if his uncle
had won at Waterloo, Poland, and Germany and Italy
would each have become a separate nation. In France,
he continued, "a liberal regime would have supplanted
the dictatorship; and everywhere there would have
been stability, liberty, and independence..."[5] Briefly
Napoleon III was making his uncle's name (and his
own) a rallying point for the deeply felt wants of the
French people and, at the same time, he was cutting
off from that name all the associations with disaster.
He was offering Napoleon I (and by implication,
Napoleon III) as the standard-bearer of democracy—
an ideal in France during the reactionary years
following the Congress of Vienna. He followed this
work with a manual of artillery which reminded the
French that Napoleon I had begun as an officer in
that branch of military service, and that Napoleon III
was studying all the problems which an emperor
needed to solve. The propaganda was continuous, but

---

[4] Louis Philippe ruled as French monarch from 1830–1848.

[5] Napoleon III wrote extensive reviews of political and military
events in late 1831 and early 1832 that included these observations.

it never became tiresome because it varied the method while keeping the object continually in view.

The next move was action. In 1836, Napoleon III and a few friends attempted to seize the French garrison at Strasbourg and, with it, to overthrow the monarchy. It was a failed attempt, but while his followers were giving him splendid publicity through the persecutions of the French government, he returned to Switzerland. The French attempted to hound him out. Napoleon III stayed on until a whole army corps was mobilized at the Swiss border. Then, having in this way convinced the French people that he was a person of supreme importance, he persuaded them that he had no private ambitions—he had only *their* interests at heart—and left Switzerland for England. In just a few years, Napoleon III had established himself as the rightful heir of Napoleon I: he had impressed all of France with his intelligence and his importance. He had broken down the anti-Napoleonic prejudice, and kept alive the strong nationalistic spirit which Napoleon I and the Revolution had created. He had made himself the center for liberal and democratic ideas.

Napoleon III's friends published portraits showing that he was the image of Napoleon I with "the same finely proportioned nose [and] the same gray eyes," noted Blanchard Jerrold in his 1874 book *The Life of Napoleon III*. Two newspapers supporting

him were published in Paris, there was a constant
stream of pamphlets, and clubs of old soldiers were
founded. The French were reminded by caricature
and by sarcastic oratory that once their monarch
carried a banner and a sword, and that their present
King, Louis Philippe, carried an umbrella! In the
summer of 1840, Napoleon III, after a characteristic
address to the French public that contrasted his exile
with the glories of his ancestor, made another attempt
to invade France. On the boat from England he
carried with him an eagle—it was really a vulture, but
it was called an eagle—the symbol of Napoleon I. He
was captured and imprisoned. In May of 1846 he
escaped from jail and, in 1848, there was a revolution
in France. For months the government of France was
alternately carried on by dictators who could not
dictate and by rioters in the streets of Paris. One man
remained the people's friend—Napoleon III. He
stood for order, which was dearly desired, and he had
written (in 1844) the book *The Extinction of Pauperism*.
Cries of *Vive Napoleon* went up in the streets of Paris.

Gucdalla's book brilliantly describes the
complicated propaganda which Napoleon III then
undertook:

> In the last week of May he made a serious move
> into French politics.... He wrote an indignant letter
> demanding his rights as a French citizen; and his
> friends had already taken drastic steps...by a

candidature opened in his name at the by-elections....
A handful of workers...were covering the town with
hand-bills, small posters, and brass medals detailing
the virtues, the credentials, the sufferings, the
principals of Louis Napoleon Bonaparte.... The
Bonapartist committee worked desperately; street
musicians were even hired to give a Napoleonic turn
to their performance and prophetic sleepwalkers
murmured the Prince's name. A great crowd waited
outside the Hôtel de Ville to hear the result. The
Prince was in, and the hats went up with a great
cheer. Louis Napoleon had arrived, in June 1848, at
his first public position in France; he was a Deputy
for Paris.

He was still, however, in exile. He let his
enthusiasts work for him while he remained in
London and heard of nightly meetings of Bonapartists
on the boulevards who offered, said Guedalla, "a spate
of little papers with cuts of the emperor and his
nephew, echoing with prophecies. Crowds paraded
the streets all day...and the Place de la Concorde was
full of men selling little tricolor flags seditiously
inscribed 'Vive le Prince Louis.'" The National Guard
was called out, and there was a small riot in the
streets. It was clear that Napoleon III was so
powerful that the government could not permit him
to take his place as an elected deputy.

In September 1848, after a terrible massacre in
the streets of Paris, Napoleon III was elected to a

seat in the National Assembly as a representative of true democracy, of the order, and of mild socialistic friendliness to the lower classes. His first speech was a statement of his devotion to the Republic. Three months later, with more than 74 percent of the vote, he had been elected president.

Over the next several years, Napoleon III re-cast his leadership from that of president to emperor. The steps by which the French mind—now accustomed to the name of Napoleon in a new significance—was prepared for the return of a Napoleonic emperor were similar. Protesting adherence to the constitution, the president usurped power, handed it back, put down rioting with a firm hand, backed a military enterprise in Rome,[6] and by its success, restored French prestige and the tradition of the first Napoleon. Slowly, he persuaded the people that the deputies and the ministers stood in the way of orderly progress, and that he needed a free hand. "The name of Napoleon," he announced, "is in itself a program; it stands for order, authority, religion and the welfare of the people in internal affairs, and for national dignity in foreign affairs." And he appealed directly to the people, over the heads of their deputies, to support him.

---

[6] During his presidential term, Napoleon III had authorized a French force in Rome to fight, if necessary, to protect the papacy of Pope Pius IX, who had been threatened by the Italian military.

He opened new railways and laid foundation stones, and issued bonuses of triple pay to regiments which cried, "Vive l'Empereur" on parade. He suggested that if the people wanted to lay a still heavier burden on his shoulders, he would be a deserter if he refused. He manufactured a foreign war in Rome and, out of it, cast himself as a popular military hero to lead the army in favor of the French Empire. In the last days of the Republic, the very coins used by the people spread the propaganda. On one side they bore the legend "Republique Française" and, on the other, "Napoléon Empereur." It was a contradiction in terms, but the prince-president had manipulated the mind of the people so that they did not notice it. Finally, he asked the people of France to put their seal of approval on a fact. He had dispensed with ministers and deputies. He had restored the eagles to the standards of the army. He was, in fact, emperor. And the people, by an overwhelming majority to which his appointees contributed something more than their votes, elected him emperor in December 1852.

Chapter 8.
The Napoleonic Touch in Alabama

AS SEEN IN THE PREVIOUS CHAPTER, the details
of the Napoleonic campaign are all connected with
the basic psychological fact that it is possible to divert
the attention of people and to create in their minds
new associations with words and things. Whether this
sort of manipulation of the public is a desirable thing
or not remains to be seen. To some it may appear as
the worst type of trickery; to another this change in
associations may seem the path of all progress. The
significant thing to the student of publicity is that it
exists, and that men's minds are being constantly
made over by removing prejudices and substituting
favorable reactions. This is the natural behavior of the
mind, and we have seen it in action in a case involving
not only the value of a symbol (Napoleon) but the
form of a nation's government. Publicity put
Napoleon III on a throne, and the carefully false
publicity of the Ems telegram, as given to the press by
Bismarck, helped to unseat him, to start the Franco-
Prussian War, and thus to prepare for the War of
1914.[1]

---

[1] In the summer of 1870, the Ems telegram was a message from the
King of Prussia to German Chancellor Otto Van Bismarck. The
telegram, which the King authorized Bismarck to release, alleged

In the field of industry, the range is more limited, the questions involved not quite so far-reaching but, underneath the details, the same principles are in operation. The supply of electric power in Alabama is in the hands of the Alabama Power Company, an organization which, in 1920, was so unpopular in the territory it served that 99.1% of the newspapers in Alabama were hostile to it. The company suffered the general disfavor, prevalent at the time, of a public which was suspicious of monopolies, disliked large corporations engaged in public service, and had, or imagined, grievances. The company had a plan in regard to Muscle Shoals which found no favor with the public. Whether the public was justified is beside the point. In 1920 the name of the Alabama Power Company was anathema.

In 1924, according to *Forbes*, which awarded the company a silver cup "for the best public relations work done during the preceding year," the position of the power company in regard to its public had so far been changed that 92.6% of the newspapers of Alabama were heartily co-operating with its program and frequently praised the company and its service to the state in their editorial columns. This change in public opinion, of which the newspapers are, in the long run, an adequate mirror, was achieved by creating

---

that a French ambassador to Prussia had acted rudely to the King. France subsequently declared war that summer.

an entirely new series of associations in the minds of
the public. What had once appeared as a grasping
monopoly, with no interest in public service, gradually
became a state institution devoted to the highest
good of the citizens.

The company made a spectacular arrival on the
Alabama scene as the enemy of the boll weevil. The
chemical most destructive to this pest (which
threatened the fortune of every cotton raiser and of
every enterprise depending upon the prosperity of the
state as a whole) was found to be calcium arsenate. As
soon as this discovery was known, cotton planters
began to use calcium arsenate in such quantities that
neither current supplies nor current production could
keep up with them. The price of the commodity
naturally soared. The company then found a way to
use an electrolytic process to efficiently make more of
calcium arsenate which, in turn, led to its wider
availability at affordable prices.

The company—now the enemy of the boll
weevil, and the supplier of chemicals at reasonable
prices—found less difficulty in persuading farmers to
electrify their plant. The next step was to establish
experimental stations in the use of electricity in farms
and in agricultural homesteads. The actual problems
of the farmer were solved by the method of trial and
error. The company appeared as a group of individuals
sharing the common life of the neighborhood it

served, not as a disembodied corporation looking out
only for its own dividends. For three years, the
company advertised Alabama in national magazines.
The advertisements were devoted to the industrial
advantages of specific localities, noting natural
advantages, labor conditions, the laws governing taxes,
and whatever else could induce manufacturers to
locate their plants there. Moving pictures, circulars,
radio broadcasting, booths at expositions, and
personal solicitation were used in the same campaign.
These efforts resulted in a jump in cotton mill
spindles from 79,000 up to 1.5 million, with other
industries like steel, cement, and wood working also
increasing.

Among other activities in the same campaign for
capturing good will, the company presented
thoroughbred stock to agricultural groups, it made
donations to educational institutions, and established
scholarships and a system of drawing employees from
the graduates. It cooperated with other agencies in
spreading accurate data on crops and farming
methods, and placed its broadcasting station at the
disposal of the various chambers of commerce in the
state. It helped restock the waters of the state with
game and food fish by throwing open its reservoirs to
the state for use as a hatchery.

In some of these activities, such as inducing
manufacturers to establish plants in Alabama, the

company gained directly in the sale of power. But, for the most part, the gain was indirect. The complex of prejudices which surrounded the name of the company had been dissipated. In its place was a new closely-woven web of ideas: the company as scientific enemy of the boll weevil, the company as participant in the progress of the state, the company as stock-breeder, the company as a friend to education, the company as a good sport, the company as an aid to the fisherman.

It is an operation comparable to lifting a cataract from a man's eye and then giving him glasses with powerful lenses. He sees things in a new light.

Part III

The Forms of Publicity—
Short-Term and Long-Term

Chapter 9.
The Stunt

THE PRECEDING CHAPTERS HAVE outlined the
scope of publicity, showing its relation on one side to
a universal habit of mankind—the habit of influencing
others—and, on the other side, to the special activity
of war propaganda. The difficulty of arriving at the
truth has been matched with the necessity for
responsible utterance, on the assumption that a
signed lie can be traced and refuted more easily than a
nameless insinuation. The twin instances of Napoleon
III and the Alabama Power Company have illustrated
the effectiveness of responsible publicity in re-
working the public mind, turning it from old
prejudices to new allegiance.

Although specialists in both advertising and
general publicity sometimes try to invent an essential
distinction between them, the common instinct to
consider them together is correct. Advertising is a
particular kind of publicity, subject to whatever "laws"
hold good for any other kind. This chapter, and the
three after it, approach publicity largely through
advertising, as it is a microcosm in which the
workings of general publicity can be suitably analyzed.

The simplest form of publicity is calling
attention. The great majority of human beings are

busy about their own affairs and, if we want them to attend to ours, to give us their money or their votes, we have forcibly to detach their attention from their own preoccupations and turn it to those which interest us. This is preeminently the field of the stunt. One of the stories common in newspaper offices tells us how Mary Garden bet the owner of a newspaper that she could get her name on the first page of his paper every day for a month.[1] With her colorful and picturesque personality figuring in the public eye, she had no difficulty until the last day when she had exhausted all her ingenuity in stunts. On the eve of the last day, she simply called in the reporters and told them about the bet. It made the front page.

Short-term publicity has to content itself largely with a call to attention from the outset. Except in the larger cities, there is no time for people to say, "You must go to the circus, we went last week and enjoyed it enormously." The suggestion to go to the circus must come from the circus itself. Ballyhoo is the life of the circus, and P.T. Barnum knew it. He bought a herd of buffalo to the New York City area and announced that they were the last surviving monarchs of the plains, and that they were being shipped to England. He corralled them on the New Jersey side

---

[1] Mary Garden (1874–1967) was an opera singer and actress who achieved widespread recognition from 1910 to 1932, primarily performing in Chicago.

and announced that they would be on free view, with
roping and riding as added free attractions, for a
weekend. The sentimental ballyhoo over these
animals was terrific. The patriotic gesture of affording
New Yorkers a last free view of the animals was
widely commented on. Crowds flocked to New Jersey
on a Saturday and Sunday and saw a tame collection of
beasts and some very bad riding. But as they had paid
no money to the view the attraction, they had no kick
coming.[2] Barnum, however, had chartered all the
ferries for the two days—the fare was then twelve and
a half cents—and still made a tidy sum of money.

Another time, Barnum bought Jumbo, the largest
elephant in captivity, from the London Zoological
Gardens. After the sale was completed, he let it be
known that he was thinking of taking Jumbo to
America. He got some of his friends to write letters to
the London papers mentioning the rumor that Jumbo
was to depart; the letters asked what the little
children would think. Immediately the little children
began to shower the papers with pleading letters
asking them to stop the dreadful Yankee from taking

---

[2] To have a "kick coming" is to have a complaint. For example, a late
19th century locomotive trade magazine said, "We all admire the
man who stands up...and kicks when he has a kick coming, but we
have no use for the man who is always finding fault..."

away their Jumbo.[3] National pride was aroused.
Petitions were signed by the yard. Jumbo appeared in
doggerel in the music halls; there were protests
everywhere and the thing became almost an
international issue. Barnum cashed in on it in London,
keeping Jumbo there longer than originally announced
in order to give every little boy and girl a chance to
ride on Jumbo's back. The ballyhoo kept up with
descriptions of the final parting from the zoo, with
the difficulties of loading Jumbo into the ship, and
with details of his food. The ballyhoo began again in
New York where, upon Jumbo's arrival, all the details
of the London campaign had been copied. Within
countless columns of free advertising, Jumbo became
a first-class attraction and remained so to his death in
1885—his name still is used as the symbol for the
elephant.

Edna Wallace Hopper, star of the Broadway
musical *Florodora,* felt that life was hardly worth living
if she did not get to the horse races.[4] But *Florodora*
was a hit, and she could not get away on Saturday
afternoons. So, one day, she bought out the entire
rack of tickets, had the house closed, and tripped off

---

[3] Circus impresario P.T. Barnum (1810–1891) purchased Jumbo from
the London Zoo in November 1881; more than 100,000 children
wrote to Queen Victoria protesting the sale.

[4] Edna Wallace Hopper (1872–1959) was a stage and silent film
actress.

to see the horses run. She was photographed going and coming and cheering the winners. Her check for $2,500 was photographed and reproduced in the papers. The publicity accruing to the show was worth ten times what it cost.

One of the earlier skyscraper hotels in New York City worked with an enterprising violinist to give New York a scientific demonstration. The violinist claimed that the vibration of his G-string, played at the proper place, would shake the hotel to its foundations, probably demolishing it. The announcement came from the violinist's manager; the hotel genially agreed to the test. A model of the hotel was made and obligingly fell when the G-string was scraped. Scientists declared for and against the predicted result of the test. On the day of the experiment, a vast crowd gathered, but it rained. There was more publicity. Eventually the whole thing ended in nothing—but, by that time, the public had forgotten the promise and the only things fixed in its mind, for a brief moment, were the name of the hotel and the name of the violinist.[5]

---

[5] In August 1903, *The Lutheran Observer* quoted an architect: "...I will venture to say you would never expect violin playing to injure the walls of a building. Yet that is certainly the case...The vibrations of a violin are something terrible in their unseen, unbound force, and when they come in contact with regularity they bear their influence upon structures of stone, brick or iron."

Stunt publicity, as all these examples indicate, is a means of creating curiosity. As readers of detective fiction know, nothing is deader than curiosity when it has been satisfied. That is why stunt publicity is effective only over a short period. The circus which comes to town for one day needs nothing more. The gaudy billboards, the exotic animals, the parade and the calliope, all concentrate curiosity which can be satisfied at once. The circus does not make its chief bid for people who come three or four times; it wants everybody to come once. The publicity is exaggerated, comic, tricky, and sometimes downright lying. But there is no check-up. The matter is not of the highest importance. If there is no proof that Joice Heth was really the nurse of George Washington, there is no disproof.[6] No one cares. Curiosity is satisfied merely by seeing how the ballyhoo artist has managed to trick you.

Stunt publicity is the open field for irresponsibility. One reads that all the girls in a revue are graduates of a convent, or that they are all devoted to reading or to their mothers. No one checks up the facts; no one investigates to see on whose authority these facts get into the papers. The Sunday newspaper

---

[6] Joice Heth (1756–1836), an African-American slave and part of Barnum's shows, was advertised in 1835 as the 161-year-old former nurse of George Washington. After she died in 1836, Barnum admitted the hoax.

dramatic sections print press agent stuff, especially if it is interesting, knowing all the time that it has been written with no intention of literal accuracy while expecting the readers to know that, too. No patron of the Ziegfeld Follies has ever sued Ziegfeld because he discovered that one of the showgirls never had the pearls she said were given to her by a Grand Duke. No one has ever tried to wreck a sideshow because the fat woman was not the fattest woman on earth.

The more limited the object, the more its publicity can be tricky. Little children buy a penny bag of popcorn advertised to contain in addition a "prize" of incalculable worth. The prize is stunt publicity—irresponsible and exaggerated. But when one comes to buy a motor car for $10,000 one looks beyond the cut glass flower holder and the trick cigar lighter; one examines the motor and gets expert opinion, tries out the car, and looks into the dependability of the manufacturer. If a manufacturer guarantees that a car will run 18 miles on a gallon of gasoline and the car runs only on ten, there is redress within the law.

Without discredit to stunts worked for legitimate purposes, it is clear that they can be employed for fraud where consistent, logical, and long-term publicity could not be used. It is, of course, the object of publicity, rather than the method, which gives a good or evil character to the work. A hospital may engage in a brief and startling campaign for funds, and may risk doing undignified things to waken public sympathy. The purpose, however, remains a good one, and the fact that the hospital continues to exist in the community gives some assurance of honesty. In contrast, a salesman for fraudulent oil stock may conduct a campaign which seems entirely ethical, yet rob all his customers.

The check on dishonesty lies in this: that no fraudulent publicity can be successful in the long run. Fraudulent stunt publicity is a sky rocket. Its flair is more brilliant than a steady light, but even a succession of sky rockets would hardly be used to illuminate a city.

Chapter 10.
The Long Run

A VIOLENT EXPLOSION WILL CAUSE a man to jump. A subdued, regular drumbeat will make him leave home and family, suffer privations, and face death in war. The explosion is stunt publicity; the drumbeat, varied with the fife, the bugle and the trumpet call, is the power of consecutive, reiterated publicity. It catches attention without startling, and it does not stop there. It holds attention, concentrating all the faculties on a desirable object, helping to create wants by showing how they can be satisfied.

A layman riding in the cab of a locomotive, deafened by the roar, noticed with surprise that the fireman and engineer were carrying on a perfectly calm conversation, apparently in normal tones, all through the trip. At the end of the trip, he asked the engineer how he managed to hear the fireman's voice over the roar of the train. The engineer replied, "The roar is the one thing I don't hear. What I listen for is any unusual noise." The blatancy of some forms of advertising in the past was discredited because as soon everyone began to shout, no one was heard. The still small voice of the advertiser who dropped all reckless claims and startling effects, and, instead, turned to the "unusual noise" made by neat typography and composition, good drawings, attractive colors, and a sufficient amount of white space to set off his type, was heard under and over the roar of stunt advertising and stunt publicity. This unusual noise was persistent, varied, and adapted to its circumstances. It held attention.

The prime value of advertising, to the advertiser, is that he writes his own headlines. The best piece of newsworthy publicity sent out is subject to the blue pencil of the copy desk of the newspaper and to the chance that a run of big stories will utterly swamp it. The familiar Monday morning press agent story is due to the fact that news items of great importance seldom develop over Sunday. But if a radio manufacturer were to announce for publication Monday that he had perfected machinery for speaking to Mars and had actually received something which might be an answer from Mars, while on the previous Sunday evening Lake Michigan had been swept by a tornado so that half of the Chicago lakefront was either destroyed or under water, the Chicago papers would probably bury the Mars story on the fifteenth page.

The *New York Times* was once offered an extraordinarily interesting story as exclusive news if it promised first-page position. The paper's managing editor replied with regret that it was the unalterable rule of the *Times* never to promise position to stories. The advertiser insures against this editorial supervision. He buys space, and frequently buys preferred space. Nor is his advertisement cut, nor, within the bounds of decency, is it censored. Before a nation of headline readers, the advertiser creates his own headline. Similarly in England, before American advertising methods were adopted, advertising copy adapted itself to the standards of news and editorials. Several of the most successful advertising campaigns were series of little editorials distinguished from those of the newspaper in which they appeared by a little picture or a signature, but thoroughly in the editorial tone.

Textbooks on advertising have been appearing in America for many years. Some of them, like textbooks on publicity, are written by professionals, and attempt to make a mystery of the business, trying to prevent the average man from seeing that advertising, like all publicity, is the application of common sense to the obvious. The technicalities are numerous, while the fundamentals are few and simple. And just as there is no mystery about publicity, there is none about that part of publicity which is paid for and is called advertising. In France, advertising is called *publicité*, with entire correctness since its object is to make things public. The root of the English word is equally illuminating: it suggests "to turn the attention toward a thing." Publicity is, in a certain degree, passive. It sends a curtain up or lets a light in. Advertising is more aggressive, paying cash for the privilege of an unrestricted appeal to the public.

The sign "Danger—Blasting Going On" is in a sense advertising because it calls attention. But the object is not one for which most people would care. Commercial advertising wants to call favorable attention. A new product often begins with a week of advertising of simply the name. On the theory that any new thing evokes curiosity, the name may not even suggest the nature of the product, and people are supposed to wonder whether "Ookums" stands for a new confection, a silk stocking, a disinfectant, or a dog biscuit. The theory is correct: "repetition is reputation" and it becomes a question only of how long the monotonous, unsupported repetition of a name will hold attention.[1] The moment the public says, "That's old stuff", the effectiveness of the advertising is gone.

But once a name is fixed in the mind, it becomes a nail on which any picture may be hung. If the unknown Mr. Johnson wishes to sell airplanes, he will have to persuade the people of a hundred things: of the stability of his organization, of the excellence and safety and speed of his planes, of the scientific

---

[1] "Repetition is reputation and reputation makes customers," has been attributed to Florence Nightingale Graham (1878–1966), the businesswomen who built the Elizabeth Arden line of cosmetics that appeared in salons around the world beginning in 1915.

character of his experts. Henry Ford had no need to do any of these things. He has recently been publishing a series of advertisements concerning the romance of flying, omitting all persuasion, because his name automatically cancels all the preliminary questions.

"What we attend to controls our behavior," says Professor Harry Overstreet, "What we can get others to attend to controls their behavior."[2] Yet we attend to many things in order to satisfy some primal curiosity and then possibly turn from these things with dislike. For instance, the shop windows which attract the largest crowds are those in which a man or woman is doing something—writing with a new fountain pen, demonstrating a sweeper, or exhibiting an unusual capacity to add up columns and figures. These draw the crowds when they are new because movement always attracts the eye and, even when the crowd is so thick that the passerby cannot see any movement, the crowd itself attracts. Perhaps, in the early days of man's life on earth, movement indicated danger—a wild beast or an enemy fluttering the underbrush. The eye remains irresistibly attracted to movement, whereas the ear has, to an extent,

---

[2] Harry Overstreet (1875–1970) was a professor who was chair of the Department of Philosophy and Psychology at City College of New York from 1911 to 1936. This quote comes from his 1926 book *Influencing Human Behavior*.

atrophied and many people are unconscious of changes of pitch or tone. But the fact that the eye attends does not always mean that the mind responds favorably. The animated shop window holds attention fleetingly unless the object shown has some inherent quality to keep people interested and to bring them into the shop to buy. The spectacle of a salesgirl putting on and taking off a tiara in Tiffany's window on Fifth Avenue might attract attention because it would be both novel and inappropriate, but it would hardly help Tiffany to sell tiaras. The crowd outside the store may be attracted by a moving ad; merchants prefer to have their crowds inside, and the most successful stores depend on taste and tact and judgment in their window displays to attract attention, and to carry attention over into favorable action.

Movement implies change. The electric sign which flashes on and off, alternately revealing the same name or figure in different colors, holds attention only against rivals which flash and then go dark. The dancing geometrical figures of the famous Wrigley ad at Times Square had movement and a slight touch of mystery.[3] One couldn't be entirely sure which figure would be the next to go up or down. But

---

[3] Wrigley's took out newspaper ads in the early 1920s that claimed their sign at Times Square—250 feet long and 70 feet high—was the largest electrical sign in the world.

the limitations remain: after a few moments the sign has to repeat itself and attention wanders. In the blaze of Broadway, it often rests with gratitude upon a small quiet sign spelled out in the pink or purple electric tubing which is so familiar in Paris—because on Broadway this is novel and restful.

Another type of advertisement which combines movement with suspense is the running story spelled in electric letters against the sky. The mechanism is so arranged as to give infinite variety, anything can be spelled out. Actually, the signs are geared to spell forty or fifty words and then to repeat them. Around Columbus Circle in New York, it is common to see people gaping at the sign of General Motors, slowly spelling out the words, outguessing the machine. At the end of each repetition of the advertisement the sign announces, "The current time now is—" and then it goes blank for half a second. People on their way to the theater through Central Park watch the sign with fascination often mingled with despair at the thought of the approaching jam of traffic, and there is a totally illogical sense of triumph when one catches the time signal just as 8:26 p.m. merges into 8:27 p.m. The sign performs a service, or answers to a need, and, at the same time, corresponds to an almost universal interest.

Excess of attention-catching has made the American public suspicious. Writers of form letters, after a thousand devices have been used to conceal the fact that the letter was not personal, have come to the open statement at the beginning of their letters, "This is a form letter," followed with an instant appeal to the interest or sympathy of the reader. Young men schooled in "putting the punch in the first line" have sometimes punched so hard that the reader wanted to hit back, an attitude presently graced with the name of "sales-resistance." The affected simplicity of omitting phrases of courtesy and the affected heartiness which makes many form letters distasteful, have turned out to be as ineffective as affectation of any other kind. Brevity, simplicity, and dignity remain firmly established, after fads have come and gone, as the best approaches to the favorable intention of a stranger. The defect of excessive brusqueness or joviality is that they set up a negative current just when a positive reaction is essential. What the salesman (or advertiser, or press agent, or politician) wants is what the psychologist calls "the yes-response technique."[4] The salesman, in fact, can ask for

---

[4] The "yes-response technique" as described in the 1969 book *Interpersonal Communication in the Modern Organization*, is characterized by the salesperson asking a series of questions that are designed to get the person to respond with a "yes" (e.g., "Do you have children? Do they go to school?," etc.). This approach, of encouraging affirmative responses, is designed to get the respondent to be conditioned to say "yes" to a sales offer.

nothing better than a nation of prospects, all of whom were yes-men who have lost the faculty of saying no.

In experience, the moment you offer a prospect a piece of land, a grand piano, or anything more dubious than a two-cent stamp, you instantly set in motion two currents: the response to your persuasion and the response to the man's own interests. The salesman is deliberately trying to divert the prospect's attention from himself and toward the commodity he is selling. The man wants a piano; he also wants to economize, to put more money in the bank this year than last, to go abroad, to send his son to college. Each of these desires is an active system of thought and feeling in the man's consciousness. The salesman who says "This piano will give you more pleasure than a radio" aids the negative response, because he brings the idea of the radio forcefully to the man's mind as a possible (and cheaper) competitor of the piano. The creation of the yes-response depends partly on excluding from the prospect's mind all thoughts except those applying favorably to the object.

The first impulse in some people is to say no to any new thing. In others, where curiosity is perhaps higher, or more easily gratified, "yes" is the quicker response. To the person of the "no" habit, the salesman directs himself cautiously, trying to get a yes response on some question not concerned with his sale and thus settling up the muscular, and as we are told, glandular activity which leads to saying yes, so that a repetition of "yes" to 50 indifferent questions may lead to a 51st "yes" which makes a sale. It is rather like the game of Solomon-says "Thumbs Up."[5]

The much-abused conversational opening about the weather, or about the scenery along a railroad, is, in essence, an attempt to establish a sympathetic contact on which future conversation can be based. It is one subject upon which the human race, in any given climate, is substantially in agreement and, at the same time, it permits the expression of a personal feeling. "Good morning," does not mean, "This seems a good morning to me and I hope it does to you." It is impersonal and makes no direct appeal to the yes-responses, whereas every variation of comment on the weather expresses an entirely personal reaction and allows an equal expression, sympathetic and agreeable, from the person addressed. After "What a day!" you may go on and suggest that it looks like a good Republican year. Your adversary may say, "Yes, thank Heaven!" or, "Yes, unfortunately." But if you had omitted the introductory remark about the weather and begun by saying, "Good morning. It looks like a good year for Republicans," you would be far more likely to be met with, "Not at all. The Democrats are

---

[5] This is a variation of "Simon says," the children's game about following commands that are only preceded with the words "Simon says."

winning all along the line." With that negative response, the chance of interesting a suspicious fellow man in your affairs, to the extent of saying yes to an order, is diminished.

The headline is the usual conversational opening in advertising, but many advertisers have used a little space for an exact parallel to the remark about the weather. The ten- or fifteen-line John Wanamaker ads, signed by the founder and devoted to general comment or moral philosophy, suggests that the store is not pressing you to buy, and that the advertisement is ready when you are ready.[6] It suggests that you and the store, as fellow human beings, can afford to chat a moment about other things. In New York theatre programs, the Rogers Peet Company[7] has half of the page opposite the list of characters, and expends a deal of ingenuity in connecting the title of the play with the subject of its advertising, making a conversational bridge between something in which the audience is already interested (to which they are responding affirmatively) and the offer made by the store.

The face of an advertisement tries to be bright, interesting, and honest—to evoke the corresponding

---

[6] Wanamaker's was a prominent department store before the Great Depression, both in New York City and Philadelphia.

[7] Rogers Peet was a men's clothing company.

qualities in the reader. The peculiar faculty in human beings of stammering when they talk to a stammerer and smiling when they are smiled at, reflects itself in the response to the printed page. The appearance of an advertisement—dignified, striking, serious, gay—is taken as a reflection of the thing advertised and sets up an appropriate response. During the high-tide of the questionnaire fad, advertisements often carried sets of questions to excite interest. The reader was challenged, and the questions were usually graded so that almost everybody could answer some of them, so that no hostility developed. In advertisements for novelties, it is usual to explain what product the new thing supplants, so that the reader recognizes something familiar, something favorably known, and can go on from that basis to consider the superior attractions of the new. Finally, the good advertisement does not overstep the bounds of nature: it omits more than it says, mentions only a few prices to give the range, notes the important technical specifications, uses one splash of figures, but avoids statistics. And the good advertisement in a series keeps some features—the color, the slogan, the type in which the company's name is printed—and varies the other appeals, so that monotony does not set in.

Consistent, repetitive publicity, of which advertising is a prime example, has a further advantage to the advertiser. It helps to establish human wants, to make them so pressing that they overbear other wants and lead to positive action—to buying the product advertised. The product itself must be capable of treatment. No amount of advertising could today make the public want sedan chairs,[8] or sand-sifters to be used instead of blotting paper,[9] or thirty-day trans-Atlantic trips on sailing vessels. But a public accustomed to eating chocolate and to eating nuts, although it may not actively crave chocolate nut bars, can be made to want them and to buy them. As in everything else, publicity is the agent.

How can a thing be shown to be desirable? To a certain extent, by logical proof of its quality. A motor car costs less than any other, goes faster, uses less gasoline, and lasts longer—it is a perfect argument. But, apart from the fact that the public would be suspicious of such perfection and would demand proof (which would at once put the motor car on the defensive), the picture of the car with a pretty girl at the wheel, driving up to the country club, would sell

---

[8] Sedan chairs were portable covered chairs that were used as transportation, customarily by the well-off, in England from the 17th through the early 19th century. Two men, one in front and one in back, used carrying poles to lift the vehicle and then transport the passenger.

[9] For handwritten correspondence, sand-sifters were used to spread sand on paper so that ink would not run or smear. Ink absorbent blotting papers eventually made sand sifters obsolete in the U.S. by the late 19th century.

more cars. The girl, the car, and the country club all symbolize fundamental human wants. The whole interest of sex is represented by the girl. The fact that she is driving to the country club indicates leisure and comfort; the club itself suggests social advancement, wealth, ease, and healthful recreation. To a great number of people, the ideal life is suggested by such a picture, and prominent in it (the focus of attention) is the motor car. At once the car becomes associated with the ideal life, with the satisfaction of the wants one has felt for years. Simultaneously, social pressure set in: if this is the make of car seen at country clubs, I will be seen at country clubs if I have this make of car—hence, it is the make for me.

The wants which are suggested by an advertisement may not be remote from the common man. A familiar billboard in England a few years ago showed a billiard player apparently hanging by one arm from a chandelier, his cue still in his hand, and a strange expression on his face. It was intended to be funny and, in itself, the drawing caused a smile. But it called to no common want, and it did not associate the object advertised with the subject of the picture. The closest scrutiny revealed that the picture was an ad for a gas mantle which claimed to be unbreakable. Contrast with this the famous advertisement "The Prudential has the strength of Gibraltar." To most people, Gibraltar is a symbol and not a fact, yet it calls up various associations: the strength and splendor of the British Empire, the phrase "firm as a rock," the dominant position of Gibraltar in control of the Mediterranean. A motor car might be incalculably strong, yet it could not call itself as strong as Gibraltar because the suggestion of solidity, inflexible determination, and immobility, which are all appropriate to an insurance company, are totally out of place in connection with the motor car. The observer of the Gibraltar advertisement subconsciously thinks of his own security, or lack of it. He also thinks of his desire for permanence in his health, his domestic life, his job, and of his desire for some powerful and trustworthy person or institution to fall back on—and the association is made.

It will be noted that the thing with which the advertiser associates his product is, in itself, familiar, desirable, and not subject to criticism. No one in America advertises a shoe or a radio with a picture of the Red Square in Moscow. Apart from its unfamiliarity, the name of Moscow starts up too many counter-currents, when the advertiser wants a smooth and powerful current in a single direction.

The indirect method of approach can be observed on the stage. In the famous acting version of *Vanity Fair*, George Arliss as the Marquis of Steyne came down the stairs.[10] The audience saw at first only his feet on the top step, then his ankles, then legs—but, by that time, an indescribable feeling of uneasiness had made itself felt, for all the characters on the stage had moved or gestured in such a way that the viciousness of the approaching figure was communicated to the audience. Chaliapin as Boris Godunov strikes terror into his audiences by striking terror into the hearts of the on-stage crowd that watches him.[11] Socony's advertisements offer another example of the indirect method. Their ads point out the natural beauties, the good roads, the historical interest of New York and New England. Socony, as the product of the Standard Oil Company of New York, is not on sale beyond a limited area, yet its advertisements appear in magazines of national circulation. Their purpose is to draw motorists into the New York area. Once there, they will be urged to buy many brands of gas, but the fact that they were at least partially persuaded to come through Socony advertisements will set up a favorable association in motorists' minds.

It was said of George M. Cohan that whenever he felt a weak spot in a play he would find an excuse

---

[10] George Arliss (1868–1946) was the first English actor to win an Academy Award. It was for the title role in the 1929 film *Disraeli*.

[11] Feodor Ivanovich Chaliapin (1873–1938), a Russian opera singer, played the title role in the Russian opera *Boris Godunov*.

to wave the American flag.[12] Al Jolson once explained his technique by saying that he told a joke and if the audience didn't laugh, he dropped a pole on his assistant's head immediately, so that the audience, laughing, thought that it had enjoyed the joke.[13] This is hokum, as Jolson said, but it reveals how the "yes-response technique," and the combination of the known with the unknown, both operate in this process of association. For that reason, advertisements often appear palpably false to human experience, yet true to human desires. Mechanical progress has made washing clothes infinitely easier than it was, yet it remains a burden. The advertisements of new washing powders show a pretty woman, her hands unwrinkled, her face lightly flushed with pleasure but showing no sign of having met steam and hot water in the morning, her dress dainty and unspotted—and behind her the clock indicates 10:30 on a sunny morning. All the sloppiness and discomforts of washing are banished, and with the thought of the new powder comes the thought of daintiness, free afternoons, and health.

---

[12] George M. Cohan (1878–1942) was a playwright, lyricist, and composer, best known for songs like "You're a Grand Old Flag," and "Over There."

[13] Al Jolson (1886–1950) was a singer and actor best known for the 1927 movie *The Jazz Singer*.

The emotions expressed by men, women, and children in the advertisements seem excessive if coldly viewed. Little children do not jump up and down and clap their hands with excitement merely because the bread offered to them is made by a certain baker. Yet mothers whose children turn away from bread do desire their children to rejoice at the thought of eating wholesome food; and the picture of a happy, healthy, and not troublesome child, so different from the actuality in many cases, becomes associated in the mother's mind, if not in the child's, with the virtues of a special kind of bread.

A coffee sold at a price low enough for all but the poorest to buy is advertised with the picture of a man in evening clothes, a butler, a silver service, and damask tablecloth and napkin. A cigarette is advertised by testimonials from opera singers, proving that it does not hurt the throat, a logical argument behind which lies the emotional overtone—opera singers, rich and famous, use these cigarettes. A face cream costing about 50 cents is praised by millionaires' wives, duchesses, and queens. The appeal to snobbery may be obvious, but the picture of the queen's table with the cold cream jar upon it creates an image of fastidiousness against which doubts as to whether the queen actually does use the cream are unavailing.

The picture of a motor car skidding against a lamppost in the rain is a direct appeal to the fear of death and disfigurement. A picture of the same car skidding and hitting a little child appeals to the paternal instinct and sets up a current of feeling—that every motorist should be compelled to use chains, skinless tires or certain brakes, or whatever the picture advertises. Men's clothes are advertised by association with youth (college men), or success in business (executives at their desks), or prowess in love (one man surrounded by three or four girls). Women's clothes follow the same pattern. House furnishings are connected with the pride of showing a beautiful home to friends, and the reverse method is used in an advertisement showing three well-dressed and obviously cultivated women looking at a teapot and saying, "Beautiful, my dear, but it's not sterling." The object advertised is associated with a normal, deeply felt, human want in every case. The manufacturer of a domestic appliance—a carpet sweeper, or a dish-washing machine, for example—can associate his product with the leisure and daintiness (as the washing powder ads do) or with social success (as furniture ads do). Or, he can address his appeal not to women, as in these two cases, but to men, showing them that the purchase of his appliance will make their wives happier, prouder, and healthier. In this case, the appeal is to the love of the husband for the wife, although the husband can only in the most indirect way benefit from the purchase. Actually, this very appeal has been found, in practice, to sell more goods than the direct appeal to women.

One of the functions of long-run publicity is to crowd out hostile or distracting ideas. Another is to supplement the suggestion from the outside with auto-suggestion. These two things interact and serve one another. The human mind can hold only a limited number of ideas at one time. Emotions sometimes come into conflict, but usually one dominates the others. If a radio set is offered to one man he may think that it will be a source of noise and irritation, another may think that he can't afford the outlay, a third that he doesn't like jazz music. The radio advertiser and publicity man keeps constantly before these reluctant people a series of pictures: a radio set in the home of a society leader, a family listening to a symphony program, another preferring to stay home from the theatre because a famous tenor is singing on the air. The advantages of the radio crowd out the fancied disadvantages; when these advantages are pushed far enough down into the unconscious, this radio is bought.

But, at the same time, when the former hater of radios goes to the store to buy his set he does not think he has been persuaded against his will. He thinks that he has independently arrived at the conclusion that he ought to have a radio. Except for those who suffer from an inferiority complex, human beings are possessed of an amount of self-confidence and resent any attack upon their own judgment. Even the consciously inferior person believes that, in certain ways, he is superior, and often goes to extremes to prove it. Therefore, when we are compelled to do something we think undesirable, our attitude is hostile. Imagine the grace with which the president of the No-Tipping Society would give a tip to a French theatre usher because he was ashamed to make a fuss in front of the girl he was with! People frequently pay overcharges at restaurants because it is a tradition that liberal spenders never look at the bill. But these actions are accompanied with a strong negative current of feeling which the salesman of objects or ideas wants to prevent.

If the suggestion leading to the purchase of a radio is all outside suggestion—from the man's wife and children, from violent assertions in the advertising pages of the newspapers, from the sneers of neighbors—the purchaser will be suspicious of everything offered. He will assume that the salesman is trying to sell him a discontinued type, or one in which the store is overstocked and for the sale of which the salesman will get a premium. He will take particular pains to note every possible defect and will fail of enthusiasm over demonstrated merits. He will

buy a cheap radio, with the minimum of equipment.
But, if the publicity has been skillful, the purchaser
will long before have absorbed all the arguments in
favor of the radio and think that he has invented them
himself. He may tentatively offer some of these sales
points to the salesman himself. He will display, with
some pride, his knowledge of the technical intricacies
of radio as a whole and of the merits of the various
types shown to him. Phrases he has picked up from
friends, arguments that became so familiar in
magazines and newspapers that they have become
part of his mental furniture, will persuade him that he
has considered everything and decided upon just the
radio set which is most suitable to his requirements
and his purse.

This is, again, an instance of repetition being
reputation. Repetition is applied to the advertiser's
activity. Before it becomes reputation, it has to enter
into the mind of the purchaser, become part of him,
so that he thinks it is his own intelligence, his own
reasoning power, his own judgment which are at work.
Here and there an individual might say, "I bought a
kind of soap because I got tired of seeing so many ads
about it." The majority of people would say they
bought that kind of soap because they thought it was
what they wanted—the best for the money, or the
best at any price. At the maximum, they may say,
"The salesman talked me into it," forgetting that, in

nine cases out of ten where a highly advertised article is concerned, the talk of the salesman is only the last word in a series which began with the printed page, continued to the conversation of friends, and came to fruition in talks customers had with themselves. In a sense, no salesman ever sold to customers anything that they didn't want. The good salesman only needs to discover what the customer secretly wanted, and then to make him buy it.

Publicity which tells the reader everything, without appealing to his own wit and intelligence, remains outside suggestion. If auto-suggestion is wanted, a little gap is left in the argument, with the implication, "a person of your intelligence will see this." In the psychologist's technical use of the word, auto-suggestion also plays a part in influencing human beings. A man who has persuaded himself that he is a new Messiah can frequently get others to believe in him; the man who doubts his own mission, however, has no followers. But even technically, auto-suggestion is believed by psychologists to be the source of imperative ideas and, in that sense, applies correctly to an idea which is strong enough to move a man from apathy to enthusiasm, from refusing to believe to belief, and from indifference to patronage. Auto-suggestion, in the case of monomaniacs, is characterized by the concentration of all of one's faculties on a single object. This corresponds to that process of driving out and excluding hostile ideas which was mentioned before. In all cases where suggestion works, whether from within or without, every opposing suggestion must be pressed down to a low level or expelled entirely. The psychologist often expresses this by saying that there must be a "narrowing of consciousness." Arthur Christensen,[14] in his 1915 book *Politics and Crowd-Morality*, says:

> If I, through constant repetition of an assertion, without the addition of proofs or rational arguments, cause a person to believe in it, a case of suggestion arises. The assertion may be so unreasonable that simple reflection would show its untenability; but the *narrowing of the consciousness* prevents such reflection on the part of the person influenced by the suggestion, and makes him impervious to objections from a hostile quarter.

This goes back, of course, to the problem of attention. The magician, when he approaches a particularly delicate moment in his act, fires off a pistol or attracts attention away from his hands. In a play recently on the stage in New York, *Cock Robin*, a fictional murder was performed in full view of the audience, the murderer moving from behind a saloon bar, taking a favorable position, and throwing a knife

---

[14] Arthur Christensen (1875–1945) was a Danish academic who specialized in Iranian philology and folklore.

into the back of his victim.[15] Yet these movements passed virtually unseen and, after the murder was reconstructed in the last act, most people in the audience did not believe that the actor had actually done what the character in the play was supposed to do. Actually, he did every night go through the exact movements, as people who went a second time saw. The reason they did not see the first time was that, simultaneously, a shot was fired, a door opened, the shadow of a man with a firearm appeared on a wall, and a girl across the stage from the murderer screamed and pointed to this shadow.

The engrossment of a lover in the merit of his beloved makes him not only impervious to criticism of her, but actively hostile. People say they are so "taken up with" a pet charity or a dinner party that they cannot bother about anything else. In argument one says, "I can't see that point at all," which is almost literally true because the mind's eye is preoccupied with its own argument. Consciousness can be narrowed from the outside, but in the end our own interests and desires serve as the great concentrating forces. They determine to what we shall pay attention, what habits we shall form, and what jobs we shall work at. And the man who wants to influence another man to his way of thinking has to enlist self-

---

[15] The play *Cock Robin* ran on Broadway in New York City from January 1928 until April 1928.

interest—to make the other man think that he is, of his own motion, doing one thing and not another.

In many cases, publicity looks to establishing habit. The general advertising of paint manufacturers, growers of citrus fruit, and makers of silverware mentions no brands or trade names. It wants people to get into the habit of painting their houses, eating oranges, and buying silverware; once the habit is established, the separate manufacturers have a background of affirmation against which to set their own appeals. Makers of yachts and pipe organs may be satisfied with a single sale to a single customer, but most industries live on the repetition of orders.

The advantage of being the first in the field with a new toy, a new breakfast food, or a new type of humor is that the first-comer sets the standard and is considered as the measure for others. In habit forming the first comer also has an advantage; it is easier for a man to repeat what he has once done than to learn a new trick. Physiologists assure us that there are tracks in the brain as easy to follow as railroad tracks, and that, to do a new thing, we must push a new track through the undergrowth. The psychoanalyst Sigmund Freud has suggested that most people live under a compulsion to repeat themselves, and criminologists have found that burglars use the same technique over and over again, down to such

details as rifling the icebox for bread and jam after
their burglary is completed. Some of the craftiest
mass murderers have been brought to justice because
they never varied their murders, and the coincidence
of circumstances in widely separated areas after lapses
of time set the police on their trail.

The habit of buying by trade names is a labor-
saving device. Instead of asking for a pound of coffee
in which such and such types are blended in such and
such proportion, at some price between 35 and 50
cents, the customer says, give me "a pound of Acme
coffee" in complete confidence that it will be exactly
what he wants, i.e., exactly like the last pound. Until
he is dissatisfied with this coffee, or tastes a better
one at the home of a friend, the habit of buying it will
persist and a rival advertiser will have a hard time
breaking his habit. This is the point at which the
citizen has his hold on the publicity agent who looks
for the long run. If the advertising is consistent, the
product must be unvarying and the manufacturer
must stand responsible for every claim made.

Advertising is one form of publicity in which
anonymity is impossible. The advertiser may try to
escape legal responsibility for a false or exaggerated
promise, but he cannot escape commercial
responsibility. He cannot sell one pound of good
coffee and one pound of bad; he cannot claim 100%
purity when his product is adulterated. The statute

laws governing advertising are still chaotic, but the law of commerce is clear and just. Shoddy, adulterated, and imperfect goods can be sold for a time. In the long run, however, they are bound to be exposed by the potent publicity of mouth-to-mouth condemnation.

The relation of publicity to responsibility can be expressed in a mathematical formula: the longer one wants publicity to be effective, the more detailed must be the accuracy of the publicity itself and the responsibility of the person behind it. The vendor of snake oil at one-night stands can say anything, and leave without giving name or authority. The manufacturer who wants his product to be bought day after day for years can tell nothing but the truth. It may be his own partial version of the truth, but such as it is, he must stand ready to prove it, to give the satisfaction he promises, or be destroyed.

Chapter 11.
The Fear Motive

IN THE PAST FEW YEARS an apparently new technique has come into advertising: the technique of threat. In a varied, sustained, and extremely successful campaign, the makers of Listerine undertook to persuade the American people that the fear of halitosis is the beginning of social advancement. Actually, the same method had been used (in the same connection) years earlier in magazines of the cheaper sort. The Listerine advertising was notable for its psychological insight, for its appearance of dignity mingled with frankness, and for a sort of courageous indifference to the jeers of sophisticated people. First, there was the discovery (or invention) of the name "halitosis" which gave both novelty and ease of discussion.[1] It was linked with a product already favorably known, and the objective was extremely personal. The suitor rejected by the girl he loves, the traveling salesman who is beginning to slip on orders, the ranking clerk over whose head a younger employee is promoted, the husband whose wife avoids his kisses—all dramatized bits of life familiar to every

---

[1] The word "halitosis" is a clinical term denoting bad breath. Listerine did not coin the term; physician Joseph William Howe used it in an 1874 on the subject of breath and diseases.

reader, suggesting something in his personal experience. By implication, some fundamental desires of all humanity were touched: desires for popularity, prosperity, love, and happiness. Directly, however, the advertising played on the fear of ostracism, of defeat, of losing ground, of becoming unpopular in old age, and of losing out.

To a great many people, although probably not to the majority of readers of advertising, there was something funny in these advertisements, but even this element contributed to publicity. The phrases "sometimes a little child blurts out the truth" and "that is the insidious thing" crept into common use. The name of Listerine might be omitted, but when the phrases and the central idea of halitosis were used in vaudeville sketches, the audience made the necessary mental association. The style of advertising was so fresh, the distribution so complete, that publicity accrued to the manufacturer without his own efforts. In addition to the outside suggestion, inter-suggestion came into play whenever people talked about the ads or joked about the subject.

The same theme was presently used by other advertisers. Those whose products were intended to correct other personal defects were frankly imitative. Others managed to give their advertisements a touch of originality. "You never said a word all evening" was the headline of an ad showing a man and woman, obviously of the prosperous class, the man in utter dejection, the woman humiliated. It was an advertisement for a book, which, one gathered, would supply topics of conversation to the average man and make him interesting. The first book of etiquette[2] advertising, which ran a course similar to that of Listerine, worked on the perplexities and worries of the socially uninstructed and drove, at the same time, at the fear of committing a faux pas. The dull man not only disgraced his wife, but lost standing with the banker and manufacturer whose business he might have won had he made a favorable impression. The girl who used the wrong fork or unadvisedly "asked him in," saying that "the folks are still awake" lost the attentions of a cavalier of a higher social rank than herself. Another advertisement indicated the lost business opportunities caused by ignorance of foreign languages; another noted the bad effect of wearing soft collars during business hours. The normal desire to have white teeth and to avoid going to the dentist was translated into the threat that "four out of five get pyorrhea" at a time when the technical name for the disease of the gum was coming into use.

Special as this advertising seems, it is based on a motive entirely familiar in publicity. For many years before the war, a group of publicists were urging

---

[2] Emily Post (1872–1960) first published the book *Etiquette in Society, in Business, in Politics, and at Home* in 1922.

military preparedness on Great Britain—specifically urging the creation of a large army—and one of the motives to which they appealed was the fear of invasion. Whenever the project of a tunnel from Dover to Calais was broached, it became a lever in this publicity campaign.[3] The English remained indifferent; in France, however, the fear of invasion is a pressing and permanent factor not only of public policy but of public opinion. The geographical situation and the national memory combine to make invasion a threat which cannot be exaggerated. Security against invasion is the prime object of French diplomacy, and sufferings from invasion is a lively element in the experience of generation after generation of Frenchmen. In England, the tradition is exactly the opposite. Until the Zeppelins began to launch bombs on London, and German cruisers bombarded towns on the east coast, no hostile force had touched the soil of England in the memory of generations, and the whole tradition of British policy was to depend on the fleet for protection (with only a skeleton home guard), and to wage its wars on the Continent. The publicists of preparedness, who were perfectly right when they spoke of the broad ground

---

[3] Leading up to World War I, First Sea Lord Admiral Fisher said that the English Channel—the body of water between Dover in England and Calais in France—was one of the "five keys [that] lock up the world."

of British obligations, were talking to deaf ears when they spoke of invasion. They were accused of creating false fears, of insulting the Navy, and of militaristic tendencies. They failed to associate their objective with the common experience of the average man, and they exposed the pitfall in all fear-motive publicity—that it if fails to frighten, it becomes ludicrous.

In the U.S., the difference in feeling between the East and Middle West on one side and the Pacific Coast on the other illustrates the same point. In a sense, California has experienced an invasion from the Orient—a peaceful one which, nevertheless, brings home to the ordinary citizen the existence of a great power across the Pacific. The Middle West knows nothing of this, and the East is contemptuous of the idea that an enemy could land anywhere on the Atlantic Coast. Along the Pacific, the threat of invasion would make for effective publicity for various causes—for another canal paralleling the one at Panama, for a larger army, for a larger navy and a vast anti-aircraft aviation program, for better relations with Japan, for a new naval ratio, for the study of the problems of the Pacific, and for a specific policy in regard to the independence of the Philippines. In the Middle West, publicity for these objects (which range from preparation for war to insurance for peace) would have to be based on other motives in order to escape the mockery of the people. To persuade the

people of Kansas that invasion was a practical
possibility, a press agent might dramatize the problem
by marching an army corps over the Rockies and, by
the speed of the march, prove that mountains are no
longer a barrier to modern armies. He could appeal to
the sentiment of unity, to national pride, and racial
exclusiveness. He could bring moral and social
arguments to bear—but he could not proclaim the
threat of invasion unless he did, in some dramatic
way, bring it home. Otherwise, the indifference of his
public would turn to actual hostility if they felt that
they were being frightened by a non-existent danger.
Publicity which overreaches itself is fatal, and the
Little Englanders (those who were opposed to
enlarging the military establishment) profited
enormously by the tactics of their opponents.

"Don't swap horses while crossing a stream" is
the slogan of political campaigners for the party in
power. There is always some sort of a stream to be
crossed, but the fear that the other party could not
conduct the work of the nation is not ingrained in the
American mind. Republicans and Democrats have
managed to win wars, live through panics, pass laws,
and sign treaties. Even in the case of an actual war,
the burden of proof is on the person making the
threat. Manufacturers who threaten to shut down
their factories if the opposition candidate is elected,
and those who predict panics if their party is turned

out of power, can only do so safely if a panic, under the other administration, is vividly in the minds of the voters.

Against the normal fear of change there is the normal desire for novelty. Those who have prospered in the past four years want the same policies to continue; those who have been hampered in business want a change. Neither side has a long historical memory; the campaigner who drags in 1837 and 1873 as proof of his party's superiority in giving prosperity to the country is on dangerous ground. He has to prove his points—and one of the tricks of debate is to force your opponent to disprove.

The fundamental peril of all fear-motive publicity is that it may become too urgent. Common experience may reject the idea that halitosis is a certain bar to success. If the public is in a frivolous mood, for example, these threats are all ineffective and they are naturally useless in persuading people who consider themselves successful and happy. The variation by Listerine, after the original series of ads (with their dramatic pictures) had firmly fixed their idea, is interesting because it shows how the fear-motive can be modulated. The dramatic illustrations—a man with a child in his arms, a salesman looking at his almost empty sales book—disappeared and a simple etching took their place. It showed a young man or young woman, entirely agreeable in almost every aspect. Underneath was a summary of the "case" according to this formula: promise of success, early successes, gradual and unexplained failure, and then return to success. Attached was a single-line statement of the virtues of Listerine. The fear-motive began to disappear and the motive of ambition, of desire for happiness and prosperity, took its place.

Possibly the advertiser felt that the public was being over-stimulated, a condition which is far more common that advertisers believe. There is, in New York, an excellent electric sign for a coffee advertised as "good to the last drop" The sign shows a tilted cup and the last drops fall from it as the sign flashes. A woman who worked at night in an office building commanding that sign, and who saw it hour after hour, once said she would never order that brand of coffee because of the effect the sign had on her. Seen for a few minutes by passersby on Broadway, it was effective; but, in the long run, with attention too closely concentrated on it, the sign over-stimulated. Danish psychologist Christensen has called this overstimulation by the name of "contrary suggestion." "On certain people," he says,

> an exaggerated or importunate recommendation of an article will act as a deterrent. They will be less inclined to tackle a book if they are urged on all sides to read it; and they find a tune unbearable, just

because it is popular.... Still commoner is the contrary suggestion aroused by a prohibition ("stolen fruit is the sweetest"). Advice not to read a book will usually only incite people to read it. If it is prohibited by the authorities, its success is assured; though here the suggestion of sensationalism is apt to co-operate with the contrary suggestion of the prohibition.

Chapter 12.
The Slogan and the Picture

THE MAJORITY OF MEN ARE visual minded. Few can remember a smell and only gifted ones a tone. Even the sense of taste, which has so much to do with appetite and nourishment, is feeble in our memory. But nearly everyone can remember what an ice cream soda or a band leader or a skyscraper looks like. We speak of the mind's eye, but never of the mind's ear, finger, or nose. What we see goes directly to the brain and makes a profound impression there. Little children, after they have begun to read, turn with distaste from books and magazines which are not illustrated. Business men, when they are being bothered with complex details, say roughly, "Give me a picture of it," or ask for a graph or diagram.

The fact that things seen are so impressive accounts for the obstinate way in which human beings associate even abstract things with images. Justice is a blind-folded woman with evenly balanced scales; England is a portly man with a rough walking stick accompanied by a bull dog; hope is a picture by Watts.[1] Images supply our symbols, and the average man thinks in symbols. Around them cluster all the

---

[1] Arthur Watts (1883–1935) was a British illustrator whose work appeared in popular magazines like *Punch* and the *Tatler*.

associations which can be played upon to make him act. Before words were written, pictures were drawn, and the source of our alphabet is in pictures. With the progress of invention it begins to be likely that humanity will return to a sort of picture-writing—the moving picture.

The effectiveness of the moving picture as publicity is being felt around the world from all quarters of which comes the complaint that the predominance of American movies is immeasurably powerful in Americanizing the world. Not only American motor cars and bath tubs impress themselves on Turks, Hungarians, and Siamese. The American codes of manners and morals, as far as the moving picture is able to interpret them, are set before foreigners for contrast with their own. The Oriental censors cut out scenes which are perfectly innocuous to Americans, but offensive to Oriental taste; they cannot, however, cut out the general sense of American life which our films give.

Films supply a medium of education infinitely more rapid than any other, and apparently as profound. For a hundred years the United States was flooded with British novels and with French and Italian sculpture, German and Russian music, and Scandinavian plays, but no one seriously felt that these arts could Europeanize America, or in any way corrupt its essential spirit. The moving picture, combining motion with the visual appeal, is instantly felt to be a danger. The need of regulating moving pictures far more than the stage was accepted even by people naturally opposed to censorship. The moving picture is always seen by a crowd and differs there from reading novels or seeing sculpture. Its cheapness means that the crowd is composed largely of the less educated and the less highly organized members of the community, constituting a difference between the movie and the play or the symphony concert. The English dramatic critic Arthur Bingham Walkley justified a theatrical censorship by saying that "an audience in the theatre has the psychology of a crowd. Its intellectual pitch is lowered, its emotional pitch raised.... An offensive play, performed before it, has an entirely different effect from that which the play would have if read separately and privately by each individual."[2] Theatre audiences, however, are often composed of the highly intelligent, many of whom have grown accustomed to resist mass-suggestion. They act as barriers to contagion of emotion. Some of them are of that peculiar constitution which makes them dislike whatever is popular, and they are likely to sit still when others applaud, or even to mock the enthusiasm of their fellows. The spectators at a moving picture are less likely to be of this contrary

---

[2] Arthur Bingham Walkley (1855–1926) was a theatre critic for *The Times* for 26 years.

type, and the majority of them would not be affected so much by the snobbish disapproval of a few. This means that the moving-picture audience is exceptionally suggestible, and that it is exposed to an instrument of suggestion far more persuasive than any other.

The moving picture has been recognized as unconscious propaganda even in the United States. Opponents of Christian morality and of the capitalist system complain that the moving picture keeps alive certain American myths and symbols. That vice is punished, that riches do not bring happiness, that "poor but honest" is sure to win, that class distinctions do not exist in the United States, that Americans are morally superior to foreigners—these, and dozens of other basic assumptions of the American masses, receive effective support from the moving picture. As direct propaganda, the movie is suspected by managers of the theaters, but they cannot easily draw the line between a scenic picture of Yellowstone Park issued by a group of railroads and a scenic film of Yellowstone Park made independently by a producer of short features. In the midst of a political campaign, the leading candidates naturally appear in the newsreel and enthusiasts applaud. The talking movie supplies an even greater variety of appeals.

One of the attractions of the moving pictures is its appearance of reality. The spectator says, it must be so because I saw it with my own eyes. As the newsreels particularly are signed by the name of the company offering them, and as they compete with rival newsreels of the same events, the prospect of faking any is very remote. The spectators always know at what moment the camera man has stepped in and said to the hero of a newsreel, "shake hands with the governor and say a few words in front of the camera." In its essential report the newsreel is accurate and responsible and even serves as a decided check on exaggeration in newspaper reports.

This reality, and the sense that every statement can be verified, carries over to the still picture. The picture which first catches the eye in an advertisement sets the tone. When the new Ford car was ready, a week of concentrated advertising began. Not only were pictures omitted, but in the publicity campaign backing up the advertising, the public was informed that pictures were "jealously guarded." Enterprising newspaper reporters managed to get one photograph and the publication of this was considered a news beat. The purpose of the whole publicity campaign was to get crowds in front of the Ford dealership windows throughout the country on the day the new models were to be shown. Only on that day, as the climax of the whole campaign, did pictures appear in the advertising. As a result of this suspense and interest, one person in every ten in New York City looked into a Ford window on the opening day and, in spite of a terrible rainstorm, the police were called on to regulate the crowds.

When Boss Tweed cried out, "those damn pictures," he paid the highest compliment to Thomas Nast's cartoons. The cartoon is effective because, unlike the real picture, it is the result of a selection. Each character bears not only a written label but a label in every line of the drawing. The Germans are said to have put a price on the head of Louis Raemaekers because every line of his drawings made the Germans fiends.[3] It is no part of the cartoonists' business to make delicate distinctions. Five oil men may be corrupt and 500 honest, but the cartoonist fighting corruption makes a picture labeled "Oil" and this picture is the image of a convict, a briber, or a murderer. Theodore Roosevelt became a pair of eye-glasses and a mouth full of teeth because the cartoonist had to simplify and to supply an image which could always be identified.

Once an image is established, the cartoonist must stick to it because, if he varies in any important

---

[3] Louis Raemaekers (1869–1956) drew editorial cartoons during World War I for the Dutch paper *De Telegraff*. No proof has been found to substantiate the assertion that the Germans placed a bounty on him.

detail, the swift recognition on which he counts will be lost. If a reader of a newspaper has to stop and ask "whom is this supposed to represent?" his mind begins to function and, to that degree, the emotional response is checked. That is why John Bull remains a country squire although the country squire's place in England has largely been taken by the slender barrister, the nervous manufacturer, or the business man. The farmer still appears as a man with a whip of hay under a straw hat. These are created images to understand that which one does not have to think about.

Printed publicity has to find a counterpart for the picture. It uses pictorial words, it selects striking detail, and it also has phrases which lag behind the times but serve as centers for association. We still say, "A cast iron guarantee," although many other metals have surpassed iron in strength and durability. Yet the most effective of all substitutes for the visual appeal lies elsewhere. There is one sense not usually listed among the five senses of perception which is as closely connected with the savage or the child as the sense of sight. That is the feeling for rhythm. Psychologists say that whatever corresponds in beat to our pulse makes an instant appeal to us. The savage is called to war and to worship by the beat of a drum, the child learns his multiplication table to a song, the round-shouldered business man walks erect and more firmly to the sound of a march. In his ideal *Republic*, Plato permitted only that music whose rhythms made men virile and banished the effeminate modes. In his ideal Italy, Prime Minister Benito Mussolini is insisting on a place for Italian music expressing the Italian spirit as a counterpoise whenever jazz is played.

It is the good fortune of writers and speakers that the quality of rhythm can be carried over into words, producing an emotional effect equivalent to that of music. The spoken word is obviously a more direct means of communication among men than the written—that is, there is no mechanical barrier between the emotion of the speaker and the emotion of his hearer. The spoken word has an infinite variety of pitch, tone, and stress by which its rhythms are made more effective. That is the beginning of the orator's power. The end is in the circumstances of his delivery. Even before he begins to speak, excitement has been created because he is addressing a crowd. Hundreds of individuals have given up their private concerns in order to listen to the orator. They have come from the quiet and habitual monotony of their homes to a public place full of friends or strangers all laboring under a similar excitement. The speaker is a person of some consequence around whose name alone congregates a number of exciting associations. The audience is suggestible in advance, and it looks up to the speaker hoping to be moved and swayed. In that condition whatever a speaker says—unless he is deliberately hostile to his audience—is tremendously effective, and if the way he says it touches the fundamental rhythms there seems to be no limit to his power.

The first sentence of Lincoln's Gettysburg address is, "Four score and seven years ago our fathers brought forth on this continent a new nation conceived in liberty, and dedicated to the proposition that all men are created equal." His meaning would have been equally clear if he had said, "Our predecessors made a new country 87 years ago, and this country was born in the spirit of liberty and took its main idea the principal of the equality of all human beings." With this version, however, the loss of emotional effect is complete. Around the words "four score" clings the memory of the biblical reference to the span of life which is totally lacking when using "87." Of the five chief sounds in the first phrase, four are full and deep, giving a profound sense of the gravity of the occasion, and the beat of the entire sentence is regular and slow.

Oratory is not only adaptable to the emotional appeal, it seems ill-suited for logical argument. People listen to debaters, excited by the contest and applauding well-made points, but their interest is aroused to a high point when one debater denounces or turns the laugh on another. A purely logical

speaker, giving facts and reasons, and not playing on
the emotions of his audience, loses attention.
Lecturers have frequently confessed that, after the
first few minutes of a speech, they pick out the least
intelligent looking members of the audience and play
down to them with the assurance that, if these
listeners are pleased, the speech will be a success.

There are no special qualifications for being a
member of an audience. Any man who can hear is
eligible, regardless of his understanding. It is common
at street corners to see tramps and loafers edge
toward a crowd around a campaign speaker without
any interest in what he says, which they sometimes do
not even hear and certainly give no signs of
understanding. They make their way into the crowd
because the crowd gives them, fleetingly, a sense of
belonging. The mere fact that people are entering a
hall acts as an attraction to others, and the mental
level of a crowd gathered to hear a lecture on an
important subject is lowered by curiosity seekers and
drifters. The crowd demands an emotional attack
from the orator. He answers them by pictures and by
rhythm. The early revivalists, preaching to their
intimate congregations of a few hundred souls, used
reason and logic. The later ones used music and
drama.

With the growth of populations, the physical
possibilities of reaching all the people vanished. In the

last 100 years, the spread of education gave to the publicist a new instrument—the printed word. The conditions of the appeal were changed. A man reads a newspaper or a pamphlet to himself. The physical excitement, the inter-suggestion of the presence of other people, is wanting. And the printed appeal can be made only to those who know how to read and, furthermore, to the extent they understand what they read. These are grave limitations on the effectiveness of any call to the emotions. The listener may be so carried away by a speaker that he will forget the most obvious contradictions. He cannot be sure that the speaker really did say "black" twenty minutes ago and then "white" five minutes ago. Unless he is one of the few critical and non-suggestible individuals, he will say yes to all the speaker's statements at the time they are made. With the printed word in his hand, the reader can go back and, at the first suspicion that the writer is not being truthful, honest, or logical, the reader will reject his appeal entirely. To an extent, all writing must at least seem logical.

The pleader whose aim is to convince has to prevent suspicion from arising. He can do this by being strictly logical, but then runs the risk of not moving the reader at all. Or, he can lull the critical faculties to sleep by repeating in print the tricks of the picture-maker. The pictures he evokes are simplified, familiar, and vivid. He "splashes" a color instead of "applying" it because the word "splash" connotes vividness and action. He avoids not only the words of the literary language but also the unfamiliar beat of literature, and clings to simplicity. He learns from speakers and from comedians that a word used once may have no effect, but if used ten times, at carefully graduated intervals, that word will provoke laughter. He uses certain phrases as landmarks so that the reader becomes familiar with them and sees that the whole discourse hangs together. Without monotony he repeats and repeats again.

In the continuous appeal to the public the same techniques are used. An English critic once said that you could always tell the story of a good novel in a single sentence. It's the aim of the good publicist to express his purpose in a sentence, phrase, or word which will take root and flourish in the public mind. Once he has created such a group of words, he uses them as a war cry—a single point around which to rally emotions and desires, a slogan which not only identifies his work, but concentrates scattered impulses and leads to action. The whole of Europe was stirred in the Middle Ages by the cry, *"dieu le veut"* "God wills")—the slogan for the crusades. The whole of America is still moved by the "self-evident truth" that all men are created free and equal. For half a century, socialists have rallied around, "the economic interpretation of history." "The party of Lincoln" and

"The party of Jefferson" are slogans under which the
Republican Party may become entirely un-Lincolnian
and the Democratic Party act in exact opposition to
the principles of Jefferson. The French Revolution
created the slogan, "Liberty! Equality! Fraternity!,"
permitting no one to point out that absolute liberty
and absolute equality were mutually incompatible.

The French critic, Remy de Gourmont, has
worked on the dissociations of ideas, showing that
certain familiar couplings—law and order, democracy
and liberty, poverty and virtue, wealth and vice—
remain powerful concepts in the human mind because
they have become, in a way, slogans.[4] It is the virtue
of a slogan that, by repetition, it becomes in itself an
object of respect, regardless of what it stands for.
Almost any noun joined to the adjective "free" has a
double appeal, since the word "free" is associated both
with freedom and with free gifts. Free love, free trade,
free verse, free air, free service, free speech, and a free
press are all subject to some rules and some
limitations. The names themselves, however, suggest
an absolute freedom, gathering around them all the
memories of heroes and martyrs. A slogan is not to be
examined and is no more to be changed than the color
of a national banner. The maker of a slogan attempts
to create a pattern, a tune to which his words

---

[4] Remy de Gourmont (1858–1915) was a French novelist, poet, and
symbolist.

naturally fit, and the proof of his success is found
when his phrase enters public circulation and other
words are set to it. "When better cars are built, Buick
will build them," has been adapted for use on the
vaudeville stage. The names of two of Sinclair Lewis'
books have become common identifications for a type
of community and a type of individual: *Main Street* and
Babbitt. "To make the world safe for democracy" was
not only varied a thousand times, but was actually set
to music. Sweet Caporal cigarettes' "Ask Dad, he
knows" and Packard Motor Company's "Ask the man
who owns one" each had at least a moment of
popularity during which every variation of phrase kept
in mind the purpose of the original. So did Kodak
Camera's "You press the button—we do the rest"
with which a variety of electrical appliances could
make a similar statement. The common phrase
"Bigger and Better Movies," became so popular that it
was instantly turned to the uses of ridicule.

This is a constant danger in slogans. If they are
exaggerated or lack distinction they can easily be
turned against their makers. Carried away by rhythm
and alliteration, an orator accused Grover Cleveland
of standing for "rum, Romanism, and rebellion." The
phrase is supposed to have increased Irish and
Catholic voter turnout, which resulted in Cleveland's
election to president. Nothing is so pathetically futile
as the sign "headquarters for snappy clothes" in the

dirty window of a small, cheap clothing store in a back street. A slogan must have some relation to fact. "Eventually—why not now?" can be applied to the product of a company which can potentially dominate its field. If the absorption point for motor cars in this country were one million a year, and one manufacturer made 750,000 cars a year, he might claim that eventually everyone would buy his cars. But the maker of a brand of shoes, knowing perfectly that he can supply, at best, only ten percent of a demand, runs a grave risk in using "Eventually—why not now?" as a slogan because in any event, however remote, it is not only unlikely that the whole country would concentrate on his product, it is even unlikely that he could supply such a demand. President Wilson's phrases, which favored abstractions, were particularly susceptible to criticism. They served as standards during the war, but when he suggested that the heart of humanity would break if this country failed to enter the League of Nations, the genuine emotion behind the phrase was broken down by ridicule and was defeated by the emotions crystallizing around an older and more specific phrase—"entangling alliances."

The slogan is always a short cut. By constant use it becomes a mechanism by which we explain and defend our actions. Personal liberty was at one time a slogan against prohibition, and one saw it on little

buttons worn by drunkards. "To the victor belong the
spoils" was used as a justification for robbery by men
who, in their private lives, would have shrunk from
the slightest dishonesty. A good slogan will even
convince people that their sufferings are necessary
and desirable since "The king can do no wrong" or "It
is the will of God."

At times, a slogan or a phrase is an argument in
itself. Its implications extend beyond actual words—
they are a criticism or an attack. For example, as the
result of propaganda by certain labor unions, Congress
passed a law making it obligatory for the railroads to
put superfluous men on each train. On the face of it,
it would seem impossible that any legislative body
should deliberately ask even an unpopular group of
corporations to employ unnecessary men, and it
would seem incredible that the public should approve.
The suggestion of superfluity, however, was never
made. Instead, the happy inspiration came to
someone to call the measure "the full-crew bill," and,
instantly, legislators and the public imagined that
trains had been running with depleted crews, and that
the railroads did not put enough men on the job to
insure safety. The railroads protested that their
present crews were adequate in every respect; but the
enchanting phrase had a running start and the bill was
passed. After the hypnotic effect of the phrase had

died down, the facts were painstakingly put before the public, and the bill was repealed.

Another case was that of the Hudson railway tubes. Enormous publicity had attended the construction of these tunnels under the Hudson River. The head of the Hudson and Manhattan Railroad Company, William G. McAdoo, had a gift for appearing before the public in an interesting and favorable light, a gift he afterwards used as director-general of the railroads during the war.[5] But he had to face the ingrown American prejudice in favor of a five-cent fare. It is a prejudice based partly on convenience, for additional pennies are a nuisance. It has little to do with the actual problem of the additional cost which would amount (in the case of a seven-cent fare) to less than twenty cents a week for the average patron. Chiefly, however, the objection to allowing street car and other transportation companies the right to charge additional fares must be derived from the ancient, wholesale condemnation of such companies which dates back to the time when muckrakers first exposed municipal corruption and brought to light old briberies and other illegalities practiced by street car corporations in the earliest

---

[5] William Gibbs McAdoo (1863–1941) assumed leadership of the Hudson River railway tunnel project in 1900. The project opened in 1908. From 1913–1918, he served as Wilson's Treasury Secretary.

days. The situation has changed; but prejudices outlive facts.

Still, McAdoo was fortunate in having a transportation system which had no background in graft and which was novel in its physical circumstances—it went under a river, and it connected New York and New Jersey. Yet he did not dare to ask for a higher fare directly. He asked only for a "readjustment" of fares; and by explaining exactly why a readjustment was necessary, won the people of both states to his side. The older companies operating elevated and subway lines in New York City are faced with the same situation—they approach bankruptcy unless a "readjustment" is made. But they cannot make the same plea: not only are they too old and too familiar—the five-cent fare is established in the minds of the riders as it was not in the minds of the Hudson tube patrons—but the whole subject has become a political issue, and can no longer be studied, dispassionately, on economic grounds. Once in politics, the five-cent fare became a slogan and dramatic (and even melodramatic) expedients have been used to keep it before the public.

In international politics, the slogan is familiar. The Kaiser's "our future lies on the water" did as much to create the frame of mind in which the war of

1914 became possible as any overt act.[6] It is interesting that the attitude of a country to another country, when friendship exists, can also be modified by a slogan which dramatizes a fact. About 90 percent of the American tourists who visit Italy return full of enthusiasm for the dictatorship of Mussolini. Only in the smallest degree is this due to any enthusiasm for dictatorship per se, and only a few tourists study the political situation, or the financial one, long enough to determine that Mussolini is actually doing Italy a great service. What all of them see and all of them say is that "the Italian railroad trains run on time!"[7] If it was a master of publicity who launched this phrase, he deserves a prize. First, the phrase suggests that the Italian railroads did not run on time before (which is true for the period of socialist control of Italy). Second, it particularly appeals to Americans accustomed not only to trains on schedule, but even to refunds on fares if certain trains fall behind. To the European, arrival on the dot does not mean so much. Although trains are accurate in their schedules, the appearance of hurry at midway stops is totally lacking

---

[6] This phrase comes from a speech in Hamburg offered by Wilhelm II of Germany (1869–1941) in 1901.

[7] In 1936, American journalist George Seldes, after visiting Italy, reported that this saying was a myth, spread by propagandists who were emphasizing the law and order efficiency of Mussolini's regime.

and no one comments on a train which arrives a quarter of an hour late. Thirdly, the phrase establishes a connection between the promptness of the trains (which implies that everything else is running smoothly) and the Fascist system of government. The fact that trains run on time in Norway, which is a democracy, and in Britain, a limited monarchy, and do not run on time in Spain, which is under a dictatorship similar to that of Mussolini, would not enter into the average mind. If trains began to fall behind schedule in the United States, the American who had been in Italy, or heard of Italy, would probably suggest that a dictatorship would provide the cure.

Mussolini is, in fact, a master of publicity. He knows that men's minds work by association. In the very name of the National Fascist Party he has created a link with Ancient Rome and stirred racial memories long left untouched. In the Black Shirt,[8] he revived and modulated a memory of Giuseppe Garibaldi.[9] Everything he does suggests an imperial character—but he does nothing to suggest himself as a King. Thus he escapes the charge of being hostile to

---

[8] The Black Shirts were originally a paramilitary wing of the National Fascist Party in Italy and, by 1923, became an all-volunteer militia of the state.

[9] Giuseppe Garibaldi (1807–1882) was an Italian nationalist who rose to prominence in the military and then in the Italian Senate.

the established King of Italy and places himself on the side of the emperors of Rome. He even plays the fiddle, and jestingly dares his enemies to say he is a Nero. The name, Il Duce ("the leader") is a phrase in which he concentrates the aspirations of his people.

Part IV

Special Applications and Cases

Chapter 13.
Publicity and Corporations

THE HISTORY OF THE AMERICAN RAILROADS in the last 25 years may be studied as a text book on the need and use of publicity. A single phrase misinterpreted had corrupted the relationship between railroads and the public. A reporter, breaking in on William Henry Vanderbilt, insisted that his New York Central Railroad owed an explanation of some policy or condition to the public. Vanderbilt replied with the four words which became a slogan for use against all the railroads in the country and later against all corporations. It was, "the public be damned."[1] Vanderbilt did not intend to imply that the New York Central was not earnestly engaged in serving and pleasing the public in the actual operation of the road, but he lived in an era when the right of the public to know was not recognized. He meant that the New York Central would pursue its own policy and keep its own counsel and abide by the

---

[1] This event, which happened in 1883, occurred because Chicago reporter John Dickinson Sherman asked Vanderbilt if it was profitable for the New York Central to run limited express trains, or was the railroad simply offering the line as a public accommodation. Vanderbilt responded, "Accommodation of the public? The public be damned!... [The limited express trains] do not pay.... As long as [the competition] will run them we must do the same."

result, and would issue no explanation to the people.
In regard to publicity, he meant at that moment
exactly what he said; in regard to the comfort and
satisfaction of the patrons of the road, however, he
meant nothing of the sort. His position against
publicity was so obviously right to himself that he was
unconscious of the phrase he had used and never
really understood why it should have caused so much
comment. He meant that the reporter's question was
not the kind of question the public had a right to ask
or the railroad an obligation to answer.

The fundamental error was in the failure to
realize that a new era was beginning. Rightly or
wrongly, change had come over the relations between
railroads and the public, and the public was eventually
to have the right to question everything the railroad
did, to examine its accounts, determine its rates, and
virtually control its profits.

The public, like the individuals composing it,
finds it easy to personify corporations. It creates
cartoons in its own mind. Out of the episode with the
reporter on Vanderbilt's private car, the public
created a caricature like a Nast cartoon with the
figure of the opulent railroad magnate smoking a fat
cigar, casually flicking ashes on the Aubusson rug[2] and

---

[2] Aubusson rugs come from a distinguished line of hand-woven work
that received particular notoriety in the French Court of Louis
XIV in the 17th century.

sneering in the face of the public. For many years, that picture represented in the public mind the owners and the directors of the American railroad system. "To hell with the public" concentrated ancient grievances and intensified the hostility which existed against the railroads. The railroads had done incalculable service to the growth of America, and had also, at times, been ruthless and, in places, dishonest. The service was forgotten and the wrongs exaggerated. That is the usual effect of a striking phrase like "the public be damned." It crystallized one system of emotions and destroyed another. The public attitude toward the railroads thus fortified made it possible for President Roosevelt to count upon almost universal support when he carried on his agitation against the railroads in the first years of this century. In the investigation of the finances of the Chicago and Alton Railroads, E. H. Harriman fell particularly under President Roosevelt's lash, and, in a letter which was made public, the president called Harriman "an undesirable citizen."[3]

Here was a new slogan reinforcing what the public already thought of the creators of great railway

---

[3] E.H. Harriman (1848–1909) was the top executive over extensive corporate operations including the Union Pacific, the Southern Pacific, and the Wells Fargo Express Company. Roosevelt made this statement in a letter that preceded an Interstate Commerce Commission investigation of Harriman's Chicago and Alton Railroads.

systems and came not only with the vigor which was
common to all of Roosevelt's utterances, but with the
immeasurable authority of the presidential office.
Backed by public opinion, Congress and the state
legislatures passed a tremendous volume of legislation
intended to put an end to abuses, and actually placed
the railroads in a position of almost complete
dependence on the government. This is the net result
of the lack of public confidence, of the belief widely
held for generations that railroad presidents could not
be trusted, and of the corporate policy of saying
nothing to the public. The effect on the railroads is
virtually a complete change from the system of far-
sighted planning and bold initiative which prevailed
from the Civil War for about half a century.

The rates the railroads charge are regulated, the
wages they pay are also determined, and the taxes are
fixed by the government. In the vast growth of
American industry in the past two decades the
railroads have had little share because the only new
capital they could attract has been by way of issuing
bonds which can only be offered on the basis of
existing equities, with future issues steadily limited.
The psychological attitude of the public is perfectly
expressed in this technical distinction between stocks
and bonds. When a man buys stock in a corporation
he not only takes a chance, he becomes a partner in
the enterprise and a well-wisher of its prosperity. But

when he buys a bond, he is taking a lien on the property and looks upon the corporation with a certain amount of suspicion, being interested only in assuring himself that he will get back his investment or capture the assets in case of default. The public, which had been a partner in the railroads, became a creditor.

A further result of this change in public feeling toward the railroads is that the roads themselves are unable to keep pace with the growth of the country. A few years ago there lay on the desk of the president of the Pennsylvania Railroad a summary of the improvements which the company expected to make next year, and two years, and 10 years, and 15 years, and 20 years ahead. The Pennsylvania Station in New York City was planned 20 years before it was opened. A railroad like the Pennsylvania would carry $10 million in vacant real estate in order to keep ahead of its requirements. It would purchase land and hold it against the time when it would be needed so as to have facilities for a track, or a siding,[4] or a station. This required floating capital and, with the breakdown of public confidence, this capital was withdrawn and diverted to other industries. It is still the principle of the American people to allow individuals and corporations to develop all their

---

[4] A "siding" is a railroad track that is designed for low-speed use and is separate from the main (or running) line.

capacities, and to grow as rapidly as they can, so long as they do not hamper the growth of others or violate the law. Yet the railroads, because they failed years ago to establish a proper relationship between themselves and the public, were, for a long period, incapable of developing as they naturally would and as the country required them to develop. The justice of legislation affecting the railroads need not be questioned in this connection. From the point of view of the railroad itself, the restrictions imposed by the government are a misfortune—and the misfortune goes back to the failure to create a favorable public attitude.

It has been the habit of American corporations, a habit slowly crumbling under the impact of unhappy experience, to keep themselves to themselves until a disaster warns them that the public has to be dealt with. The railroads in 1905 began a tentative approach to the public and, although they have not yet succeeded in obliterating the old picture, they are creating a new one. The railroad, at any rate, has ceased to be the ogre at the top of the American Jack's beanstalk. Publicity used to be conceived as an umbrella, to be put up only in case of rain. A year ago, when an oil man was approaching trial and senatorial investigation, he took a newspaper man out of the press gallery at the Capitol and made him his press agent. This was a confession not necessarily of

consciousness of guilt but surely of a wrong attitude
to the public in the past.

The new practice of publicity is based on the
idea that the public should be continuously informed
so that, if a crisis does occur, a corporation can count
on the public to make up its mind with full control of
the facts. Roger William Riis and Charles Bonner, in
their 1926 book *Publicity: A Study of the Development of
Industrial News*, cite as an example of the lack of
publicity the plight of the Aluminum Company. It is
not necessary to pass any judgment on this company
in order to understand its situation in regard to the
public. Riis and Bonner say:

> By 1924, the Aluminum Company had obtained a
> monopoly in its field. It had done this by virtue of the
> ability and acumen of its management, which had
> been so outstanding that one of the company's heads
> became the chief financial officer of the United
> States. The company occupied an unassailable
> position. Its market was assured and increasing,
> competition it had none and able men were directing
> its policies.

> In 1924, however, the company came under fire as
> a "trust." This word had carried opprobrium 15 or 20
> years before, but it had lost so much of its fatal
> import that the company's directors were
> comparatively unmoved when the Federal Trade
> Commission began its investigation. The quiescence,
> it turns out, proved highly dangerous.

...Let us suppose that, when first the Federal Trade Commission began its investigation, the directors of the company had summoned a publicity man and consulted with him...

...The publicity man might have said..."What you have to do now is to get the point of view of the people around the country. So far, they don't even know that you are being investigated. They don't know that there is a suggestion of your violating any laws. Their present ignorance is your chance. Tell them yourself, at once. Tell them before the other fellow tells them. Get to them with the accurate version of it before your enemies get to them with distorted versions. But get to them before it is too late."

The management of the average company would sneer at such advice. It seems like playing into hostile hands. Why broadcast facts that are better kept secret?

But nothing on earth can keep such facts secret...

The company should have stepped before the public and announced through the press that it was being investigated on the charge of being a trust. It should have explained that perhaps it was a trust; it would leave that to the Federal Trade Commission to decide. If the commission decided that it was a trust, then the company would take any corrective measures that might be recommended.

In the meantime, the company should have raised in the newspapers and magazines the question of whether a trust is inherently evil. It should have pointed out that its great organization and great control of raw materials and markets made possible cheaper and better aluminum pots and pans for every housewife's kitchen. It should have drawn this connection tight with every American home. It should have discussed frankly whether it had not benefited more people than it had harmed by its alleged violation of the law. In this there lies a case for which powerful arguments can be advanced...

But what these authors say is insufficient. From the moment an investigation began the company was on the defensive. It might put up a thousand of the best umbrellas in the world, but it could not prevent the rain from falling. The newspaper headlines were bound to repeat the words "admit" and "confesses." It was possible and probably desirable to hurry into print with a statement such as is suggested above and make it as positive and affirmative as possible. The desirable thing would have been to start this publicity 10 years earlier.

A positive attitude can be effectively used to counteract attacks. In 1915, the heads of many great corporations were called before the investigating committee headed by attorney Frank P. Walsh, who was a cross-examiner of exceptional ingenuity.[5] It was

---

[5] Frank P. Walsh (1864–1939) was a progressive attorney who worked as an advocate for workers. He became head of the Commission on Industrial Relations in 1913.

his function to put his witnesses on the defensive.
When John D. Rockefeller, Jr., was called in
connection with the coal strike in Colorado, he
appeared in the morning and it was certain that
Walsh would make the testimony of the opening
session appear entirely unfavorable to Rockefeller.[6]
After the preliminary questions, Walsh asked one
directly bearing on the strike. Rockefeller replied that
particular question was answered in a statement
which he had prepared, and asked permission to read
it. Walsh refused. Rockefeller then said that, at the
moment he had taken the stand, his statement
covering the present question and, as far as he could
judge, all questions relating to the labor situation in
the Colorado mines had been handed to the press. As
far as rousing public criticisms of Rockefeller's
methods was intended, the first day session was a total
failure because the newspapers carried his affirmative
statement—which was as complete and frank as he
could make it—in a preferred position, and the
fragmentary cross examination in a secondary one.

The same tactics were followed by William
Wallace Atterbury, vice president for operations for

---

[6] The Commission on Industrial Relations investigated deaths that
accompanied an April 1914 strike against Colorado mines owned by
Rockefeller's Colorado Fuel and Iron Company—an event known
as the Ludlow Massacre.

the Pennsylvania Railroad.[7] Months before he was called to appear before the Walsh commission in August 1912, he had issued an order requesting every official of the railroad to go back over the files and note every labor dispute which was in any way subject to criticism. The officials of the railroad knew that Walsh would ask them to admit that there exists at the Broad Street station in Philadelphia a private arsenal containing 5,000 rifles and appropriate ammunition.[8] It was easy to foresee the newspaper headlines in which Walsh would wring from Atterbury a confession that the Pennsylvania Railroad had such an arsenal with the implication that it was to be used to shoot down strikers. The company determined to admit nothing, but, in accordance with its new conception of publicity, to announce everything. A pamphlet was prepared in which every important dispute between the railroad and its workers was dissected, with both sides of the argument given as fairly as possible. On the subject of the arsenal, there was no attempt at concealment.

---

[7] William Wallace Atterbury (1866–1935) was a Brigadier General during WWI and, from 1925–1935, was the president of the Pennsylvania Railroad.

[8] During that same Walsh commission hearing, a Pennsylvania Railroad official confirmed that the Broad Street Station housed 90 guns—their purpose, he said, was to arm railroad police officers to prevent a further rash of attacks on post office safes in stations along the railroad's line.

Although the question had not been raised, the
Pennsylvania Railroad announced that, in order to be
prepared for every eventuality, to protect the
enormous property in which thousands of American
citizens had invested, and to safeguard the lives of its
passengers, it kept always ready an adequate defensive
arsenal. The pamphlet was given to the press just
before Atterbury took the stand and effectively cut
the ground from under Walsh's feet. The public
actually learned a great deal about the Pennsylvania
Railroad—particularly that, although it had disputes
with labor, it was seriously endeavoring to settle these
disputes in a spirit of fairness to the workers and to
the stockholders. There were no admissions and no
confession.

A testimony of a present judge of the United
States Supreme Court on the legitimacy of such
publicity may be taken. In 1913, the railroads appealed
for an increase in freight rates. Their chief opponent
was Louis Brandeis.[9] Before the Interstate Commerce
Commission (ICC) met to consider the appeal, the
railroads sent a letter to the ICC informing them that
they intended to carry on a campaign of publicity

---

[9] Louis D. Brandeis (1856–1941) served on the Supreme Court from
1916 to 1939. Prior to his appointment to the court, Brandeis was a
leading advocate for reform, including criticizing railroad rate
increases as signs of inefficiency, and working against the
consolidation of ownership of the railroads.

based on the hearings, and asked if the ICC saw any objections. The ICC replied that they had no comment to make. Day by day, the testimony of the railroads before the ICC was summarized, interpreted in simple language, and sent to the newspapers. The same testimony in a slightly more elaborate form was sent as a bulletin to all the people in the United States who might have serious interest in the subject. The result was that chambers of commerce all over the country began to pass resolutions favoring the plea of the railroads, and Congress was bombarded with letters. The campaign was so successful that the late Senator Robert La Follette brought it to the attention of the Senate and published, in a 349-page issue of the *Congressional Record*, all the publicity matter sent out and all the letters and resolutions that answered it.[10] The senator considered the campaign a nefarious attack on the activities of the ICC, although nothing appeared in the publicity which had not been submitted under oath before the ICC itself. Brandeis was asked to criticize this campaign. Specifically the question was put to him, "Do you see anything which we are doing that we ought not to do?" Although

---

[10] Senator Robert M. La Follette (1855–1925), a progressive Republican, was a major critic of the railroads. He called this rate campaign by the Pennsylvania Railroad a "monument of shame" within comments that accompanied the reproduction of the campaign materials in the *Congressional Record* of the 63rd Congress, 2nd Session, 1914, Volume LI, Part 8, pp. 7735–8093.

opposed to the railroads, he replied, "If I were in the railroad's place I would do exactly what they are doing." He added that his only regret was that no one on his side had the money or power to do the same thing and that the interests on his side were therefore not so fully presented to the public. This is, of course, one of the gravest problems of publicity and one to which neither the upholders nor the critics of publicity have yet discovered a satisfactory solution.

These examples of corporation publicity have been drawn from the experience of corporations already under fire. They can be supplemented by examples of the more effective publicity used in ordinary circumstances. Some time ago, the Bethlehem Steel Company determined to increase its capital as soon as the investment market would take its stocks or bonds. The difficulty there was not a government investigation nor any public hostility. What the bankers reported to the company's president, Eugene Grace, was that the public had a picture of the company in the back of its mind, and that certain elements in this picture (e.g., labor unrest) would not be favorable to investment. They said to Grace, "During the war, the Bethlehem Steel Company was so notably engaged in making munitions that its other, normal activities were pushed into the background. Charles Schwab[11] touched the public imagination as few men ever touched it, but now the people were reading of the Washington Conference which calls for a degree of disarmament.[12] People have understood that you build warships and that you have navy yards, and they know that the shipbuilding business is at a very low ebb. Everybody knows that you and Schwab are great men, but, with these ideas in the back of the people's minds, you haven't sufficient public friendship to create the confidence which you ought to have for issuing securities."[13]

The first step in the considered program of altering the public attitude toward the Bethlehem Steel Company was setting before the public the facts about the relationship between the company and its workmen. No organization which is constantly threatened with strikes or hindered in its productiveness by discontent and sabotage can expect the confidence of investors.

---

[11] Charles Michael Schwab (1862–1939), in tandem with Eugene Grace (1876–1960), ran Bethlehem Steel.

[12] The Washington Conference, which ran from November 1921 until February 1922 was called by President Warren G. Harding. The U.S. and nine other nations, mostly European, discussed, among other items, arms control. It is considered to be the first arms control conference of wide international scope.

[13] This is not a direct quote but, instead a simulated "single voice" of the banking industry.

The satisfactory situation in the Bethlehem Steel Company was set before the public not merely by printing facts, but by the use of picturesque and dramatic incidents. With this as a foundation, the company proceeded to recondition the public mind. The buoyant enthusiasm of Schwab for his war baby was played down, and the economic soundness of the institution correspondingly played up. In newspaper articles, and in special bulletins distributed to bankers and investors, the false picture of idle shipyards was erased and a true story of the transformation of these yards into a great and highly profitable ship-repairing industry took its place. The sword was literally being beaten into plowshares, for the Bethlehem Steel Company was successfully manufacturing agricultural implements as well as cars, locomotives, and other products which looked not backward to the war, but forward to the industries of peace. The facts had been available for many months, but they were ineffective until they were known. When deliberate publicity made them known, the resistance of bankers and small investors was overcome and the Bethlehem Steel Company had no difficulty in floating a loan of $30 million.

The advertising of the Bell Telephone System has a special point of interest because that system is virtually a monopoly, meeting no competition in its own field, and competing for business only against such other mediums of communications as the telegraph and the postal systems. From time to time in various cities, the Bell Company has to meet two distinct forms of criticism. One is that its service is unsatisfactory, and the other that its rates are exorbitant. Yet, for the most part, the relations of the company to the public are agreeable. The company, having no rivals, is hardly subject to the temptations of other industries. It may be assumed that the company operates within the law and has nothing to fear except legislation which would prevent it from expanding.

The direct advertising of the company consists largely of pictures and text dealing with the human elements involved in the creation and operation of the system or with the simple emotions which using the telephone can satisfy—reaching out while stuck in a snow storm or within an isolated village or making a telephonic appeal for help after a tornado, poles and wires down and a crew of Bell employees already at work keeping the service going. Other ads show instruments of precision handled by expert mechanics to make the delicate instrument, or an anxious father or mother telephoning to a son at college, or an enterprising sales manager making ten sales in ten minutes by long distance. Nowhere in its direct advertising does the company stress the fact, known to every traveler, that the American telephone system is infinitely superior to any privately or publicly operated system abroad. In Bell's advertising in periodicals of national circulation, the question of rates and legislative interference do not occur. Rather, in this advertising, which has a rare combination of dignity and interest, the public is only invited to new uses of the telephone and to a greater familiarity with a thousand human details of its operation. It is a long-sustained and constructive system of making the public friendly to the company by making the public know about the company. The publicity, beyond advertising of the Bell System, satisfies the American interest in science and invention. The Trans-Atlantic telephone operating at a loss—to which the British government-owned telephone system violently objects—is carried cheerfully by the American system because it dramatizes the claim of the company to annihilate time and space. The company associates itself with the public mind with radio, telephotography, and with the prospect of television. In the public mind the telephone company, unlike some institutions giving public service, figures not as a mossback, self-satisfied and unprogressive organization, but as one expressing perfectly the spirit of American progress.

The creation of a favorable attitude toward a corporation can hardly be accomplished by informing the public only of its major activities. The fact that a railroad carries millions of passengers in safety and millions of tons of freight with dispatch lacks novelty and interest for the public. Statistics have to be dramatized and facts soaked in human interest before they are palatable. Some years ago, on an extremely cold day in January, the general manager of the Pennsylvania Railroad instructed the foreman of track gangs[14] that, whenever a train was approaching, the foreman should not only blow a whistle to warn his men to get off the track but should see to it that the men actually did get off. The reason was that on cold days the men wore ear muffs. Care for the safety of employees is a matter of routine with railroad executives; it is, in fact, almost a matter of self-protection. But this is not known to the general public, and the fact that the general manager of the Pennsylvania Railroad was aware of ear muffs worn by members of track gangs 1,000 miles away effectively dramatized the interest of the company in its employees. A purely moral idea was given concrete form, and the spirit of the institution was embodied in a humane action. The general manager's routine order, to which he himself attached no particular

---

[14] A "track gang" is a crew of railroad workers responsible for maintenance on a section of railroad track.

importance, was carried as an interesting news item and inspired editorials throughout the press.

Publicity for a corporation includes the activities of the corporation. Within any corporation there are bound to be divergent policies. For example, the question arose whether plate glass or crystal glass should be used in the windows of passenger coaches of a certain railroad line. The operating policy was to save $100,000 a year by putting in crystal glass. The policy toward the public was in favor of plate glass because crystal glass distorts the vision and plate glass does not. It was entirely proper for the operating officials to state their point of view, but when the question was referred to the company's advisor in public relations he replied, "You have no choice. You cannot put window glass which distorts vision in the cars of the railroad that carries 300 million passengers a year." The policy adopted by the railroad—the adoption of plate glass—was, in itself, a piece of publicity because passengers accustomed to squinty windows elsewhere contrasted with them the clear vision they had on this railroad. Announcing the fact that plate glass was being used was publicity also, but was publicity based on policy.

A shipper who has entrusted a carload of goods to the railroad may wonder why his customers have not received the goods and, therefore, calls the local freight agent to demand specific information on the progress of his shipment. There is no law compelling railroads to inform shippers of the progress of their goods. But the railroads have established an elaborate bureau with a large amount of personnel who send and receive reports on the routing of freight. This is so that, if you have shipped a car from New York to St. Louis, you will be advised when the car is in Pittsburgh, when it is in Indianapolis, and when you can expect it to reach its destination. Unless some dramatic incident or human touch should be given to this bureau, it would not make publicity in a narrow sense. That is, in the sense of getting an item published in the newspapers. But the bureau itself *is* publicity because it makes known to every shipper the fact that the company does not cease to be interested in his shipment when his order is taken; instead, it follows through and keeps him informed of daily progress.

The fate of the railroad is often in the hands of the public. In great things the public attitude affects legislation; in small things it may affect the verdict in a damage suit. The general policy of the railroad and the service it gives are its first lines of attraction. They have internal lines of support. The Pennsylvania Railroad has about 175,000 employees, each one of which can be made a focal point of friendly interest in the company, interpreting the spirit of the institution and the public. The employees of the Pennsylvania

Railroad are scattered over a great part of the United States. They are of many races, of many levels of education, of divergent interests, occupations, and traditions. The one thing that joins them together is the receipt of pay checks from the same employer. If that was all, they would hardly be conscious of being a group and could not act as a group does. They may be physically organized but their emotions would be chaotic. But when any employee sees an advertisement of a crack train,[15] or of a group of freight carriers of the Pennsylvania railroad, and if this advertisement speaks not only of the company's achievement, but of the intelligence and loyalty of the men, he begins to take pride in the institution for which he is working. A number of manufacturing concerns have recently used in their advertisements photographs of individual employees. Often these are expert craftsmen; sometimes they are men of long service with the company. Although one out of a thousand can be singled out for this type of publicity, the one stands for the thousand and each individual feels that he is an essential and appreciated worker in an institution worthy of respect and pride. A considerable amount of institutional advertising is really intended not so much for the general public as for the employees.

---

[15] A "crack train" it the fastest express train between two stops.

The "house organ" publication is another instrument in the creation of group feeling. It is often spoiled by the intrusion of direct company propaganda. In the newspaper issued for the employees of the Pennsylvania Railroad, no company propaganda of any kind is allowed. This newspaper is the counterpart of a small-town weekly, telling the neighbors news about each other. The theory is to get into its columns mention of every man on the railroad who does anything of the least consequence. If a foreigner is naturalized that fact is recorded in the paper. An Italian proud of his new citizenship, pleased to see his name in print, will send a copy of the paper home to show his people in Italy that the great Pennsylvania Railroad is aware of his existence. He will also feel proud of the fact that 175,000 other employees have been called to take notice of him and, thereafter, he will be more interested in similar items of news concerning others. In this newspaper there are no pictures of company officers, no items of policy, nothing that can interfere with its specific purpose, which is to recognize the interest of the employees in each other. With that as a foundation, the railroad issues an entirely separate publication in which, with perfect frankness, the management of the railroad gives to the men its views of controversial questions as they arise and, without any insinuation or concealment, explains its purposes and policies.

IVY LEDBETTER LEE
WITH BURTON ST. JOHN III, PH.D.

Chapter 14.
The Public Utilities Campaign

IN THE SPRING OF 1928, the Federal Trade
Commission (FTC) investigated certain activities of
various public utilities with special attention to their
methods of publicity.[1] The report on this
investigation is a terrible example of how not to do
publicity. Omitting all consideration of ethics, the
methods exposed are definitely inappropriate to the
present condition of public opinion, and to the
attitude of the public toward corporate activities. The
mere fact that these activities had to be brought to
light, and were not themselves *in* the light, condemns
them from the point of view of intelligent publicity.
In a few instances, the publicity used was intelligent
and legitimate; in a great majority, it was of the type
which has given publicity a dubious reputation.

---

[1] The facts and quotes presented in this chapter related to the FTC
investigation are selected from the early stages of an 84-volume
report from the FTC on the NELA's (National Electric Light
Association's) use (and abuse) of domestic propaganda. For more,
see the U.S. Federal Trade Commission (1928), *Annual Report of the
Federal Trade Commission for the Fiscal Year ended June 30, 1928*.
Washington, D.C.: Government Printing Office; and Gruening, E.
(1931). *The Public Pays: A Study of Power Propaganda*. New York: The
Vanguard Press.

The first thing to notice is that, although the National Electric Light Association (NELA)[2] had a publicity organization since 1921, its work was fragmentary in every case until some sort of opposition developed outside. Walter E. Long,[3] an official in a public policy committee of the Pennsylvania Electric Association, testified that the attitude of Pennsylvania Governor Gifford Pinchot[4] in relation to giant power compelled his organization to intensify its campaign. Further witnesses indicated that the threat of the government investigation brought their fund for publicity work from $750 up to $140,000 in a few weeks. This would indicate that, although these public utilities had been carrying on some sort of campaign to establish friendship with the people they served, they did not think that they could trust this friendship in any crisis.

The greater part of this publicity was done behind the scenes. The chief counsel of the FTC

---

[2] NELA had been formed in 1885 to represent the interests of the electric power industry.

[3] Walter E. Long was elected president of the Pennsylvania Electric Association in 1914. The more significant power broker behind NELA was its founder, Samuel Insull (1859–1938), who held several power companies in the Chicago area.

[4] Gifford Pinchot (1865–1946) was first elected as Pennsylvania Governor in 1923. Previously, he was the first head of the U.S. Forest Service from 1905–1910, known for advocating planned use and preservation of the nation's reserves.

asked a witness, "Do you mean that it is honorable
and lawful for a man paid by your committee to go
before a committee of the legislature and oppose a bill
without disclosing the fact?" The witness replied, "I
consider that lawful." On the question of honor, the
witness did not commit himself. Had the investigator
been an expert in publicity he might have asked
whether the witness thought that a method of
doubtful integrity would, in the end, prove effective.
Among the means of publicity used by the utilities
was the subsidizing of people who had access to the
public. Thus, college professors giving courses, in
which the problems of public utilities and government
ownership might be discussed, were employed as
lecturers, and were paid sums, in addition to their
expenses, which appeared to be excessive.
Newspapermen were put on a regular salary list of
which their employers were not necessarily aware.
Writers formerly identified with radical movements,
and men formerly occupying positions of high trust in
the government of the United States, were either
subsidized while writing books or paid lump sums for
doing so, and the fact that these payments were made
could not be known to the reading public. In many
cases, salaries were drawn for doing opinion surveys,
the exact nature of which was not explained in the
testimony, and also for doing historical research.

NELA naturally took a great interest in the textbooks used in schools and colleges. One of their officials wrote that he would "assist in editing the matter used in putting utility economics courses in state colleges." Another testified that the business of driving out textbooks unfavorable to the public utilities was left in the hands of local company officials because, "The men who are actually in the field and are locally acquainted could accomplish more by carrying the complaint directly to the school boards than could be done by any general campaigns against the books." In New England, the testimony indicated that electric light companies not only offered jobs to college undergraduates but offered "reasonable compensation" to professors and instructors who would study utility operations with them.

The methods of concealing the source of the publicity sent out were various. As one official put it in connection with textbooks, the work was to be done "in a manner well safeguarded from suspicion." In addition to concealing their own connection with the activities already noted, public utility companies would send out editorials to favorable journals and then use these on the clipsheets sent to other newspapers which would, naturally, consider these editorials as independent expressions of opinion. The exact testimony on this point was:

Q. Well, isn't it a fact that there is a considerable quantity of the news material put out by your association which finds its way into the news columns of local papers?

A. It certainly does. If it didn't we would be a failure on that particular phase of the work.

Q. And if you didn't do that you would stop putting it out?

A. Exactly.

Q. And a considerable quantity of it is put out in the news columns without the source of where it originated from showing?

A. Yes, even though the figures are backed by statements not disassociated from the original sources.

Concerning the ways in which this favorable news matter reached newspapers, the testimony is direct. One witness testified that "he urged the utilities to advertise in the newspapers, especially the country papers, because he thought they would be more likely to be friendly and to publish their news matter." In Iowa, according to a report which was read into the testimony, the newspapers published news and other matter agreeable to the public utilities which would have cost $80,000 at advertising rates. In the same report, the industry's publicity committee claimed responsibility for increasing public utility advertising in Iowa by 1,000 percent. Further

testimony indicated that local managers were
instructed to establish contacts with newspapers in
their territory:

> Q. In the next place you say that careful
> consideration should be given to regular
> advertising in each of the small papers within the
> territory covered by them?
>
> A. Yes, sir.
>
> Q. And you put considerable emphasis on regular
> advertising?
>
> A. Yes, sir.
>
> Q. That was as a means of promoting relations
> between the newspapers and the local
> committees?
>
> A. And promoting increased use of electricity.
>
> Q. And promoting increased use in the newspapers of
> the material sent out?
>
> A. Yes, sir.

So far, all these forms of publicity have been
underground, if not underhanded. They worked under
the old conception of publicity as a surreptitious
means of getting control of public opinion. In most of
these cases, the companies involved concealed their
interests and avoided responsibility for the statements
which they actually put forth. At the same time, a
certain amount of publicity, in a later conception of

the term, was used. An effort was made to make every employee a point of contact between the companies and the public. The employees were not only told what the companies were doing, but why they were doing it. In addition to specific training in courtesy, employees of many companies were instructed to anticipate complaints by "looking for trouble" before the customer was even aware of it. Further, many companies carried on substantial campaigns of selling stock to their customers, the purpose being not only to attract capital, but to attract the sympathetic interest of the general public.

In a customer-ownership plan, the NELA, representing 228 companies, had 15.5 million customers, of whom 1.4 million had bought 15 million shares. The ratio of stockholders to customers is roughly one-to-15 and, for every user of electric light and power, approximately one share is held in the hands of the general public. It was definitely intended that these customer-owners should not only stand against government ownership, but also radiate such confidence in a friendliness toward the companies so that hostile legislation would be met by counteracting impulses from the public. The public utilities of the United States stand particularly in need of public confidence. This is due partially to their peculiar relation to the public which they serve every day in immediate contact. The grave problem for the public utilities is to persuade state legislatures to lift the ban which forbids savings and trust funds from investing in public utilities. The companies, therefore, have to prove themselves well established and not only law abiding, but clear of every suspicion. It is often said that the perpetual threat of hostile legislation and of government ownership forces the companies into difficult positions. But it is precisely this threat which friendly relations with the public can banish.

The publicity which hides itself is a contradiction in terms. It may be temporarily effective, but it always runs the risk of being exposed—and the moment it is exposed, the fact that it concealed itself brings with it an imputation of wrong doing.

Chapter 15.
Publicity and Finance

OTTO KAHN ONCE SAID THAT there was a feeling on Wall Street that no issue of securities was a success unless it was sold before it was advertised.[1] The implication is clear. Both the institution offering securities and the bankers handling the issues must have, in advance of advertising, an effectively mobilized public opinion since advertising alone, in the experience of bankers, is insufficient for a sale. As the *Wall Street Journal* once told European bankers trying to float loans here during the war, in America "publicity is one of the recognized foundations of credit." It is therefore a little odd to find that, even in America, financial publicity has been largely placed in the hands of the least trustworthy. Knowing the British attitude toward advertising, one is not surprised to learn that the London Stock Exchange forbids its members to advertise in any way. The London Stock Exchange member may not even put his card in a financial publication—he may publish simply his name and address. He may not send a circular of his firm to anyone who is not already a

---

[1] Otto Kahn (1867–1934) was a prominent investment banker and philanthropist who was known for his leading role in supporting the arts.

client of the firm. He may not send out market letters, such as our New York Stock Exchange houses distribute. He may not do anything which is in the nature of what we call advertising; and the same thing is substantially true of all stock exchange firms on the continent of Europe. In New York, the stock exchange, through its committee, maintains a very strict scrutiny of all financial advertising, and forbids any advertising which will be in the nature of recommending stocks for speculative purposes, anything in the nature of tips, and anything predicting the future course of the market. Anything of that kind is forbidden. A great many otherwise perfectly proper advertisements are forbidden by the committee of the New York Stock Exchange.

The result of this prohibition is that most irresponsible and blatant advertising is done by the less responsible houses—the bucket shops, and those who have fake securities to sell, and oil securities that represent hopes rather than assets.[2] The most persuasive financial advertising, that which is really designed to get a buyer, is done on behalf of the less responsible ventures. What is the result of that? It is that the people who are ignorant, who have the least knowledge of investment, who have their savings

---

[2] A "bucket shop" was a location that takes bets on movements within the stock market, but handled no stock market transactions. Most states have long declared them illegal.

accumulated for the first time in order to begin to be investors, derive their first knowledge of advertised securities from houses which have the least legitimate claim upon their attention.

For generations the financial symbol of the United States has figured in the public mind under the name of Wall Street. Wall Street is supposed to have wanted peace or war, or the triumph of a political party, or the defeat of a bill in Congress. Wall Street has been the place where speculators made millions and the small investor was robbed of his shirt. Wall Street was, in short, one of those dangerous symbols around which emotions cluster and crystalize. It has been noted that symbols lag behind fact—the last Emperor of Austria was the head of the Holy Roman Empire although that empire (itself neither holy, nor Roman, nor an empire, as British Ambassador to the U.S. James Bryce puts it) had not existed for centuries. The Wall Street symbol may have been accurate at the time when trading and investing was limited to a small number of people. Conditions have changed. The flotation of Liberty Bonds during the war made the United States a nation of investors. At about the same time, great corporations began to seek out the small investor partly for financial reasons and partly in pursuit of a new public policy. As corporations were first subjected to hostile publicity, and later learned to develop publicity on their own account, they realized that among their most precious assets was a public in partnership with them.

Yet the symbol of Wall Street persists. It still means, in many minds, a small group of rich financiers opposed to the public interest. Still, the excitement caused by the trading of at least three or four million shares daily at the beginning of 1928, and the participation of thousands of small speculators during this period, have done much to create a new idea of the stock exchange in the public mind. The "stock exchange" as a phrase is beginning to supplant Wall Street as a phrase. Yet it is probably that incautious small investors, when they lose, revert to their old idea of Wall Street which has been bred in the bone.

For generations, Wall Street has not lacked publicity, but most of it came from the outside and was hostile. It is only within the last 10 years or so that the stock exchange as a body broke through its own reserve and began a system of public education. It took several years to persuade the governors of the exchange that such publicity was necessary. Like many other institutions, the stock exchange waited until it was under fire and the Hughes commission in 1909, followed by the Pujo Investigation, finally compelled publicity.[3] The necessity was great. One of

---

[3] New York Governor Charles E. Hughes led a committee in 1909 that investigated speculation in securities and commodities on

the primary functions in the stock exchanges is to
offer to investors and to speculators a group of
brokers of established integrity. The great enemy of
the honest broker is the bucket shop, not chiefly
because the bucket shop is a rival in business but
because every fraud practiced in connection with
investing or speculating is held against Wall Street as
a whole and not against the criminal bucketeers
whom Wall Street is most anxious to destroy. The
difficult task of dissociating things, once they have
become associated in the public mind, had to be
undertaken by the stock exchange itself. On one
occasion, a Western senator took the time of the
Senate to deliver a long speech mostly on the crimes
of the stock exchange against his own state. Every
item of his charge should have been directed against
the bucket shops; the stock exchange had no
connection whatever with them, as the senator was
compelled to admit when the publicity committee of
the exchange gave him proof.

In addition to this defensive publicity, the
exchange went on to the creation of friendly relations
with the public. As a result of supplying practical
material for use in courses on economics and finance,
the exchange's publicity committee was able to help

Wall Street. In 1913, Congressman Arsène Pujo of Louisiana led a
congressional committee investigation of the concentration of
financial power on Wall Street within money trusts.

colleges create special courses on dealings in securities and, at the same time, colleges cooperated by sending lecturers into the Wall Street district to speak to employees there. Teachers of economics and writers of textbooks have found the stock exchange eager to help them with historical and technical data.

This is, of course, only a beginning in publicity. What the exchange wished to do was to persuade the investing public that the interest of the public and of the legitimate investment banker and broker are identical. The investment banker particularly wishes to encourage conservative buying. The legitimate broker wishes to encourage general interest in stocks, and to prevent fraud and misrepresentation. To accomplish this, it is necessary to educate the public in the fundamentals of finance and to teach them discrimination between fraudulent and honest stocks. A former governor of the stock exchange, William Van Antwerp, has compared its activities to that of the government under the pure food law. This law, said Antwerp, "enables a man to know what he is buying. It does not certify that the thing he buys is good for him; that is left to his intelligence." The stock exchange, he said, "...cannot protect investors and speculators against the consequence of their unwisdom in buying unprofitable securities, but we can and we do attempt to reduce their risks." This is the basis for the check on brokers' advertising. The

mere fact that there are evils in speculation compels
the stock exchange, said Van Antwerp, "to maintain a
standard of business morality higher than that
ordinarily applicable in the commercial world at
large."[4] A seller of real estate may say that his
property is certain to triple its value in two years, or
may point out that the adjoining property has so
increased in value. But no man can make such
predictions about speculative investments and,
therefore, the exchange forbids its members to give
even an implied assurance of profit.

About fifteen years ago, *The Outlook* magazine
was able to say, quite correctly, that there are millions
of people in the United States who do not know the
first principles of investment. One reason was that,
confusing investment and speculation and having no
standard by which to judge wild cat promotions or
legitimate enterprises, the majority of people
withdrew from the whole business of investment as a
dangerous and unprofitable thing. Even entirely
honest corporations were in the habit of offering
stock with only a sketchy indication of their financial
situation and prospects. The *Chicago Tribune* at the
time pointed out that Blue Sky laws and government
superstition could often be evaded or forgotten

---

[4] These quotes come from Van Antwerp's remarks before the
Associated Advertising Club of the World meeting in Philadelphia
in the summer of 1916.

whereas, "the law of supply and demand cannot be repealed or dodged and all corporations offering their securities to the public are subservient to it."[5] Noting that great corporations were beginning to use publicity, the *Tribune* predicted that those concerns which insist on secrecy would gradually be retired from activity.

The operations of bankers and brokers are a mystery to most people, and most of the financial statements issued by them are so cluttered with figures and involved in technical terms that the average reader turns from them with displeasure. The average person, when encountering the doctor's prescription in Latin ascribes the mystery of that language to the doctor's superior knowledge, but the mystery of the financial statement seems deliberately invoked to hide something vaguely unfriendly. Even the first steps in investing often leave the beginner with a sense of dismay. A syndicate puts out an issue for a foreign loan operating through bankers as centers of distribution. While the loan is being offered the interest rate is established, some facts about the foreign government are tabulated and, with the assurance that this particular loan is a good investment, the beginner buys his securities. The

---

[5] A 'blue sky law" is a state regulation that requires the registration of all stockbrokers and brokerage firms. Kansas passed the first blue sky law in 1911.

moment the issue is sold, the syndicate is closed up, the investors' money is transferred to a foreign government, and a banker goes on to something else. The people who buy the issue have it on their hands to worry over, or to be happy over, depending on circumstances. Neither the syndicate nor the banker gives them any further information concerning that issue or concerning the progress of the foreign government behind the issue. If the securities go down, the small investor feels that he has been played for a sucker; he suspects that the syndicate and the banker did not lose in the transaction. He positively resents the difference in attitude between the days when he was a prospective buyer and the days after he bought. If the facts, even the disagreeable facts, were sent to him, if those who sold the securities followed through and indicated some interest in the investor's future, his feeling toward another loan would be infinitely more friendly.

Foreign loans now constitute an important part of the investment business in this country and, so long as America dominates the money market, their importance will keep pace with a gradual restoration of Europe. Yet banking houses engaged in floating foreign loans have shown an amazing inertia in their dealings with the public. A few years ago, the French government was offering $100 million through its famous American agents. This loan was to be taken up eventually by the public but no effort was made to enlist public interest until two weeks before the issue was made. The publicity work in this case had excellent results, but was unsatisfactory to the man who had it in charge. At the end of it, he was told that in less than six months another issue of the same size would have to be made. He said to the bankers, "let us begin now with our publicity so that we shall create a different atmosphere for the next issue." The bankers replied that no contract had yet been signed, and they could not go into any expenses in advance. The organizer of publicity suggested that the French government should underwrite this publicity, even if it were only to send one man to France and let him act as a source of favorable information concerning France for the American people. The representative of the French government replied that propaganda was politically unpopular and could not be put into the budget. To the publicity man the situation was impossible. He traced it back to false assumptions, and to lack of good business habits. The assumptions made by both the French government and the American bankers were that publicity could be whipped up at the last moment and that it needed to apply only to a single effort. The habit of remaining constantly in relation with the public was one which that particular banking house, and many others, had never formed. Seeing a priceless opportunity slip away by the mere lapse of time, the publicity man made a sporting offer to the banking house. With the understanding that the house would employ his organization if and when the loan was authorized, he undertook to finance the publicity campaign himself and he promised them that his fee, which would look very large for two weeks work, would cover the expenses of six months. The offer was accepted, and the second loan was floated in circumstances which justified the experiment.

Chapter 16.
The Banishment of the Trusts

IN THE SECOND VOLUME of *Our Times*, Mark Sullivan's account of what occupied the public mind in America at the turn of the century, many pages are devoted to the institutions known as "trusts."[1] More than once, Sullivan seems to despair of making younger readers, who did not share the passions of the period, understand how absorbing the topic was in those days. He has no such difficulty in describing the early days of aviation, or the change in the social freedom of women; as a keen observer of contemporary interests, however, he is aware of the fact that the trust has passed out of existence as a factor in the public mind. The name has no currency; although great combinations exist, they are no longer the focus of popular passion. Yet, as late as 1912, Woodrow Wilson was appealing for votes on the platform of what he called the New Freedom, part of which, at least, was freedom from the power of huge industrial and financial concentrations.

The history of anti-trust agitation is concerned with much greater forces than any the professional

---

[1] Mark Sullivan (1874–1952), a journalist from the muckraking era, wrote the six-volume *Our Times* as a popular history of the United States. The volumes were published from 1926 through 1936.

publicist can set in motion. Publicity in every sense
was a factor in whipping up and allaying the public
excitement. But the story of the trusts is an example,
mostly, of the concentration and dispersal of
attention. It shows how economic questions can be
injected into public discussion, and how these
questions can withdraw themselves. In certain phases,
it points to a continuity of interest on the part of the
public—in others, to instability. It was in connection
with the trusts that the public first appeared as a
recognized third party in disputes between capital and
labor, and over 90 percent of the votes of America
cast their ballots for presidential candidates who were
opposed to the trusts (e.g., Bryan, Roosevelt, and
Wilson).

The high tide of opposition to the trusts was
between 1899 and 1908. Pools and combinations,
however, had come into being shortly after the Civil
War. The South Improvement Company (out of
which grew the Standard Oil Company) was formed in
1871 and set the pattern for later organizations.[2] By
1888, there was an epidemic of investigations of the
trusts—the name had entered common speech six
years earlier as a term of odium and dislike. In 1899,

---

[2] The South Improvement Company, which lasted only a year, was
formed as an effort by John D. Rockefeller to combine the
Pennsylvania Railroad with other railroads and oil and natural gas
industries.

almost all the basic commodities of life were trustified
to some degree: glass, copper, rubber, oil, agricultural
implements, school slates, castor oil, coffins,
wallpaper, and dental tools among them. Kansas
passed the first state anti-trust law in that year and,
before the end of 1891, 14 other states had followed.[3]
In 1888, both the Democratic and the Republican
parties had declared against the trusts in their party
platforms and, in 1890, the federal anti-trust law, the
famous Sherman Act, was passed, with less than one
quarter of one percent of the members of both houses
voting against it.[4] In 1892, various trusts were
dissolved by judicial decisions. The popular temper
was so exasperated that acts to punish trusts were
introduced in various state legislatures, in defiance of
their own constitutions, and, on one occasion, a man
accused of stealing oil from the Standard Oil
Company admitted the crime and was found not
guilty by a jury!

Between 1893 and 1895 the trusts dwindled. The
panic of 1893 slowed up industrial amalgamation and
withdrew those trusts that existed from the center of
the stage. With the resumption of business in 1895,
legislation against the trusts again became common,

---

[3] See Millon, D. (1990). The first antitrust statute. *29 Washburn Law Journal 141.*

[4] In the Senate, the Sherman Act passed 51-1 and, in the House, 242-0.

and William Jennings Bryan linked monopolies with the gold standard of coinage in his first campaign.[5] Yet the trust, for the next four years, was a legal and industrial problem more than a popular one. It was driven into the public mind when, in 1899, Bryan felt that the free silver issue was insufficient for his campaign and chose the trust issue as the center of his platform. In the same year appeared Edwin Markham's *The Man with the Hoe and Other Poems* to which Sullivan justifiably devotes a whole chapter of his book as a symbol of the political and economic mood of the time.[6] Incredible as it seems now, the average man took Markham's words "slave of the wheel of labor" as applying to himself. Cartoons by Frederick Burr Opper[7] and Herbert Johnson[8] showed the pathetic little figure of the "common people" serving as a golf ball for the swing of business interests or as harnessed to the sleigh in which corpulent meat

---

[5] Bryan campaigned in favor of silver as being the basis for America's monetary standard, maintaining that gold was concentrated in the hands of corporations.

[6] Edwin Markham (1852–1940), an American poet, was best known for the poem "The Man with the Hoe," which offered a portrait of the hardship of the laborer in the field.

[7] Frederick Burr Opper (1857–1937), considered a pioneer of American comic strips, was the originator of the widely-popular Happy Hooligan strip and also drew numerous political cartoons.

[8] Herbert Johnson (1878–1946) was best known as a cartoonist for the *Saturday Evening Post* magazine.

and coal trusts sat at ease. When defenders of the
trusts spoke of the inevitable workings of natural
economic law, Bryan cried out, "Is God or Nature
responsible for the...trust? Is God or Nature
responsible for private monopolies?"[9]

The trust question was in politics and was to
remain in the public eye for many years. In 1900, 28
books and 150 magazine articles dealt with the
subject. Roosevelt, as a political accident, since he
first came to the presidency without the direct choice
of the people, handled the trusts delicately at the
beginning. Author and humorist Finley Peter Dunne[10]
wrote essays featuring the fictional Irish immigrant
bartender Mr. Dooley, who imagined Roosevelt
saying, "Th' trusts are heejous monsthers built up be
th' inlightened intherprise iv th' men that have done
so much to advance progress in our beloved country.
On wan hand I wod stamp thim undher fut; on th'
other not so fast." And, alluding to the fanatical anti-
trust agitator, Dooley imagines Roosevelt saying, "Th'
haggard face, th' droppin' eye, th' pallid complexion
that marks th' inimy iv thrusts is not to me taste."

---

[9] These are excerpts from comments Bryan wrote for the *New York Journal* that reflected on Markham's "The Man with a Hoe" poem.

[10] Finley Peter Dunne (1867–1936) offered the Mr. Dooley columns for over 30 years, featuring the fictional character's observations in a heavy Irish accent and dialect.

Bryan, however, made the most of the issue, and
in 1902 President Roosevelt took two steps of prime
importance. That year, he started a suit against the
Northern Securities merger, and he settled the coal
strike.[11] The first led the country to believe that great
combinations were no longer immune from
prosecution and, when the Supreme Court reversed
an earlier decision and declared the Northern
Securities merger illegal in 1904, faith in the process
of law displaced cynicism and despair. The coal strike,
in which the U.S. president opposed president George
Baer[12] of the Philadelphia and Reading Railroad,
introduced the public as an interested party in labor
disputes. Although J.P. Morgan saw the public aspect
of the coal strike, many conservatives considered that
Roosevelt was striking at the root of our civilization
by interfering between the coal miners and the
operators. Wall Street was generally supposed to be
hostile to Roosevelt. When the suit against Northern
Securities was ended, Joseph Pulitzer, publisher of the
New York World, and an enemy of Roosevelt (as of

---

[11] Northern Securities was a holding company consisting of major
railroad operations held by John D. Rockefeller, J.P. Morgan and
Edward Harriman. The coal strike concerned anthracite coalfields
in eastern Pennsylvania; Roosevelt initiated a fact-finding
commission that acted as an arbitrator and successfully facilitated
the end of the strike.

[12] George Baer (1842–1914) also served as spokesperson for the
anthracite mining owners during the 1902 coal strike.

Wall Street) said, "he has subjugated Wall Street," and it was clear that the president had taken the trust issue away from the Democrats.

Yet, in 1904, Roosevelt, accurately representing the popular state of feeling said, "Sooner or later, unless there is a readjustment, there will come a riotous, wicked, murderous day of atonement." And it was not until April 14, 1906 that the edge of his lance was turned against the agitators themselves in the famous speech of "The Man with the Muckrake." A year later, a significant episode showed how the wind stood. The president was speaking of "malefactors of great wealth" and others in a speech at Provincetown, Massachusetts, and came to this sentence: "From the standpoint of our material prosperity there is only one other thing as important as the discouragement of a spirit of envy and hostility toward business men, toward honest men of means; this is the discouragement of dishonest business men."

The audience applauded at this point. The president stopped and said that he was glad they had applauded then, but, by failing to applaud earlier, they had shown that they had missed his attitude entirely. Deliberately he restated his proposition: "Every manifestation of ignorant envy and hostility toward honest men who acquire wealth by honest means should be crushed at the outset by the weight of a sensible public opinion."

There was tremendous applause. "Now," said the president, "I will go on."

President Roosevelt's "Square Deal" for big business as well as for the common people had worked a change in public sentiment. The concentration of hostility against wealth, however honestly acquired, was becoming formidable, as the president saw. Pledges were circulated similar to the following, which was proposed as a solution of the whole trust problem: "I will, so far as I am able, avoid every transaction likely to yield a money or property profit to any person worth more than $100,000."

The trust-busting campaign was linked in the public mind with the popular sport of muckraking. Municipal corruption, exposure of the methods of the trusts, and pillorying of individuals went on remorselessly. The air was full of rumors about "the system," "the octopus," "combinations in restraint of trade," graft, and boodle. The phrases, "tainted money," "frenzied finance," and "social privilege" came into use. Magazines lived on muckraking and employed men and women of the highest capacities to investigate and expose corruptions. This was publicity with a vengeance—but the corporations made very little effort to meet fire with fire. A few books and magazine articles appeared defending trusts, addressing, for example, the theory of trusts, their legal rights, and so on. But the fixed policy of most of the great corporations seemed to be silence. In 1899, John R. Dos Passos,[13] a lawyer, said, "the cry of publicity, in our estimation, is entirely unwarranted by the law and the facts." Publicity, at that time, meant chiefly access to the financial books of the corporations, a check on manipulations of stocks and profits. Oddly enough, Elbert Gary, the president of U.S. Steel, and John D. Archbold, vice president of Standard Oil, were both favorable to this sort of publicity, but as late as 1912 the Canadian system of publicity (created by Prime Minister Mackenzie King) was still so novel in America that magazine articles explaining publicity had to be written by the articles' sponsors.

The trusts kept silent in the years of the most furious attacks. The policy of secrecy laid down by John D. Rockefeller Sr., was maintained by nearly all who imitated his methods, although this secrecy was known to exasperate public feeling. As the railroads, in a similar situation, could hardly expect fair play from a jury in a damage suit, corporations faced such laws as the Missouri enactment that "no individual or corporation belonging to a trust having for its object the control of prices could recover any debt." Instead,

---

[13] John Randolph Dos Passos (1844–1917) practiced corporate and brokerage law, and was considered an expert on trusts. He was the father of John Roderigo Dos Passos, a well-known 20th century American novelist.

in Missouri, if such a corporation needed to recover debt it had to appeal in court, forcing it to produce its books.

Investigations and prosecutions during the Roosevelt Administration compelled corporations to take up a new attitude. Slowly and reluctantly, they began to take the public into their confidence, tentatively employing publicists, making clear their intentions. At the same time, the success of the Roosevelt policies, the activity of trust-busting, the exposure of corruption in some cities, the election of honest officials, and the change to the commission form of government all aided in changing the public attitude. Policy on one side and publicity on the other were beginning to break down the trust-bogey.

Yet in 1912, as has been noted, Wilson could still point to great concentrations of wealth and power as a danger to the country and when, in 1914, he spoke of an "atmosphere of accommodation and mutual understanding" his enemies considered him as a renegade to the people's rights.[14] They said that business men did not condemn monopoly, as he claimed; that big business, instead, had merely found other means of accomplishing its ends than those forbidden by the government. This was the situation

---

[14] This phrase was used in Wilson's address to a joint session of Congress on the issue of trust and monopolies, given on January 20, 1914.

in 1914 when the war broke out. In spite of the clamor about international financiers—and the charges against Wall Street and the munition makers—the mind of the world turned away from old preoccupations and to new excitements. Just as it was physically impossible to publish war news and domestic news all on page one of the newspapers, it was impossible for the average man to keep war interests and domestic interests on the first page of his consciousness. In the four years of the war there was ample time for the disappearance of old grudges against monopolies. The danger was that, in the reaction of the peace, old hatred would be inflamed. By that time, facts and publicity combined had created the specter of Bolshevism. The publicity was partly war propaganda and reflected the bitterness of the Allies at the desertion of Russia; it was partly the defense of one system of living against another.

The result in America was extraordinary. In so far as Bolshevism was opposed to wealth, it was the enemy of concentrated wealth; it was communism against capitalism. At the same time, it was opposed to the private wealth even of the comparatively poor man; it was the proletariat against the great middle class. Instantly a new alliance was formed in America. Great concentrations of wealth became the allies of the moderately prosperous man—not his enemies. The American Federation of Labor, which had grown in popular approval during the war, became a weapon against the International Workers of the World and all communistic groups. Attacks on wealth now came not from bishops, presidents, and educators, but from enemies of the Republic sworn to overthrow the capitalist system, not to improve it. It was felt that, in this struggle, wealth was on the side of democracy. That the threat of Bolshevism was deliberately used in many instances to further private ends is probable. It became a stereotype, a symbol, and no one was allowed to question it. The Red took the place of the Hun, who had taken the place of the trust as the object of public hatred. The amount of dispassionate reasoning was about equal in the three cases.

The public today, as in the days of St. Paul, is always seeking a new thing; when the public is stirred, a clever manipulator can always use the crowd by setting before it a hateful object upon which it can discharge its anger. It would seem that the public, however, has only a definite quantum of hatred and that this cannot be spread over too many objects. There was not enough hate in Germany to cover France, Russia, and America—it concentrated especially on England—and in the Allied countries, there was not enough hate to cover Austria and Turkey.

So, after the war, Bolshevism served as a whipping boy. Before the accusation was recognized as ridiculous, it covered a multitude of minor sins; whatever one man did not like in another he called Bolshevism. The public concern with domestic affairs was turned to a sort of crusade for the preservation of democratic institutions against foreign principles. With the disappearance of the Red Menace (as a present and all-embracing force), new objects acquired hold on the public mind. Prohibition was one, fundamentalism was another. Economic problems, especially when prosperity reasserted itself, were secondary.

The power of wealth is not now considered a menace in itself. In 1928, the idea that a large monopoly necessarily raises the cost of living, or destroys independent competitors, or works illegally, would hardly affect an average American audience. Its concern at the moment is in the relation between wealth and the integrity of the American judiciary. The trust, as a danger to the freedom and prosperity of America, has vanished from the public mind.

Chapter 17.
Political Campaigning

THE MOST STRIKING FEATURE of American presidential campaigns is their unsuitability to the dignity of the office and to the importance of the issues involved. The stampede of delegates in convention is the picturesque expression of the campaign spirit; it is known, however, to be an outworn device, and is confessedly artificial and hollow. The connection between "demonstrations" and the character of candidate and office is hard to discover. The campaign managers who supply delegates with cowbells, arrange for music at appropriate moments, appoint floor leaders and parade marshals, provide flags, and, in general, stage manage these demonstrations are not, however, blind followers of tradition. If the demonstration had no publicity value, it would cease to exist.

The publicity value, is, in part, associated with those campaigns in which the demonstration for candidates was spontaneous and immediately useful. Where a contest is being fought, when the choice of candidate has actually to be made on the floor, the strategic importance of a demonstration is great. The loyal delegates, springing up in every part of the convention hall, moving through crowded aisles and in various directions, multiply the effect of their numbers—as, in the movies, crowds running in the design of the figure eight seem larger than they actually are. The delegate sitting by, unless he is definitely hostile to the demonstration, is moved by the basic human desire to be with the crowd, with the largest and happiest crowd; he wants to imitate others. The demonstration, then, was originally intended literally to sweep neutral delegates off their feet, by giving the impression of the power and confidence in victory.

Even when there is no contest, shows of enthusiasm are sometimes genuine—as in the case of a president being nominated to succeed himself. While there is no proof that the loudest demonstration is connected with success at the polls, election in November sets a seal of approval on demonstrations in June; the fact that the defeated candidate was also cheered is forgotten. The demonstration, is therefore, associated with success. Outside the convention hall, the demonstration is a symbol of power and of popularity. The logic is weak: the fact that a man is popular with those who like him is supposed to aid in making him popular with those who do not like him. The emotion is, however, sound. It is in the technique of repetition.

In 1928, the nomination of Herbert Hoover for president was assured on the first day of the Republican convention, a vast majority of the delegates having announced their purpose of nominating him. Yet, on the fifth day, a demonstration lasting three quarters of an hour was staged. The contagion of enthusiasm in the hall was superfluous. In actual fact, however, it was not effective, as the single body hostile to Hoover, the farm bloc, remained unmoved. The absence of such a demonstration would, none the less, have been perilous. The candidate's career was unsensational; he was known to be more interesting as a thinker and administrator than as a "personality" (in the flamboyant sense of the word). He had held no elective office, his direct personal contacts were few. Additionally, it was feared that he would not be a good campaigner. In response to these concerns, the demonstration indicated to the outside world that the delegates not only had chosen Hoover, but liked him and believed in his success. It linked his nomination with many successful ones of the past. Memories of triumphant campaigns attended the singing of "Hail! Hail! The Gang's All Here!" (a stereotype at conventions). The new candidate was incorporated into the familiar background and assimilated to all the traditions of his party.

The demonstration covered certain dissections and discrepancies. The one serious fight on the platform concerned farm relief; it was fairly met. But the campaign managers would prefer the unenlightened voter to believe that the decision left no wounds. At the same time, the outburst of enthusiasm was meant to prove that the candidate had expressed his intentions on all subjects of importance and that these intentions were approved by the delegates. Actually, Hoover had declared himself on only very few subjects and his promises were generalities.

The political rally (of which the demonstration is a typical part) corresponds in tone to a camp meeting. One hundred years ago, foreign observers linked these as the great holidays of the backwoods—the two things which brought isolated pioneers together. The excitement of being in a crowd after months of solitary life seemed to foreigners to parallel emotions of their own religious festivals and holidays. The torch light parade, the oratory, the banners, and all the paraphernalia of direct appeal go back to this period. Although no one remembers on what platform President William Henry Harrison ran, or against whom, that fact that miniature log cabins were used in his campaign has become a fixed point in the mind.[1] Modern campaigns seem still to assume that Americans are living in isolation, at great distances

---

[1] William Henry Harrison (1773–1841) was the first president to actively campaign for the office during the 1840 presidential contest. His party referred to him as the "log cabin and hard cider" candidate, positioning him as a man of the people.

from towns, and that the congregating of a crowd is a rare pleasure. The new media of publicity are used— print, movies, and radio—but the old impulses of the ballyhoo are strong. The nearer a campaign approaches a circus, the better satisfied are its managers.

One reason is the average voter is not qualified to judge the major issues of politics. He is qualified perhaps to say what he wants: war or no war, tariff or free trade, wine or no wine. But he has made no study of the tariff, of industry, or international affairs. The platform of each party expresses a judgment, and the campaign speakers explain that judgment in simple terms to the voters. For the most part these explanations are, naturally, appeals to prejudice. The campaign manager wants the voter to think only of one thing—to vote for his candidate. There is no pretense whatever that the electors whom, legally, the voter chooses, have any discretion; they are specifically linked with the name of the candidate. Out of this rises the enormous publicity about persons in a campaign. At the beginning of the campaign, it is common for the candidates to say that they wish to make their appeal to the voters on the grounds of policy, not of personality. The campaign managers wink slyly. One of them is quoted as saying in 1928, "We'll feed them the old pabulum."

Before the candidates are nominated, the ground is laid. To undermine the reputations of the leaders of the opposition, congressional investigations are started. The surveys of the past four years are of service to the party which is out. The investigations of campaign expenses work both ways. Every effort is made to create in the public mind a new system of associations. Candidates are linked with special interests, with the money power, with corruption whenever possible. The process continues through the campaign. Every visitor to the candidate's office is marked down. If a politician under a cloud comes to pay his respects, the candidate is supposed to be beholden to him. If a financier endorses a candidate, the meaning, for the public, is that the candidate is the tool of finance. In the 1928 campaign, both sides used these tactics. After receiving the Republican nomination, Hoover was pictured as receiving the crown from Senator-elect Vare,[2] and, before the Democratic convention, that party's presidential hopeful Al Smith was continuously associated with the ancient ill-fame of Tammany Hall.

On the side of each candidate an enormous publicity is used to show him in as favorable a light as

---

[2] William Scott Vare (1867–1934) was a Republican U.S. Senator-elect from Pennsylvania for over two years. His election was marred by accusations of ballot stuffing, eventually resulting in the Senate not agreeing to seat him.

possible. His appeal must be all things to all men. The candidate as a poor boy risen to high position has always been used, as it corresponds to a stereotype about America in the American mind and is particularly useful because the honesty and simplicity of rural life is always assumed to be a safeguard against corruption. The candidate may pitch hay, receive a university degree, go to church, kiss a baby, and be inducted in an Indian tribe. The more popular these things make him, the less necessary it will be for him to discuss his platform. For every statement he makes can be turned as a weapon against him. Wherever a controversy exists, the candidate runs the risk of alienating one man while he is winning over another. But there is no risk for a candidate so long as he does purely personal things and lets his speeches consist largely of patriotic appeals.

The candidate is advertised and sold to the country more or less as a surprise package. He is sold on the secondary qualities, on the great personal interest he evokes, although no political observer would say that these qualities are even essential in the making of a good president. The severity of both Woodrow Wilson and Calvin Coolidge lent itself with little grace to exploitation—yet they received enormous popular votes. In spite of this, campaign managers stick to the ballyhoo system. They know perfectly that the badges and buttons worn in parades carry the picture of an individual, not an abstract argument. The appeal is to the emotions. It counts on the shortness of public memory and on the ease with which crowds are moved. Yet, to an extent, political campaigns are parts of long-run publicity. It is important to win a single election, and it is also important to consider later contests. The best publicity for a political party is the prosperity of the country when that party is in office, and each party is responsible for its actions. Platforms and pledges are sometimes cynically offered, or so vaguely expressed that they are hardly binding. It becomes a question for campaign managers to what degree they can run counter to the commercial morality of the country, by offering for sale goods which are not as advertised. If a party had to create its entire voting strength each time, the effort would be colossal. Actually, it goes into a campaign with the certainty of holding the body of its voters, unless such an exceptional case as the Progressive bolt occurs. What the party has to win is an undecided fraction of the voters in certain states. It can appeal to the undecided emotionally or logically, but its loyal voters have to be held through emotions and through satisfaction rendered in the past.

The tricks of publicity are used in campaigns to produce excitability, to create an unreasoning yes-response. The voter is made to believe that he has chosen a candidate, and to believe also that this candidate assures prosperity. All through the campaign, and especially as Election Day approaches, managers in despair over the poor showing of their candidates announce the certainty of victory—so that those who waver may be inclined to vote for the ultimately successful man. The significant issues are clouded over. The voter chooses not so much a group of principles as an individual, although half a dozen other individuals in each party could have been made equally acceptable to him. In that sense, campaigns are a form, not a reality. The persistence of old-style publicity indicates that the public has not been studied in connection with its political life, and it seems possible that the application of a newer technique might bring about a type of campaign more suitable to the importance of national elections. It could not be a technique separated from the emotional appeal, but that appeal might be more effectively used not to conceal the realities of the campaign but to emphasize them.

Part V

Publicity and the Crowd, Justice, and the Public Relations Advisor

Chapter 18.
The Crowd and the
Egregious Man

THE LATIN WORD FOR "CROWD" is "grex," from
which the rarely used English word "egregious" is
descended. It means "one who is outside the crowd,"
and in modern usages it is applied almost exclusively
to fools. In a word-association test, the response to
"egregious" is almost always "ass" and only writers
with a cultivated feeling for the original meaning of
words say "egregious merit," or "an egregious
diplomat." In recent years, the study of crowd
psychology has become popular and phrases like
"group-consciousness," "instincts of the herd," and
"mob psychology" have ceased to be scientific terms
and become counters in daily use, usually without the
scrupulous exactitude of the original scientific
meaning. The result has been a vast misunderstanding
of the relation of the individual and the crowd. The
fact that we use the word "egregious" not to mean
exceptional in a favorable sense, but with the
connotation of stupidity, would be taken by hardy
individualists as a sign of degeneration. The very
words "crowd" and "herd" are terms of contempt, and
when one says of a man that he runs with the herd,
one denies him all individuality and character.

Yet there is a sense in which the egregious man is not only a fool, but, in all probability, a madman. Living in civilized communities is an exercise in association with others. The hermit and the misanthrope go off and live alone; the madman and the criminal are put in solitary confinement. The reason is very much the same: none of them can live on terms with their fellow men. Mutual interest and understanding create groups; self-interest and incapacity to understand others create solitaries.

Anti-democrats have labored over the distinction between the exceptional man and the "boob," or common man, to such a point that the issue has become obscured. One of their favorite philosophers is Friedrich Nietzsche, and they speak of him as if he were an aristocrat in every respect.[1] Yet he was thoroughly a man of the herd in a hundred ways. He was one of the select herd which admired German composer Richard Wagner at one time and one of the smaller herd which turned away from him later. He was also one of the herd that liked Italy; one of the great herd that despised socialists; one of the smaller herd which held Christian ethics in contempt. Charles Darwin, likewise, belonged to several herds, among them the Philistine herd which cannot appreciate the

---

[1] German philosopher Friedrich Nietzsche (1844–1900) is considered by scholars to have had a major impact on schools of philosophy that study postmodernism and existentialism.

arts. Renowned attorney Clarence Darrow belongs to the herd opposed to capital punishment, journalist H. L. Mencken to the herd opposed to eugenics.[2]

All of these classifications sound more friendly if one uses the term "group" instead of "herd." However, if a group which blindly and without knowledge denies the theory of evolution is to be called a herd, it is both morally and logically justifiable to call the group which blindly accepts evolution a herd also. If the Republican voters on Election Day are a rabble, simply because they are swayed by mass instincts, so are the communists—a smaller rabble, to be sure, but essentially of the same character.

There is a supposition, without foundation in experience, that only the less intelligent and more numerous sections of humanity are given to following the leader. Five hundred thousand people may accept as gospel the syndicated articles of Frank Crane, 100,000 those of Glenn Frank, and 25,000 those of H.L. Mencken.[3] The 25,000 may all have superior brains, education, a sophisticated outlook on life, and a thorough civilization, but they form a cohesive

---

[2] Clarence Darrow (1857–1938) was a prominent attorney and high-profile member of the American Civil Liberties Union. Journalist H. L. Mencken (1880–1956) wrote articles and essays for *The Baltimore Sun* and the magazine *The American Mercury*.

[3] Presbyterian minister Frank Crane (1861–1928) and University of Wisconsin President Glenn Frank (1887–1940) wrote essays for magazines.

group, are stirred by group emotions, and respond as any other group responds to stimulation. They do "the right thing" as religiously as the most conventional people, and do it because it is the right thing—only their right is other people's wrong. They are "no" men and the others are "yes" men, and to say "no" because that is what you are told to say is as unindividualistic as to say "yes."

It is the business of publicity to help in the creation of groups: the group that buys a new kind of safety razor, the group that goes to the first night of a spectacular movie, the group that waits outside the theatre to see the first group go in, the group that votes for joining the League of Nations or for abstaining, the group that believes in disarmament or a federation of the world, the group that eats no meat, the group that rides in street cars, and thousands of other unconscious associations of human beings. It was the function of the *Sacra Congregatio de Propaganda Fide*[4] (which has given us our word "propaganda") to further the creation of a group faithful to the Catholic Church, and historians have credited to it the creation of something more: a unity, perhaps the only

---

[4] In English, the Sacred Congregation for the Propagation of the Faith. This was a congregation for missionary work formed by the Catholic Church in 1622.

unity Europe has known since the destruction of the Roman Empire.

If we banish from our minds all the ideas of mob rule and pictures of crowds at a lynching, the idea of the herd or the group is not so formidable. As far as we know, the history of mankind and civilization implies grouping. It also implies the breaking up and reforming of groups. If publicity is an instrument for making groups or crowds and, as Everett Dean Martin says, in his 1920 book *The Behavior of Crowds*, "the habit of crowd-making is daily becoming a more serious menace to civilization," it should also be remembered that publicity is equally effective in breaking down groups.[5] Both the first and the second iterations of the Ku Klux Klan were diminished in authority and power by publicity, and the growing value of this social organ of defense against crowds is shown by the comparative rapidity with which the later Klan was undermined. Furthermore, publicity carried on by an ex-president, professors, and even poets threatened at one time to break up a political group which had existed for 50 years in the United States, when the progressive party was formed and captured an overwhelming majority of the Republican Party's electoral and popular vote.

---

[5] Everett Dean Martin (1880–1941) was a minister and social psychologist who wrote on the subjects of crowd persuasion, adult education, and religion.

In forming or breaking down groups, publicity is an instrument. It is the converter of power. The power itself must inhere in the ideas to which publicity is given. Recent enthusiasts for advertising and publicity operations have suggested that these agencies are themselves creative. This does not seem to be proved. If it were true, publicity would be able to invert the habits of mankind; actually, it can only modify them. Of two things which are more or less desirable to human beings it can make one preeminently desirable. But publicity can never make suicide desirable to the majority of human beings. It can only help make men willing to give up their lives in defense of their honor, their families, or their country. And, in these cases, it is not publicity which creates a new feeling in men but the thing for which it acts—honor, or loved ones, or country.

Wherever publicity operates, it reaches its greatest point of effectiveness when it touches a group or a crowd. In recent years, a determined attempt has been made to discover why this is so and, although investigators do not agree on some of the fundamental principles, a few things are accepted by all of them. A modern pioneer in this work is the Frenchman Gustave Le Bon whose 1895 book, *The Crowd*, may be taken as the starting point.[6] The two

---

[6] French author Gustave Le Bon (1841–1931) studied and wrote on psychology, sociology and medicine.

things which Le Bon has established are: first, when
people are in a crowd they behave differently from the
way they behave when they are alone, and, second,
that this difference in behavior is due in some way to
the unconscious.

Observers of religious camp meetings from the
18th century time of Methodist founder John Wesley
to, more recently, evangelist Billy Sunday, testify to
the fact that those who came to scoff remained,
instead, to pray. Something in the atmosphere broke
down their hostility to the preacher and, in spite of
their determination, they succumbed. Had they met
the evangelist alone in a room they might have spent
hours discussing the truth of revealed religion or the
literal interpretation of the story of creation, but it is
extremely unlikely that they would have been
converted. In the biography of all the great
evangelists, the fact that they made conversions en
masse is noted. After the violent excitement of a
revival meeting, they gathered penitents into smaller
groups for the final stages of conversion, but the
solitary convert is almost an unknown phenomenon.

The existence of a crowd makes people do things
they would otherwise not dream of. It is almost
inconceivable that anyone would go to a bull fight if
he had to witness it alone. Americans who express the
profoundest horror of bull fights are carried along by
enthusiasm when they reach Spain and, although they

expect to be nauseated by the spectacle, almost invariably sit out the killing of five or six bulls, with the attendant horror of the gored horses. Americans then often have a violent reaction after they leave the arena and get out of the crowd, a reaction which manifests itself often when they are most alone, in their dreams.

"It is easy," says Le Bon in *The Crowd*, "to prove how much the individual forming part of the group differs from the isolated individual, but it is less easy to discover the causes." He continues:

> The individual forming a part of a group acquires, solely from numerical considerations, a sentiment of invincible power which allows him to yield to instincts which, had he been alone, he would perforce have kept under restraint.... A group being anonymous, and in consequence irresponsible, the sentiment of responsibility which always controls individuals disappears entirely.
>
> .... We see, then that the disappearance of the conscious personality, the predominance of the unconscious personality, the turning by means of suggestion and contagion of feelings and ideas in an identical direction, the tendency to immediately transform the suggested ideas into acts; these, we see, are the principal characteristics of the individual forming part of a group. He is no longer himself, but has become an automaton who has ceased to be guided by his will.

According to Le Bon, the conscious mind of the individual ceases to operate when he becomes part of the crowd and, under the influence of suggestion, the unconscious, which he shares with his race and his nation, takes its place. Sigmund Freud, however, suggests that when we enter a crowd our own repressions come up to the surface, and William McDougall[7] notes that people who normally are very restrained in showing their emotions will break into roars of laughter or will cry out loud at the theatre if a tremendous outburst of applause frees them from restraint. In all these cases, emphasis is put on the arrival, at the front, of emotions which are usually kept in the background.

Another Frenchman, Gabriel Tarde,[8] has studied the crowd and found that its dominating characteristic is imitation. The English writer Walter Bagehot,[9] whose work on politics influenced Woodrow Wilson to a great extent, had arrived at a similar conclusion a generation earlier. He said that, in the most primitive societies, imitation was a ruling

---

[7] William McDougall (1871–1938) was a social psychologist who published numerous books, including the 1908 text *An Introduction to Social Psychology*.

[8] Gabriel Tarde (1843–1904), a French sociologist and social psychologist, wrote about several subjects including on crowd behavior and the diffusion of inventions.

[9] Walter Bagehot (1826–1877) founded the *National Review* in 1855 and, in 1860, became editor-in-chief of *The Economist*.

force, that it continues to this day, and speaks of "the
necessity which rules all but the strongest men to
imitate what is before their eyes and to be what they
are expected to be."[10] According to him, an accident
may make a certain way of dressing or holding one's
fork, or thinking about politics, predominate. After
that, the instinct to imitate makes it the correct thing
to do. Most men, he says, would rather be accused of
wickedness than of awkwardness, because
awkwardness is a bad imitation of the right thing.

Tarde goes much further. According to him,
society can be reduced to a process of imitation,
which is a kind of repetition, plus a process of
invention. The individual invents something. If it's
not opposed to the natural instincts of humanity, the
crowd imitates it. Progress obviously begins with an
invention, but the stability of a group or a nation
depends on its capacity to imitate. "...Society is
imitation," said Tarde.[11] This brings up the famous
comparison of human beings to a flock of sheep. If
one sheep leading the flock stumbles over a stone, it is
said that all of those directly behind him will also
stumble; if one shows terror, a whole flock quietly
grazing will run in panic. Harvard President Abbott
Lawrence Lowell has criticized the emphasis which

---

[10] This quote is from Bagehot's 1872 book *Physics and Politics*.

[11] This quote is from Tarde's 1903 book *The Laws of Imitation*.

Tarde puts on imitation. Although the tendency is genuine, he says, Tarde makes too much of it, and he quotes Graham Wallas' remark that "if a sheep, being bitten by a fly, scratches its ear with one foot, the sheep feeding beside it does not do the same."[12] That is, there is no definite instinct of imitation. It is because the sheep experience the same emotions that they do the same things.

Another brilliant analysis of crowds has been made by Wilfred Trotter in his 1919 book *Instincts of the Herd in Peace and War*.[13] Trotter believes that, just as the forms of life develop from the single-celled amoeba to the millions of cells making up a human being, single individuals follow the same biological tendency to come together in groups. This tendency he calls the "gregarious instinct," and ranks it as one of the fundamental impulses of human beings. This instinct makes a man sensitive to the behavior of his neighbors and makes him want to be like his neighbors so that he can remain in the herd with them. It also changes his mental makeup, quite as Le

---

[12] Abbott Lawrence Lowell (1856–1943), was president of Harvard from 1909–1933. Lowell cited an excerpt from Graham Wallas' (1858–1932) book *The Great Society*, published in 1914. Wallas was co-founder of the London School of Economics in 1895. Quotes from Lowell in this chapter, and in chapter 19 come from an unattributed source.

[13] Wilfred Trotter (1872–1939) was an English pioneer in neurosurgery who also wrote on crowd psychology.

Bon suggests. A man in a crowd accepts any suggestion from the crowd whether it be "lynch him," or "make him king." The crowd is strong and irresponsible. If a mob burns down a house, 99 of the 100 men composing that mob will think themselves innocent, and will be sure to escape punishment. Therefore, whatever the crowd suggests has authority. Trotter believes that all morality and all ideals are due to the influence of the herd and that our private feeling of right and wrong—our conscience—can be traced back to our fear that others will disapprove of us and edge us out of the crowd in which we feel safe and happy.

Trotter, Le Bon, and Tarde all describe the crowd in terms which are hardly flattering. According to Le Bon, a group never reasons; it is impulsive and changeable. Whatever idea possesses it becomes so imperative that it must be acted on at once, even at the risk of life. It believes itself omnipotent. At the same time, it is exceptionally open to any influence and will believe anything, no matter how absurd. All its feelings are simple and exaggerated. The crowd thinks, if it can be said to think at all, in images—that is, it associates but it never criticizes. The crowd is always extreme. In an instant, a suspicion becomes a fact. Since it is extreme itself, the crowd demands the extremes of stimulation. An orator talks loudly, uses the most vivid images, repeats the same thing over and over. The music which affects a crowd must have the simple beat and rhythm of the military march and the melody of the most sentimental song.

The crowd knows absolutely what is right and what is true. It is extremely intolerant and, at the same time extremely obedient. It adores violence and power. It desires to stand in awe of its leaders and to be swayed. It is conservative, cruel, brutal, and destructive. In one respect, however, Le Bon finds an admirable quality in the crowd: It can be moved to action on behalf of high ideals and it is capable of self-sacrifice. That is, morally, an individual may rise to a higher level when he associates with a crowd, but mentally he always sinks to a lower level. Finally, the crowd is influenced by the magic power of words— not so much by their meaning as by their sound and their associations. This is because the crowd never wants the truth; it wants only an illusion, and never makes the slightest effort to distinguish between the two.

According to Trotter, the crowd man is intolerant and afraid of being alone. He distrusts his own powers and feels secure only when he is backed up either by the physical presence of other people or by their moral support. The voice of the herd has a profound capacity to persuade the individual. It can make him bow to a tyrant and to hug his own miseries to his bosom. The crowd is given to mob violence and to panic and, at the same time, wants to be led and hardly cares whether the leader is properly qualified. Finally, the crowd-man wants the other members of the herd to recognize him—to admit, as the Hairy Ape says, that he "belongs."[14] Although these characteristics are found in men at a low mental level, Trotter believes that they continue to influence man at every stage of development. The suggestions put forth by the herd affect the individual not only when he is in a mob or stricken by panic but, as Trotter maintains, are in effect "always, everywhere, and under any circumstances."

These various descriptions of crowds are not mutually contradictory. Tarde's imitation, Le Bon's contagion and suggestion, and Trotter's gregarious instinct, all work together and all of them consider chiefly the emotional and unconscious factors in social life. It is only natural that the most famous of modern students of the unconscious also have studied the crowd.

The psychoanalysts whose interest is chiefly in the inferiority complex point out that the individual's sense of being inferior is compensated when he joins a crowd. All crowds, says Martin, claim to be infallible. "Where the crowd is, there is tyranny," says Martin,

---

[14] *The Hairy Ape*, a 1922 play by Eugene O'Neil, centers on a laborer's quest for belonging in an era of industrialization and the rise of the wealthy class.

"Tyranny may be exercised through one agent or through many, but it nearly always comes from the same source—the crowd." The tyrant-crowd, which is always growing in strength and showing its power, gives to the inferior man the sense of superiority which he craves. Alone a man may doubt his own wisdom as much as he doubts his own capacities. The moment he joins the crowd these doubts vanish and the crowd imposes its whim as the universal law. The crowd mind, says Martin, "should best be classed with dreams, delusions, and the various forms of automatic behavior." Its controlling ideas are like complexes, he says, or fixations, and crowds only think as paranoiacs think. The typical crowd men, he says, "show something of [the] narcissus complex".

Freud himself has studied the crowd in some detail. He places in a position of supreme importance the one factor which all the others neglect—the leader. Following his wide construction of the meaning of love, he suggests that in a crowd the individuals are bound together by love for the leader and love for the members of the group. In the Catholic Church, for instance, (and in a great army) each individual believes that the head—Christ (or the Commander in Chief)—loves him as much as he loves any other individual. In his 1921 book *Group Psychology and the Analysis of the Ego*, Freud said that:

> All the demands that are made upon the individual are derived from this love of Christ's.... There is no doubt that the tie which unites each individual with Christ is also the cause of the tie which unites them with one another.... The Commander-in-Chief is a father who loves all his soldiers equally, and for that reason they are comrades among themselves. The army differs structurally from the Church in being built up of a series of such groups. Every captain is, as it were, the Commander-in-Chief and the father of his company, and so is every non-commissioned officer of his section.

A religion or an army is a highly organized group. In dealing with groups which are more chaotic Freud makes an equally startling criticism. Whereas other writers have claimed that panic is one of the typical activities of a crowd, Freud says that panic never sets in until the group spirit has been destroyed:

> Dread in an individual is provoked either by the greatness of a danger or by the cessation of emotional ties; the latter is the case of neurotic dread. In just the same way panic arises either owing to an increase of the common danger or owing to the disappearance of the emotional ties which hold the group together; and the latter case is analogous to that of neurotic dread.... It is impossible to doubt that panic means the disintegration of a group; it involves the cessation of all the feelings of consideration which the members of the group otherwise show one another.

It would seem then that, in Freud's estimation, the group is the enemy of chaos and panic and is sustained by mutual love. Continuing to insist on the importance of the leader (for which a personified idea may be substituted), Freud says that hypnotism operates in the formation of a group but in a limited way, just as love operates without any direct sexual tendencies. Primary groups, he says, are those which have not been organized beyond the simplest characteristics of individuals, and his definition of such a group is that it consists of a number of individuals who have selected the same object as their "ego ideal" and, as a result, have identified themselves with one another.[15] In a group, says Freud, justice and equality must prevail. "No one must want to put himself forward, everyone must be the same and have the same," he says, "...This demand for equality is the route of social conscience and the sense of duty." Following a conjecture of Charles Darwin's that the earliest form of human society was a loosely organized tribe ruled over by a despot, Freud attempts to upset Trotter's essential idea in the following way:

> Do not let us forget, however, that the demand
> for equality in a group applies only to its members and
> not to the leader. All the members must be equal to

---

[15] In Freudian theory the "ego ideal" is that part of the individual who self-imposes concepts of ideal behavior that have been formed by both parental and societal standards.

one another, but they all want to be ruled by one person.... Let us venture, then, to correct Trotter's pronouncement that man is a herd animal and assert that he is rather a horde animal, an individual creature in a horde led by a chief.

If further investigation proves that Freud is right, his ideas will profoundly modify all future conceptions of the essential nature of the crowd. Freud believes that the primitive instincts and early habits of mankind persist to a great degree in the unconscious of civilized human beings and dictate their actions, although they may be overlaid by reason (or what we pretend to be reason). If there is no gregarious instinct, and if crowds come together under the compulsion of superior beings, we have a new cause and a new explanation for the way the crowd acts. Nevertheless, Freud's description of the crowd, apart from its origin, is not altogether hostile to Trotter and Le Bon. He recognizes the extreme suggestibility of the crowd and its thirst for obedience as well as most of the other characteristics named before.

The transition between the mob and the highly organized group (such as a nation), is a chief point of interest in the work of William McDougall, whose 1920 book *The Group Mind* starts with the crowd in a state of chaos and carries it on to the development of a national mind and character. He begins with a brief survey of current ideas about crowds which he says land us in a paradox. "Participation in group life degrades the individual, assimilating his mental processes to those of the crowd, whose brutality, inconstancy, and unreasoning impulsiveness have been the theme of many writers," writes McDougall. "Yet only by participating in group life does man become fully man, only so does he rise above the level of the savage."

According to McDougall, the first essential for the formation of the crowd is that, "the attention of all is directed to the same object; all experience in some degree the same emotion, and the state of mind of each person is in some degree affected by the mental processes of all those about him." Three thousand people walking along Michigan Avenue, each one bent on his own affairs, do not make up a group in any sense and they are hardly a crowd. But if a fire engine dashes down the street, a focus of interest is created. Even a deaf man would see others staring or running and become aware of their interest and thus share it. One hundred people passing a street corner orator might become a group if he was talking about the cost of living; if he was talking about the possibility of life on Mars, however, they might all pass by and refuse to group themselves. An American trying to deliver a speech in English in Red Square in Moscow or on the Bridge of Nations at Constantinople could hardly create a group around him even if the subject he spoke of was one of vital concern to every passerby. There has to be a basis of common feeling and common interest before a group or crowd can be created. The greater the degree of this common experience and feeling, the closer the crowd will cohere, and the more intense will be its effect both on the individual members and on the leaders.

The feeblest little joke takes on the proportions of high humor and many public speakers, at first surprised by their success, have gradually succumbed to the crowd's enthusiasm and come to believe themselves great wits. Mark Twain tells of an occasion on which he was particularly anxious to make a great success at the beginning of a lecture tour. He was afraid that his humor would not be considered funny and arranged with a woman friend that, whenever he looked up toward her box, she should laugh. Her laughter was peculiarly agreeable and infectious, but Twain's speech was enormously successful and he had no occasion to turn to her. Toward the end, he brought in by way of variety a pathetic incident for which he wanted the sympathy of his audience. Delivering the tale with an agony that was comic in itself, he felt his eyes being drawn irresistibly toward his friend and, as he came to the heartbreaking point of his anecdote, he looked at her. She laughed and, to his horror, the whole audience burst into guffaws heartier than any he had won by his funny stories. It is easy to see how a speaker of small character would thereafter debase the incident in order to make the crowd laugh.

The suggestibility of a crowd is also recorded in connection with the first performance of a play called "A Little Bit of Fluff."[16] There was an almost hysterically nervous person in the audience and one of the characters set him off into uncontrollable laughter every time he spoke because his manner unintentionally suggested an effeminate man. The play ran for several years in London, and the effeminacy of the character became more and more marked. The contagion had spread not only through the first night audience, but to all the following audiences who had heard that the play was extremely funny (it came to New York and the New York audience, having no one to work them up, was totally unmoved by it and the play failed disastrously). This intensifying of emotion which makes things seem extremely funny or extremely important is, as McDougall says, one of the attractions of the crowd, as it is, to some people, one of the attractions to getting drunk. And, like getting drunk, says McDougall in *The Group Mind*, "the repeated enjoyment of effects of this kind tends to generate a

---

[16] "A Little Bit of Fluff" was a British comedy by Walter W. Ellis, first offered in 1915 in London, and later turned into a film in 1928.

craving for them," which accounts for the fact that city mobs are more fickle and more excitable than country gatherings.

McDougall has found in one principle

> ...a full and adequate explanation of such collective intensification of instinctive excitement. The principle is that, in man and in the gregarious animals generally, each instinct, with its characteristic primary emotion and specific impulse, is capable of being excited in one individual by the expressions of the same emotion in another...

The emotions most easily excited are the primary ones, those connected with coarse and simple sentiments, because they are the ones common to all the members of the crowd. Each emotion has its corresponding instinct in such combinations as fear and flight, anger and pugnacity, disgust and repulsion. But a crowd selects among these coarse emotions those which are held in universal esteem. McDougall thinks that "each member of the crowd acts in full publicity," and therefore suppresses instincts which he might indulge in privately, but is ashamed of in public. Nevertheless, the crowd acts without regard for individual suffering and enjoys scenes of brutality. The individual in the crowd loses self-consciousness and, at the same time, his personal responsibility is swept away. In short, says McDougall, "We may sum up the psychological characters of the unorganized or

simple crowd by saying that it is excessively
emotional, impulsive, violent, fickle, inconsistent,
irresolute and extreme in action, displaying only the
coarser emotions and the less refined sentiments..."

Although he believes that the individual in a
crowd acts under full publicity and substitutes
sympathy for the principles adopted by Trotter,
Tarde, and Le Bon, McDougall's opinion of the
primitive crowd, as shown in the paragraph just
quoted, does not differ essentially from the others.
The distinction of his work is that he carries on from
that point and shows under what conditions the
behavior of a crowd can be raised to a higher plain.
The first condition is that there should be some
degree of permanence in the group. This may be
either because the same people make up the group, as
in a local church, or because the same institution
exists although new people come into it, as in the
Catholic or any other established church. The second
condition is that the members of the group should
have some idea of the nature and composition of the
group and of each other; the reason this is important
is that it creates "a sentiment for the group which
becomes the source of emotions and of impulses to
action." The third, which McDougall thinks may not
be absolutely essential, is a relation with other groups
in conflict and rivalry. An American naturally thinks
of the hostility shown to baseball's American League

by the older National League and the fears expressed
that the new league would destroy baseball. In
experience, the existence of the two leagues has not
only intensified popular interest, but has given the
players in each league greater interest and pride in
their work. The fourth condition is the existence of
traditions and customs, and the fifth condition is
organization—the group must be organized as a whole
and the members in it have special functions and
duties. The perfect type of such an organization is a
patriot army, and the difference between this type
and the crowd is significant. Notes McDougall:

> Such an army exhibits the exaltation of emotion
> common to all psychological crowds. This
> intensification of emotion enables men to face danger
> and certain death with enthusiasm, and on other
> occasions may, even in the armies of undoubtedly
> courageous and warlike nations, result in panic and a
> rout. But in all other respects the characteristics of
> the simple crowd are profoundly modified. The
> formal continuity of the existence of the army and of
> its several units secures for it, even though its
> personnel be changed at a rapid rate, a past and
> therefore a tradition, a self-consciousness and a self-
> regarding sentiment, a pride in its past and a tradition
> of high conduct and achievement...

Chapter 19.
The Crowd and the Public

IT IS UNANIMOUSLY AGREED THAT the crowd debases the individual mentally and excites him emotionally. In so far as they retain the qualities of the crowd, groups, communities, cities and nations are therefore ruled by their emotions. Sir Charles F. Higham, the English publicist, in his 1920 book *Looking Forward: Mass Education through Publicity*, stressed "the value of the emotional appeal" with an important reservation.[1] He quotes Webster's definition of emotion as "a moving of the mind or the soul," and asks his readers to distinguish between emotion on one side and, on the other, "agitation, trepidation, perturbation, passion, excitement, and mental weakness generally." These states of feeling, he says, "may be bodily or mental; emotion, strictly speaking, is of the mind alone."

Far from making the matter clear, this reservation is confusing. In common speech, the mind is considered the center of reason, the brake on the emotions—and the emotions are associated with the passions. It is quite true that an emotion can be

---

[1] Charles F. Higham (1876–1938) was an advertising consultant in England during World War I and Member of Parliament from 1918–1922. He wrote numerous books on publicity and advertising.

worked up in favor of reason or in favor of any
reasonable object. The mobs of the French
Revolution worshipped the Goddess of Reason in
violent and passionate orgies. But when we say that
people are guided by their emotions we mean that
their passions dominate them and direct their action
with full or partial contempt for the intellectual
process. Higham takes as his perfect illustration the
emotional appeal during a defensive war; but, as
everyone knows, it is in wartime that all the restraints
which reason imposes on the emotions are banished.
"In times of moderate security," in his 1922 book
Public Opinion, Walter Lippmann reminds us, "the
symbols of public opinion are subject to check and
comparison and argument." That is to say, there is a
possibility that public opinion will, in some way, be
modified by the process of reasoning, provided there
is no special excitement of the emotions. The
politician knows this and tries to prevent it. The
country, according to the politician, is always in the
gravest danger. Unless his party is returned victor,
commerce and industry will be destroyed and, in all
probability, the sun will cease to rise and set. Both the
threats and the promises of the political orator are
efforts to undermine the calm security which people
naturally fall into and, by exciting their emotions,
prevent their audiences from using any reason
whatever.

Reason, we are told, developed late in the structure of the human animal. It is still woefully feeble and untrustworthy because of its habit of abdicating to the passions. The emotions, on the other hand, are built on the foundation of primitive man's earliest responses. They are powerful, but they, too, are untrustworthy because they are so easily swayed, because they are changeable, and because, being powerful, they can only be excited for a comparatively short time. It seems incredible that on the substructure of a feeble reason, standing on the quick sands of emotion, man has been able to establish governments, churches, banks, and ideals which have lasted for centuries.

The publicist with a feeling of responsibility has to consider both the elements of reason and passion, and to pick his way carefully. He is responsible, on the one hand, to his client, employer or to the cause for which he works; on the other hand, he has a responsibility to the public, to treat it fairly, and not to degrade it. If he appeals only to the reasoning faculty, he runs the grave risk of losing his effect.

Considering that mankind is supposed to be instinctively blood thirsty, and that the dominant classes have not only blessed wars but, it is charged, have deliberately brought them about, the success of pacifist propaganda is remarkable. Whatever governments may do, millions of human beings have for themselves outlawed the idea of war as an instrument of policy. Yet the least effective argument against war is the entirely reasonable one that it pays neither the victors nor the vanquished. The practical man Benjamin Franklin said that there was never a good war nor a bad peace; the proof that even the most successful war is ruinous has long been available. Yet the logic of pacifism is totally ineffective, and the intelligent pacifist manipulates the horrors of war, the chicanery of diplomats, and the moral beauty of international good will to accomplish his purpose.

All the logical arguments on both sides of the war debts problem are mere space fillers in comparison with the tremendous emotions called upon. Statistics proving that Europe cannot pay—and, that if she does pay, American trade will be ruined, are not nearly so persuasive as the single plea that the Allies fought America's battle and now America is forcing them to pay while Germany is permitted to flourish. The opposite statistics, that the Allies can pay, merely fortifies the covert emotional appeal to the American's sense that he saved the Allies at the last moment and now they are refusing to pay an honorable debt.[2]

---

[2] The United States government provided loans to the Allies prior to America's military involvement in World War I. After the war's end, the United States insisted that the debts be repaid, but the vast majority of the loans were not repaid.

If, at the other extreme, the publicist appeals exclusively to the passions, he runs a double risk. He may excite the public to a temporary outburst of actions, but he will find himself caught in a mill-race. He will have to feed the public stronger and stronger stimulants in order to keep them at the pitch of excitement. He may create hysteria—but hysterical people escape from all control. For example, in the great revivals which ran through the United States in the 1830s, the appeal to the emotions was intense and created a variety of hysterical outbursts. The revivalists themselves tell how they returned, after the lapse of a year or so, to the scenes of their labors and found people abandoning religion in favor of strange messianic cults or returning to "a cold and backslidden state."[3] The revivalists provided no discipline for the emotions they aroused. In many cases, the converts had not even a regular church to attend during the intervals between the visits of evangelists. No appeal was made to their minds, and no regular channel was provided for their emotions. It was all excitement, fermentation, and explosiveness which resulted, in many cases, in social and moral evils.

---

[3] The term "cold and backslidden state" appears prominently within *The Successful Soul-Winner: A Summary of Finney's Revival Lectures*, published in England in 1926. Charles Finney (1792–1875) was a minister in the American Presbyterian church and a leader of a Second Great Awakening across the United States.

The story is told of a riot during the Paris Commune.[4] A great crowd was rushing upon the barricades behind which some soldiers were stationed. Some distance behind the crowd ran a single man. A friend on the sidewalk shouted at him, "Don't follow them." The running man said, panting, "I must follow them; I am their leader."[5]

During the post-war election in England, Prime Minister Lloyd George announced that he proposed to make Germany pay the entire cost of the war. Among the figures mentioned was 24,000 million pounds ($120 billion). When he was asked what he meant by suggesting such a figure, since it could never be collected, George is said to have replied, "Twenty-four thousand million pounds! My dear fellow, if the election had gone on another fortnight, it would have been fifty thousand millions."[6] The appetite of the public grows by what it feeds on, and the man who begins by feeding it stimulants must make the dose stronger and stronger or lose his effectiveness entirely.

---

[4] The Paris Commune was a socialist and revolutionary government that ruled France in the spring of 1871.

[5] This quote has widely been attributed to Alexander Auguste Ledru-Rollin (1807–1874) a French politician who went into exile after the failed 1848 French Revolution.

[6] This quote, attributed to George during the Versailles Peace Conference in 1919, has not been substantiated by scholars.

The publicist who is unwilling to stupefy the
public by dry logic or to debauch it through hysteria is
not left entirely without resources. It is not his
business essentially to uplift the public, but he can
appeal to the emotions without overexciting them,
and he can work upward in the scale of human desires
instead of downward. He knows perfectly that, in
addition to wanting a few fundamental gratifications,
men also desire the approval of their fellows and
peace with their own conscience. We have seen how
the idealist President Wilson worked on the emotions
of the American people. He appealed to the common
wants: to national pride, to fear of an enemy, to the
desire for glory, to horror of war. But he did not stop
there. He fused and sublimated all of this into an
intense emotion for justice—one of the highest and
most complicated emotions which humanity can
experience. Pacifists in the United States accused the
war leaders of setting loose every base passion, and
pointed to the ways in which the war emotion was
allowed to serve as a cloak for hatred and tyranny. As
far as this is true it means only that the men who
carried the president's ideas into action
misunderstood them. The fact to which hundreds of
impartial observers testify is that the president
created a profound idealism in the American people.
That idealism may be criticized as being in itself
illogical and impotent. The fact remains that, without

losing hold of fundamental emotions, the president organized them into a highly complicated ideal.

In comparison, the publicity of Napoleon the First is illuminating. He was extraordinarily sensitive to the movements of public sentiment. He had an intelligent man prepare a private newspaper for himself alone, and took the utmost precautions not only to learn what the public felt but to make it feel what he wanted it to feel. He came upon the French scene after a period of intense disorder during which national pride had been whipped up by the creation of a people's government, by waging a defensive war, and by successfully dealing with internal and external enemies. Napoleon's great service to France was in consolidating the victories of the revolution, and he is said to have known that the Napoleonic Code would outlast the Battle of Austerlitz.[7] But, carried away by his own military prowess, he began to appeal to the French as the symbol of military glory—he was *la glorie*. To maintain himself, he could not be satisfied with peace and justice and security. He had to win more and more glory and eventually he had to lead France to Waterloo.

---

[7] The Napoleonic Code was a French civil code that was put in place in March 1804, replacing feudal laws in France. The Battle of Austerlitz took place in December 1805 and is considered by historians to be Napoleon's greatest victory.

If publicity desires an instant conversion or an immediate action, and if it has no feeling of responsibility to the public, it can go to any extreme. If, on the contrary, it desires to establish a new way of thinking and to make a fundamental and lasting change in the way people live, it has to reckon with a long-standing habit of mankind—the habit of reasoning. The reasoning may be imperfect and frequently inoperative, and its results may be constantly upset by a gust of passion, but it exists and it modifies human actions for a very simple reason. To an extent, men learn by experience. If a man is told to walk over a cliff and does so and breaks his leg, and if the second time when he is told he refuses to go, the man is making a comparison between the past and the present. If he learns not to buy stock from wildcat brokers or milk from dirty cans he is, in a very primitive way, using his reason. Experience corrects the mistakes into which our emotions lead us.

War-weariness and defeatism were due to many physical and psychological factors. Among them was the public sense of having been deliberately misled. The promises made in 1914 were not fulfilled, nor were those made in 1915 before the battle of the Chemin des Dames.[8] It was not only suffering which

---

[8] The Chemin des Dames (the "ladies path") is an area of France just north of Paris where both French and British troops engaged in a

caused French regiments to mutiny after this disaster; it was also the feeling that their leaders had known in advance that this battle could not win the war, and yet had promised them that it would. The German thrust in April 1918 came much nearer reaching Paris than any movement since the beginning of the war, yet no publicist, however irresponsible, dared to cry out "on to Paris." Experience had killed that particular appeal to the emotions. Reason had set in.

Abbott Lowell has distinguished between two kinds of opinion. There are those which are formed by a gradual growth such as the American belief in universal compulsory education or the change of opinion in the North regarding the Reconstruction policy after the Civil War. And there are opinions formed by a more or less conscious choice between alternatives. Comparing these two, he says that they are alike. They are, he says,

> The result of the attractions of the sun and the moon upon the earth. Our orbit is determined almost entirely by the sun, the moon from its small size having comparatively little effect upon it. But the moon, in spite of its small mass, has, because it is near, a greater influence than the sun upon the tides.

The tides of emotion are also acted upon by whatever is near—self-interest and the primary desires

---

major offensive against the Germans which resulted in large casualties on both sides.

of mankind. But, in the long run, it is the sun which determines the seasons, and it is the experience of humanity which dictates its course of action.

Chapter 20.
Publicity and Public Opinion

IN THE DAYS WHEN PUBLICITY WORKED directly upon the people, the connection between crowd psychology and public opinion was clear. In *The Iliad*, there is a character almost as important as Achilles or Odysseus, although he has no name other than the Greek word "tis" meaning "a person," or "someone." Tis is a little like Mrs. Grundy[1] and a great deal like "what people will say;" he is the Greek chorus representing sound common sense and the general public. Hector and Menelaus both worry over what Tis will say concerning their actions.

Tis held his influence because public opinion was not organized; it lacked the machinery for making itself effective. Telemachus, the son of Odysseus, seeing Penelope's suitor wasting his father's estate, called together neighbors, friends, and the people of Ithaca to put an end to the shame, but there was no effective way of bringing public opinion to bear. Centuries later, in the more highly organized community of Athens, the dramatist acts as publicist.

---

[1] Mrs. Grundy is an archetype for someone who is a conventional person concerned about proper behavior; the term derives from a character in Thomas Morton's 1798 play *Speed the Plough*.

Aristophanes[2] was a dramatist with a purpose; his comedies were defenses of the conservative elements in the Athenian state and, in one of his plays, he urged the people to give amnesty to citizens implicated in a revolution. The Athenian orator and dramatist held uninterrupted contact with the people. If they were a mob, a herd, a group, or a crowd, he adjusted himself to them directly, and could see his results in the marketplace the next day. Aristophanes could talk to virtually all the people he wanted to influence at one time, and, after they left the amphitheater, he could consult with 10 or 20 percent of them in the course of a few days and discover what his effect had been. Whereas Pierre Beaumarchais,[3] acting like an Aristophanes at the end of the monarchy in France, could affect public opinion only in so far as he touched the chosen few. The general public of many millions had to be reached slowly, and the discovery of what their opinion really was could not be made at all because there was no organization through which it expressed itself.

The publicist today—preacher, politician, advertiser, whatever he may be—is trying to influence the public opinion of 50 or a 100 million people. In

---

[2] Aristophanes (446–386 BC) was a comedic playwright.

[3] Pierre Beaumarchais (1732–1799) was a French polymath—he was a playwright, inventor, diplomat, and musician.

practice, the leaders of our two great political parties
try to keep faithful and to win over only some eight
million voters. A fifteenth of the population stands
for the general will in a presidential election. But even
this fraction of the whole public is scattered over the
entire area of the country and represents every
possible shade of opinion, tradition, every variety of
habit, racial background, education, and every degree
of wealth and social position. This diversity of origin
and habits suggests that a public, as we know it today,
is totally different from the crowd public of the
Athenian marketplace. Morris Ginsberg,[4] in his 1920
book *The Psychology of Society*, has said that, because
the modern public rests not on physical personal
contact, but on such indirect means of
communication as the newspaper and the radio,
individuality can be better retained and thus
individuals are less suggestible to group emotions. He
points out aspects that work against a crowd mind.
An individual can belong to only one crowd at a time
but he generally belongs to several publics. For
example, if he reads a conservative daily and a liberal
weekly he is a member of two publics which tend to
neutralize each other. Finally, various publics may
generate their own organizations that may create rules

---

[4] Morris Ginsberg (1889–1970), a British sociologist, is considered a
    seminal figure in sociology and was a founding member of the
    British Sociological Association.

of debate concerning issues and evidence—such approaches may work against the mob mind.

Ginsburg does not, however, accept the argument that, because of these differences, publics are entirely different from crowds. Merely because the modern public is larger and more complex than the ancient crowd, its prestige is greater, and the fact that hundreds of groups in widely separated areas believe the same thing makes that belief almost irresistible. Secondly, he says, there is publicity which uses cumulative suggestion that

> ...is practiced on the public on an enormous scale at all times, though perhaps this fact becomes more obvious in times of crisis, when powerful emotional and instinctive tendencies come into play, reduce the critical faculty of individuals, and lower them all to a common level in which all that is distinctive and personal is lost or submerged. Though therefore the mentality of the public is, at any rate in normal times, more rational and less explosive, it does have many elements in common with that of the crowd in the narrower sense of that term.

Yet public opinion is not exactly crowd opinion. The public expresses itself through certain organizations and institutions. A political party, a custom house, a church, a parade, a day in honor of the dead, are all expressions of public opinion. The police force is also an expression of public opinion, and it is when the police fail to deal promptly with criminals that the looser organization of a posse is formed by the public. When the police deal with a criminal in a way contrary to public opinion, a lynching mob springs up. "When the public cannot create an organization, it generates a crowd," says Ginsberg.

For a public opinion to exist at all the public must be, roughly, what McDougall calls an organized group. It must have many minds acting in common and aware of each other with at least a beginning of a common purpose. The opinion of such a public is the result of the interaction of at least its best minds and the diffusion of ideas through the mass. Opinion is not merely the instinctive response to any emotional appeal. In spite of shouting "To hell with Yale," even the most collegiate of Harvard undergraduates does not in his opinion consider Yale in any degree damnable. Opinion, says Ginsberg, "stands for that mass of ideas and beliefs in a group or society, which has a certain stability and is not a mere series of momentary reactions, but is yet not based on clearly thought out grounds of a scientific character."

The reason that public opinion is important in a democracy is not that it is infallible or even generally right; rather, it is important because it is public. "Public approval and disapproval is a tremendous force, and though not always enlightened it does nevertheless act as a check on the designs of those who wield power in society," says Ginsberg. He points out that the power of public opinion can also lead to new ideas struggling "against the apathy, indifference and sullen opposition of the mass of mankind." This is all the more reason that "efforts should be directed towards making it enlightened and open to reasoned persuasion."

It is as an instrument of enlightenment that publicity operates on the public. Its function is to shed light. The more clearly a public sees a fact, the more specifically the public interest is shown to exist, the more the public will act upon the facts. The danger of democracy is that the public will deputize its thinking—that democracies will always think by deputy so long as they can vote in person. Yet it is only by governing itself that the public can learn to govern, and only by thinking that it can learn to think. Publicity sheds light upon the subjects for thought and, by doing so, arouses interest which, by trial and error, arrives at government.

Chapter 21.
Finding the Facts

Walter Lippmann points out in his book *Public Opinion* that there exists the "intolerable and unworkable fiction that each of us must acquire a competent opinion about all public affairs." This, he says, is said to be the underlying assumption of democratic government. Norman Angell, in his 1927 book *The Public Mind*, alludes to this fiction when he calls the average man "Babbitt as manager of civilization—in his spare time."[1] Lippmann suggests that the press is incapable of doing much for the organization of public opinion, the defects of which it "intensifies and reflects." Public opinion he says, must be organized not by the press, but for the press. He notes:

> It is possible and necessary for journalists to bring home to people the uncertain character of the truth on which their opinions are founded, and by criticism and agitation to prod social science into making more usable formations of social facts, and to prod statesmen into establishing more visible institutions. The press, in other words, can fight for the extension

---

[1] Norman Angell (1872–1967) had worked for the *St. Louis Globe-Democrat*, the *San Francisco Chronicle* and the *Daily Mail*. In 1929, he became a Member of Parliament and, in 1933 won the Nobel Peace Prize.

of reportable truth. But as social truth is organized today, the press is not constituted to furnish from one edition to the next the amount of knowledge which the democratic theory of public opinion demands.

How to perfect the recording of forces and to supply instruments of knowledge is the problem, says Lippmann. His solution demands new conceptions of democracy and new organisms. The remedy, he says, "lies in social organization based on a system of analysis and record, and in all the corollaries of that principle; in the abandonment of the theory of the omnicompetent citizen, in the decentralization of decision, in the coordination of decision by comparable record and analysis." Recording and analysis are largely the work of experts. Democracies, accused of the cult of incompetence, are supposed to sheer off from experts. In the degree that the expert ceases to be a theorist and becomes a technician, he gains respect and, in many walks of life, the technical expert has been added as a sort of governor, adjusting differences between other forces. His great advantage is the possession of accurate knowledge. In the organization of the British Admiralty, there is a First Sea Lord who, with the admirals of the fleet and the experts attached to them, determine technical policy. They might conclude at a certain time that they could attack and wipe out all the other navies existing in the world, but they would be helpless to move a single vessel without the approval of the First Civil Lord who, working with the cabinet, determines policy. This separation of fact-finding and policy is typical of the organization of the British Government. The British Foreign Office has a permanent civil service whose sole function is the accumulation of knowledge. The control of policy remains in the hand of the Secretary of State for Foreign Affairs and so, ultimately, with the cabinet responsible to the House of Commons. Of these officials, it is truthfully said that, in pursuit of their business, they uproot in themselves all prejudice, including the temporary prejudice evoked by a war. They are patriotic Britons, and conceive it the highest service to their country to report whatever they can find, however opposed to their country's interests or welfare, in order that their political chiefs may control policy in full possession of fact. Lippmann, in *Public Opinion*, compares these men with an American ambassador who said that he never reported anything to Washington which would not cheer up the folks at home, and adds ironically "he charmed all those who met him, helped many a stranded war worker, and was superb when he unveiled a monument."

The ambassador's error is one made constantly in a democratic government—it is a confusion between the functions of accumulating knowledge and determining policy. If the ambassador to Great

Britain, for instance, had failed during the war to inform the U.S. President of the state of mind prevailing among British laborites, he might have furthered the policy of considering all organized labor as a menace to victory. But he would have failed to give the president a background for discussing with English Foreign Secretary Arthur Balfour a statement of peace terms acceptable to British labor. Such a statement was made by negotiations between the prime minister and the labor leaders at the beginning of 1918, and President Wilson was asked by Balfour to intensify the effect by making a similar statement. Had the president been consistently informed by our representatives abroad that the idealistic and conciliatory attitude of British labor was inspired by Pro-Germanism, and that the labor elements were negligible in the prosecution of the war, he would have lacked entirely the necessary materials for deciding his course of action.

This is a hypothetical case. An actual one is that of the secret treaties between the Allies made public by the Bolsheviks at the end of 1917. These treaties were certainly among the least desirable arrangements from the point of view of the United States. Each one represented a bargain made in desperation, and many of them violated both the spirit and the letter of the published aims of the Allies. They were all contradictory to the American interpretation of the war and to the objects of America's collaboration. They were harsh facts and those who benefitted by each of them intended that they should be fulfilled.

When the president returned to America to defend the treaty he had signed at Versailles, he declared that he had never heard of these treaties before they were placed before him at the peace conference. The truth and bearing of this statement have both been challenged. The substance of the treaties had been published, at least in pacifist journals in the United States. It is quite possible, however, that ambassadors and private individuals, wishing to spare the president difficulties, had thought it best to keep from him facts which would not only have disturbed him profoundly, but would have compelled him to change his entire policy toward the Allies. The result of this well-meaning concealment of vital information was that the president went to Paris in the belief that the Allies had accepted the Fourteen Points, and with them the American peace ideals, and found himself confronted by the fruits of the very secret diplomacy he had promised to destroy. Knowledge and policy had been confused.

Certain industrial developments indicate that these two functions can be separated. In a great many industries, competing manufacturers have joined in associations whose purpose is to benefit the industry as a whole. One of their activities is visible in a comparatively new type of advertising and publicity—persuading the public to use paint, without specifying any brand of paint, or to eat Oregon apples without specifying any trade name. An activity less apparent to the public eye, but infinitely more important, is the collection of data available to all. It is said that in the manufacturing of motor cars there are no trade secrets. Although competition between the various makers is so keen that it often leads to price wars, the scientific processes and technical devices of manufacture are common property. All the knowledge and the experience of each company is at the disposal of every other company, and this includes European as well as American manufacturers.

Policy remains individual, determined by experience, initiative, and self-interest. The collection of facts is made as impersonal as any human agency can make it. Similar work is done in a few branches of social science. Bureaus of vital statistics are common in city, state, and national governments. A few years ago, an epidemic of infantile paralysis struck a city which was then in the midst of a boom and was spending millions in advertising to attract new residents. The municipal bureau reported the epidemic with exact figures to the city council. By doing so it fulfilled its function. The fact that the city council made every effort to suppress the news of the epidemic is a matter of policy. Few people with children of their own would agree that the policy of suppression was justifiable. Apparently, most of the real estate owners and other interests in the city thought that it was useless to start a scare when the medical authorities would certainly be able to stop the epidemic in a few weeks. In the end, as it turned out, the newspapers of a rival city gained access to the facts and published them, putting the city which had suppressed them on the defensive.

The publication of facts with the intention of impartiality is carried on by certain leagues and unions which publish, for example, the record of a candidate for re-election, giving his yes and no votes on important legislation. The intention of many of these organizations is, in essence, propaganda. They are interested in the election of honest men with a high ideal of service to the public, or in preventing short weight or adulteration of goods. Yet the method, when properly carried out, provides nothing but such fact as could be sworn to under oath.

The intelligence department of an organization is its safeguard against propaganda. Lippmann, who desires to see such departments created and coordinated into a bureau of the government, mentions the Division of Far Eastern Affairs of the State Department. It is obvious that if the State

Department merely wanted to know what China and Japan wanted officially, it would need only to turn to the ambassadors of these countries. Yet these ambassadors are, in their essence, propagandists—in the old phrase, "they lie abroad for their country."[2] Instead of depending on them, and upon Americans who also have special interest in the Orient, the State Department maintains a staff whose special function is not to determine policy nor even to discover facts supporting the American policy, but merely to submit data to the Secretary of State. "The more faithfully the Division represents what is not otherwise represented, either by the Japanese or American Ambassadors, or the Senators and Congressmen from the Pacific coast the better Secretary of State he will be," says Lippmann. "He may decide to take his policy from the Pacific coast but he will take his view of Japanese from Japan."

Lippmann suggests a permanent intelligence section for each of the 10 departments represented in the U.S. Cabinet and, as a fundamental condition, desires the independence of these sections from Congress and from the secretaries of the departments. He maintains that if such a section were only

<hr />

[2] This expression is attributed to Sir Henry Wotton (1568–1639), an English diplomat and author. The full quote attributed to him is, "An ambassador is an honest gentleman sent to lie abroad for the good of his country."

supported year by year it could not function. The major portion of the staff at least should have tenure of office for life and conditions of work at least as favorable as those of a scientific research worker in a university or a great industry. These sections would have the right to examine all documents and to question officials and outsiders. They would take the place of the sensational investigations which are now frequently used for political purposes just before an election. The 10 sections would work together and exchange data.

It is possible, furthermore, that this deputized scrutiny can be transferred to other fields. A consumers' league might be able to hire an expert who could cooperate with, say, The Bureau of Standards (weights and measures) for the analysis of every commodity offered for sale in a given community. In such a matter as drugs there is no need for an expert. Drugs, for the most part, carry their chemical analysis on the label and are sold with the guarantee that they conform to the specifications of the United States Pharmacopeia. There is no such standard for paints, breakfast food, cloth, and rubber tires, although the purchasing agencies of the government submit every commodity offered to them to the most exhaustive tests. The public is not as careful in its purchases as the government, and lacks instruments for measuring quality.

If a community could create the post of public analyst, it could check, among other things, the ideas offered to it. The public would have to be certain that its analyst—or intelligence section—had the freedom of a scientist and the pride of a technician, and that he was possessed of knowledge, or of the means to acquire knowledge, and was free of prejudice and immune to bribery. Such an ideal official or staff of officials could expose to the public whatever was hidden and insidious in the propaganda continuously directed toward the creation of the public attitude. There would be little to do in regard to open and responsible publicity for this analyst function, because it carries its purpose like a badge of identification. If the public, however, is incapable of discriminating between open and concealed publicity, if it cannot judge the former on its merits and defend itself from the latter, it might be able to accomplish these ends by creating a purely fact-finding agency as a guide to conduct.

An alternative to governmental intelligence sections is the proposed government publicity department. English and American writers have both proposed that the government undertake publicity on its own behalf. The conditions in the two countries are however not identical. Traditionally, the Englishman admires his Navy because it is "the silent service." Whole departments of government work in entire isolation from public knowledge, public criticism, and public interest. Before the war, especially, it would have been unthinkable for the government to issue explanations to the public. Defenses of policy were made in response to a question in the House. His Majesty's opposition was the watch dog; but the result of a question in the House was, after all, only a reply printed in the course of reports on Parliament. Appeals to the public were few and far between, and it was the habit of the prime minister indirectly to inspire editorials or to give news to *The Times* or any other paper which was supposed to represent the government's attitude. Publicity was used, of course, but not what is technically known as publicity. This tradition was modified during the war and during the recent general strike in England. But the habit of working in a vacuum undisturbed by public opinion persists, and the habit of not expecting publicity remains strong in the public.

In America, the position is entirely different. Not only do individuals have their press agents, departments have special organizations to attend to their publicity and to tell the public what they are doing. The number of these runs into the hundreds in Washington, D.C., and suspicious senators have protested that the public money should not be spent for publicity. Even if no special functionaries existed, the various departments of the American government would still maintain an active and energetic publicity campaign.

The correspondents' meeting with the secretary of state and with the other cabinet officers, the meetings with the president, the bulletins issued by the various departments, are all publicity. It is said that the American policy in South America, for example, is misunderstood and that the government ought to have a special publicity department to avoid misunderstandings. Yet, the president, the state department, our ambassadors, and our representatives in the Pan-American Union have all done publicity for our policy toward Latin America. The visits of Will Rogers and Colonel Lindbergh were elements of publicity.[3] In fact, the publicity concerning our Latin America policy has been enormous, and if that policy still causes us difficulty, it is more reasonable to say that it is understood and disliked than to say it is not understood. On our relations with Canada, virtually nothing is said for generations. There is no publicity in the strict professional sense. Yet our relations with Canada are an example to the whole world of mutual

---

[3] In the mid-to-late 1920s, American humorist Will Rogers (1879–1935) and world-renowned aviator Charles Lindberg (1902–1974) both engaged in high-profile tours in the Americas. Rogers, from 1925 through 1928, toured across the U.S. and into Mexico. From December 1927 through February 1928, Lindbergh toured 16 countries in Latin America.

friendship and understanding. The acts of a government are often its best publicity and, when these are construed unfavorably, the chief officials of the government are the men whose position, prestige, and authority make them the best agents of publicity.

Just what a governmental counsel in public relations would add to the existing powers is hard to discover. The easy thing to foresee is that a bureaucracy of great effectiveness would be created for the benefit of the party in power. An organization instructed to find out facts may be impartial, but one created specifically to explain and defend policies cannot be. It must represent the party temporarily in power and, by doing so, must contribute to keeping that party and its policies in the position of dominance.

In theory, not only the president but every congressman is supposed to represent the whole country. Actually, we know that many of them represent special sections, special interests, and only that part of the electorate which has put them in office. They have already an enormous advantage over those who are out of office. It seems unnecessary to fortify them further by giving them, at public expense, an organization by which they can entrench themselves and undermine their enemies.

Chapter 22.
Publicity and Justice

THE ACT WHICH BROUGHT THE UNITED STATES into existence was a declaration to the public and an arraignment of King George III before the bar of enlightened public opinion. By a coincidence, the American colonies won their independence from Great Britain at the same time that the press of the mother country won its independence from tyrannous interference. Publicity and democracy have gone hand in hand.

Today, some serious critics wonder whether democracy is safe from publicity, and others whether democracy can be made safe for the world. Re-examining the ideas of the Revolutionary Fathers, some observers blame upon the mistakes of democracy all the ills of the world; others think of democracy as in itself an instrument for good, corrupted by outside forces of which publicity is among the worst. They note the excesses of the French Revolution, and base their opposition to democracy on the actions of mobs. They point out that a century of democracy and education did not save either Great Britain or America from the disasters of the war, and that democracy has been steadily (though not always openly) repudiated in favor of fascism, dictatorships, proletarian committees, inner cabinets, and the like. Others claim that the modern state has grown so unwieldy that democracy, in the sense of government directly representing the bulk of the citizenry, no longer can work, and that the capitalist system compels the formation of small groups of insiders who actually rule. Journalist and British politician Norman Angell, aware of all these difficulties, adds that even these rulers, incompetent to save themselves or their countries from destruction at best, are subject to mass opinion at its worst. Democracy is on the defensive.

A century ago, every book criticizing the existing order ended with a plea for education. Education was supposed to be the philosopher's stone of the alchemist which would turn everything it touched to gold. The cure for the ills of democracy was a hot or cold application of more democracy in a new place— i.e., in education. It would be self-satisfying to follow this scheme and announce publicity as the cure-all of democratic ills, especially of itself. The claim made here is more modest. The cure for the abuses of publicity lies in responsible publicity. It especially lies in the public appreciation of the difference between noxious and legitimate publicity. Moreover, publicity is an essential instrument in democracy; it is not, however, a sovereign remedy. Just as no medicine operates under conditions which itself prolongs the disease, just as no serum will stop an epidemic if the water supply remains infected, so the reforms of democracy will remain unavailing if the purifying process of publicity is omitted.

Angell's point, cited above, is peculiarly interesting because it takes the discussion a little way out of the realm of partisan prejudice. He examines both sides of a famous argument. The first is that, since business runs the country, public folly is of no particular importance; the opposite view is that the abolition of the capitalist system would automatically free the mind of man from social error. For many years, Angell had preached that war was economically unprofitable and believed that international capital would prevent a world war. The world war came and he realized that, powerful as it was, capital could not stand against war feeling. He now proceeds to explode "the quite unneeded myth that the capitalist has some unexplained interest in the promotion of war."[4] This Marxist view, he says, "that the wars which produced the present economic chaos were deliberately designed by capitalism for its purpose does not stand investigation, and defies nearly all the facts." It is, in short, a myth, a slogan, an emotional center unrelated to logic and reason.

---

[4] Quotes from Angell in this section come from an unattributed source. They parallel similar observations Angell offered in his 1921 book *The Fruits of Victory: A Sequel to the Great Illusion.*

Capitalism, according to Angell, is also unable to put an end to public folly. In Europe, it is faced today either with revolution in some form or a lowering of standards and efficiency—a general social failure which may be the beginning of the end. Angell's remedy is discussion. It is neither education alone nor publicity alone, but a thorough use of both of them to create "a way of thinking." Himself a publicist, he believes in the benefit to society of letting every man state his case freely and recalls the days when democracy was called "government by discussion," only to note that this conception is being obliterated. "There is no general realization of the fact that without...free discussion and the habits and disciplines which it sets up, public opinion in a democracy never can be sane and understanding, capable of good collective decisions, never can be anything but violent-minded, subject to panic, [and] unbalanced..." (It is worth remarking that British journalist Walter Bagehot, whose contribution to the idea of crowd imitation was noted earlier, considered discussion the center of progress in a democracy and a safeguard against imitation carried on too long).

Woodrow Wilson wrote, in his 1913 book *The New Freedom*, "The sole purpose of democracy is that we may hold counsel with one another, so as not to depend upon the understanding of one man, but to depend upon the common counsel of all." Yet taking

counsel is one of the most difficult things to do in a
democracy. Casting a vote is not taking counsel.
Wilson used to say that reading popular novels was a
good way to gain an insight into the interests and the
workings of the common mind, but it could hardly be
called a systematic reference of questions to the
minds of all. Even if some system of reference were
devised, there would still remain the grave question of
the basis upon which counsel could be common.

The mind of the average man, if it heeded every
call made upon it, would be monstrously overtaxed.
The man who can barely make ends meet in a country
store is, by the fictions of democracy, supposed to
make up his mind about rural credits and farm relief,
the advisability of installment buying, the proper
attitude of his country toward Mexico, the precise
angle of elevation permissible for a naval gun, and the
intricacies of the tariff. At a minimum, he is expected
to choose between two men who have made up their
minds, one in direct opposition to the other, on those
questions—and to choose in such a way that his own
interests are best served.

The publicity dealing with these problems is
pointed up, made dramatic for him in the newspapers,
over the radio, and in the movies. But it does not
begin to exhaust the calls made upon the average
attention. Every manufacturer assaults him through

advertising in weeklies, on billboards, and by circular letters. Educational institutions, new religions, organizations opposed to licensing dogs, insurance companies, banks, pacifists, fraternal orders, chambers of commerce, all ask his interest and his aid. The press acts as a filter and passes on to its readers only such items as may have intrinsic interest; the mere cost of mailing circulars keeps the level of appeals down a little. But the moment anyone is intensely interested in anything which needs public support, the barrage of publicity descends again upon the average man.

This publicity is one-sided—all publicity is. And the serious question about the pressure of publicity is not its bulk, but its partiality. When Hamlet, mortally wounded, turned to his friend Horatio, he did not ask him to present an impartial account of his death to the world. "Report me and my cause aright," he says, and, knowing that he will live hereafter in the opinion of mankind, he bids Horatio, "Absent thee from felicity awhile, and in this harsh world draw thy breath in pain, to tell my story." Tell his story, he says, the story of what he has done, so that he is justified to mankind.

So long as a person has any interest in the presentation of fact, fact will take color from interest. One way of preventing this is to forbid interested parties from appealing in any way to the public. It would hardly be necessary to note the impossibility of such a veto if the proposal for legal restrictions on publicity were not so frequently made. Those who want publicity to be censored, regulated, and approved do not, as a rule, follow their own premises to the logical conclusion. In connection with publicity, the power to regulate implies the power to destroy, for it will always be possible to forbid any publicity by imputing anti-social motives. In the present state of democracy, however, it is impossible to forbid the discussion of any subjects which the people want to discuss. It is, apparently, possible to forbid the discussion of evolution in certain schools, because the voters have so decided. But no agency exists which can, in conformity with the desires of the public, say what is to be spoken of, what facts brought out, and what prejudices exploited. The proposal to regulate is based largely on the common conception of publicity as a special function—articles in the papers, for example, and speeches over the radio. Properly conceived, a hundred other human activities, from a smile to a bribe, are concentrated on the same purpose as printed publicity, that is, the purpose of influencing men's minds.

The reverse method of treating the partiality of publicity is to recognize it and to make a virtue of it, to allow the fullest publicity to everyone, representing every side. The *New Republic* recently said in an editorial that, in the 1924 campaign, Republican orators were heard over the radio at least three or four times as often as Democratic, and probably eight or ten times as often as supporters of Senator LaFollette. "The Federal radio law of 1926 provides that when any candidate is given time on the air from any station, an equal opportunity must be afforded his opponent," it said, also offering the reservation that "It would be expecting too much of human nature to suppose that the owners of radio stations will be impartial as between the party with which they are affiliated, and its opponent." Even in the field of politics, then, where a tradition of free discussion exists, the question of assuring equal opportunities is serious. The moment economic principles are touched, it becomes even thornier. The great broadcasting stations in 1928 put the Republican and Democratic conventions on the air. The Socialist Party, however, which asked to have its proceedings broadcast, was informed at the last moment that one of the principal stations in New York would give them a single hour. The situation is hardly bettered by the existence of a socialist broadcasting station which is too remote and too feeble to reach the country at large. Under the laws of the United States, the Socialist Party is recognized as eligible to nominate and present candidates for office; legally, it stands on a par with the other great parties. Yet in practice it cannot make itself heard.

There is a law governing the French press which compels a newspaper, when it has published an attack on a man, to publish his defense in the same column of the same page, and at the same length as the original article, in order to avoid suit. The system makes for caution on the part of the newspapers and for a beginning of fair play. But everyone who has been attacked in the press knows how unsatisfactory a letter of protest to the editor must be. A man editing a single column every day may keep up a personal vendetta, by implication or direct statement, to which the person attacked, having no comparable organ of publicity, cannot reply. The man whose publication comes out every month is at the mercy of the weekly, the weekly at the mercy of the daily, and even the daily may not be able to live down the attacks of the man who owns morning and evening papers both. As for the private individual, who has no organ of publicity except his voice and an untrained pen, his plight is desperate. Yet, if a newspaper undertook to allow every individual to state his case in response to every time he is mentioned, the paper would lose all interest for the general public. If every minority was to be heard on every subject, discussion would never concentrate into action. And if no minority is heard, justice becomes a farce, as it would be in a law court with only one side allowed to plead.

The law court suggests one of the ways of preventing injustice. Every word offered in testimony is sworn to, under oath. Each witness is identified before he is allowed to testify, and opposing lawyers always bring out the relation of the witness to the principal and his possible interest in the verdict. There is a penalty for perjury and, the moment a witness refuses to answer, the jurymen suspect that the reason is prejudicial to his case. At the same time, the jury, knowing the witness's interest, discounts his testimony and checks it against the testimony of others. It is in the power of the public to compel publicity of every sort to approach this legal ideal. It can, simply by refusing to listen to other publicity, compel all who make appeals to the public to accept responsibility, and to state their true names and their true interest in the facts presented. All pleading is special pleading; in court, the witness and the lawyer both avow their connection with the plaintiff or defendant. In publicity, so far, public opinion has not compelled the pleader to do the same.

The moment the public begins to reject anonymous and irresponsible publicity, the pressure will be partly lifted. The propagandist who claims to be non-partisan and is discovered receiving checks from a single party, and the professor who happens to

believe firmly in a bill before Congress but also
happens to be receiving money from the promoters of
that bill, will find their activities curtailed simply by
the indifference and hostility of the public. The
public has only to discriminate.

The fact that an organization spends a great deal
of money on publicity is sometimes held as ipso facto
evidence of an intention hostile to the public interest.
This is entirely natural when the campaign is
underground, when the source of money expended
and the purpose are both concealed. Against open,
responsible publicity, the suspicion is as ill-directed as
it would be against the Ford Motor Company for
advertising. Some years ago an advertisement from
Bethlehem Steel Company featured the signatures of
their top executives Charles M. Schwab and Eugene
Grace. It was an explicit statement from the company
of their position against the creation of a government
plant for making armor. The interest of the company
was patent: if the government went into the business,
the company would lose contracts. Whatever the
advertisement said on the general advisability of
government operation of armor plants was naturally
discounted by the open self-interest of the signers of
the statement. Through inadvertence in preparing the
advertisement, some errors appeared in it. Secretary
of the Navy Josephus Daniels pointed them out in a
severe statement and newspapers everywhere

corrected the inaccuracies of the advertisement. The errors hurt Schwab and the Bethlehem Steel Company seriously, but within 24 hours of their appearance the public was not only aware of the truth, it was perhaps even over-impressed with the importance of the errors which had been committed. The obligation to be accurate was never more strikingly made clear; the advantage of responsible publicity, even if it makes mistakes, was firmly established. English philosopher and scientist Francis Bacon noted over 300 years ago that "Truth comes out of error more easily than out of confusion." The only part of the episode which Schwab could not understand was the protest by the *New York World*, a protest directed not so much against the publication of inaccuracies as against their publication in the form of an advertisement. Had the errors appeared in the form of an editorial inspired by the Bethlehem Steel Company, without any indication of the source, or been transmitted to the public by a secretly paid speaker, it would have been more difficult to make the truth known. The fact that the errors were displayed, even unintentionally, was the decisive thing in exposing them.

The same thing is true of a deliberate misstatement. Openly made, over a signature, it stands a thousand chances of exposure and only one of slipping by unnoticed. Every statement made with

interest on one side challenges the interest of the
other side. Every claim made in advertising is, in a
sense, an attack on all other claims for similar
products. Many years ago, a shaving cream was
advertised with the slogan "will not dry on the face."
A rival manufacturer put forth the same claim, in the
same words. One of them happened to use quotation
marks around the slogan and the other retorted with
"the truth needs no quotation marks."[5] In 1928, the
New York World published an analysis of newspaper
circulation, giving the *Herald Tribune* a figure lower
than that claimed by the latter. The figures were
instantly challenged and the challenge was again met.
The makers of advertising, realizing what the public is
beginning to do in any case, cry out, "Compare!"

The exposure of misstatements and of concealed
partisanship is one of the great services newspapers
can render their readers. As they grow in power,
newspapers become more and more independent of
advertisers, more and more skeptical of publicity. It is
peculiarly in their power to bring to light the
manipulations of publicists who themselves shun the
light. The extent to which they do this is bound to be
limited by two things: the affiliations of the
newspaper owners and the interest of the readers. If
the owner of a newspaper is a large stockholder in a

---

[5] This slogan was used by Colgate's Shaving Stick in the early 1900s.

corporation, he may wish unfavorable news about that corporation to be played down or omitted, unless his conception of the function of a newspaper compels him to publish whatever is news, regardless of his personal feeling. Secondly, if, for example, the readers of the paper do not care whether an intrigue is on foot to re-establish czardom in Russia, there will be little point in exposing the machinations of propagandists.

There again the rivalry between individuals acts as a safeguard for the public. A newspaper whose owners and editors strongly oppose government operation of power plants might have tried to omit altogether from its pages the news of the government investigation into the public utilities publicity campaign. Still, the fact that other papers were giving it headlines made for the danger that readers would happen on these other papers and wonder why they had not been kept informed. This compelled the publication of some of the report. The space given, the tone of the headlines, and the editorial comment, might all belittle the importance of the news, but the news, ultimately, cannot be suppressed.

Newspapers have often complained about press agentry, asserting that it was merely advertising without payment. The remedy has always been in the newspaper's own hands. Refuse to publish press agent "dope." Expose the press agent's hand behind the

publication of his work in other organs. If the
publicity man cannot stand publicity, he will be
destroyed. A secondary advantage to the public would
be the diminution of the flood of publicity and the
increased reader interest of whatever the editors did
permit to appear. For if the newspapers resolutely
determined not to publish anything which was not
inherently interesting, the press agent would have to
work all the harder to make his material acceptable.

In practice most newspapers make at least one of
these two defenses against the publicity offered them.
They do little in the way of exposing secret
propaganda, but they do stop whatever is
uninteresting. A great deal depends upon the
newspaper's own strength and its resistance to
pressure. An advertising agency, aware of the
inefficacy of advertising without other publicity, may
prepare articles dealing in some way with the product
about to be advertised. A contract for space is signed
with a newspaper, nothing being said about the use of
publicity matter. A week later, the advertising
manager of the paper may come to the city editor's
desk with a piece of copy sent out by the agency from
which he has just received a fine contract. He will
offer it to the city editor for use in the paper. The
agency has exerted no direct pressure; it has not made
the use of this publicity a condition for granting the
contract, it has merely offered a story. In a big

newspaper office, the chances are two-to-one that the story would only miss the wastebasket because it fell on the floor. But a small paper, trying to attract national advertising, trying to get on the preferred list of newspapers patronized by the great agencies, might feel differently.

The special automobile and radio sections of some newspapers seem even to the casual reader to be built up on the basis of so much for so much. Advertisements each seem to carry a certain amount of reading matter with them: news of changes in car design or of changes in personnel, or an interview with the maker of a new type of radio. Hardly anyone is deceived. Yet, in the sections on books and theatre, nothing of the sort operates. In metropolitan papers, the suggestion that a publisher's advertisement is conditional on the appearance of a news notice, a favorable review, or any mention whatever of his books, would be impossible. Editors, in fulfillment of their duties, review whatever books are most interesting to the public. They cannot play favorites among publishers, and the reviews a publisher gets are generally proportioned to the interest and importance of the books he publishes. Producers of plays have again and again withdrawn advertising from certain newspapers as a protest, they said, against the prejudice of the drama critic. They have, however, often restored their advertising because they found the newspapers hardened against any pressure and because they needed the newspapers more than the newspapers needed them.

Pressure exists. The utilities companies, even if a local manager had never cultivated a contact with a newspaper manager, would still have been putting the pressure of a large advertising contract upon the editorial writer of the paper. The opponents of private ownership of utilities in the state of New York could not pay for the writing and publication of a book giving their point of view, nor could they print over 100,000 copies of such a book and, by gifts or other pressure, introduce it into the schools. The established systems of property, industry, marriage, and education have an insuperable advantage over every change proposed as they have every advantage except novelty. The majority of a newspaper's readers are, in some way, attached to the prevailing system; they may suffer under it and be deluded by it, but they depend upon it. The newspaper serving them serves also those who make the system: the law-abiding citizens, the financiers, the politicians in power or about to come into power. Naturally they respond to the pressure of facts.

Against that pressure, the pressure of self-interest, there is no defense, and it is even questionable whether a defense is desirable. The steps of the Capitol are public property, but if one man has the happy idea of running a motor car up and down them to the accompaniment of moving picture cameras, and if the stunt gets into the papers and into the movies and everybody thinks that the motor car has proved exceptional stamina and flexibility by going up and down these steps, no harm seems to have been done. Yet the imagination and the initiative of the publicity man who thought of the stunt has exerted a pressure on the news reels and the newspapers—a pressure more powerful than money alone. If the Bell System were in competition with another domestic telephone and advertised itself as the only company with direct communication to London, this again would seem thoroughly justifiable. Yet it would have been the power and the money behind the Bell System which persuaded the British Government to allow it an exclusive contract.

If every school child, on leaving school, were presented with a stick of candy wrapped in a paper bearing the words "The right wing communists love you," there might be protests against communist propaganda because communism itself was considered a menace, but the method of propaganda would have to be admitted. Yet the left wing communists might feel that their richer right wing opponents, who could afford candy, were exerting pressure which they themselves could not afford. Indeed, rich corporations can hire skilled publicity men; poor ones have to make do with amateurs. Power begets power and weakness, weakness. If this is injustice, publicity has its share in it.

There is, however, a point at which the one-sided pressure of publicity becomes obvious. The fact that school officials allowed text books concealing propaganda to enter their schools is instantly seen to be hostile to the institutions of democracy. One reason is that the means were secret and seem dishonest. Another is that, even if the books bore the legend "issued under the auspices of the Acme Electric Light Company," the mind of the student would be insufficiently trained to discover the connection between this legend and the statements in the book. In a hundred ways, the school system is propaganda. It is propaganda in favor of the United States, of its system of government, of its customs and ideals. Yet the mind rebels against the thought that the schools should be made the instrument of private propaganda. It seems right and desirable to say in schools, "Opinion about the proper ownership of utilities is divided; some people want private and some public ownership. The arguments put out by each side are thus and thus." It seems wrong that one side should, without being held responsible, present its case.

The pressure seems unsocial when it is secretly exercised, when it touches those who cannot discriminate, and when money or power are used to corrupt basic institutions. It seems wrong also when there is no opportunity for check or verification. If a nation, party, or company has it in its power to prevent access to the facts. If it will not submit to letting the facts be checked by outsiders, the publicity based on these facts can go to any lengths against the public good and there is no defense. Publicity which reiterates a challenged statement without offering any proof of its truth, and trusts to the unlimited expenditure of money to drown out accusations, shares this unfavorable light. Opponents of publicity have said that its function, when caught in a lie, was not to withdraw the lie, but to repeat it. It is, on the contrary, part of the function of publicity to make the public aware of lies and to teach it how to discriminate between the fraudulent and the true.

As mentioned at the start of Chapter 9, a signed lie is ultimately of more service to the public than an anonymous truth. The lie can be caught, traced back to its propagator, and refuted; the fact that it appears with a signature is a presupposition of innocent intentions. But the anonymous truth may be intended to build up confidence, preparing the ground for the launching of an equally anonymous lie. The anonymous possible truth finds its way into even the best of our newspapers, especially when the source of accurate information is blocked. Naturally, correspondents, aware of their editors' prejudices, look for every scrap of news conforming to the paper's policy. The number of times the Soviet government in Moscow was tottering to a fall, the number of times Vladimir Lenin and Leon Trotsky[6] were reported dead, testify not so much to the newspapers' dishonesty and deliberate intention to do harm as to their eagerness to publish every scrap of possible news which can please their readers. The way anonymous reports carry across continents, receiving accretions as they go, is illustrated in one of the more recent of Trotsky's "deaths." The streamer headline of a New York evening paper announced simply that Trotsky was dying. The big first-page headline said "Banished Russian leader reported shot and dying." For the people who bothered to read further, the opening paragraph said that "an unconfirmed report of mysterious origin...was circulated throughout Europe and America today." From London came an entirely circumstantial account, telling exactly where the bullet lodged in Trotsky's spinal column, when the shooting took place, and expressing doubt only as to whether the assassin, who was a student, was a

---

[6] Vladimir Lenin (1870–1924) was a Bolshevik revolutionary who was a leader in the successful attempt to overthrow the Russian Czar in 1917 and led the Soviet Union until his death in 1924. He was joined by Leon Trotsky (1879–1940) who later led a failed revolt against increasing bureaucracy in the Soviet Union and was subsequently exiled.

Caucasian or an Armenian. A nation of headline
readers would have had Trotsky dead long before
these mazes of international correspondence had been
threaded. That is, unless they were too accustomed to
his death to believe it again.

Headlines are all anonymous. The newspaper,
theoretically, stands behind them, and the pride of
the copy desk is to extract from a news story a
headline which does two things: gets the gist of the
story accurately represented in a few words, and has
punch. In many cases, if the two conflict, punch wins
the day. Even if the story corrects the headline, the
invaluable first impression remains. Thus one reads
"Packers Make Billions," although the story which
follows indicates that the packers were making a
miserable three percent on their investment.

Headlines make public opinion more often than
editorial writers. For no dishonest purpose, headline
writers are anonymous and their succession of
anonymous accuracies makes all the more dangerous
the slipping in of an anonymous falsehood. Headlines,
in controversial matters, are dictated by policy. If a
candidate makes a speech, a favorable newspaper will
put into its headline his most serious charge against
his opponent; a hostile newspaper, in contrast, will
put in his most courteous acknowledgment of his
opponent's qualities. The public cannot expect the
newspaper to carry a warning sentence above each

headline. The public has to provide its own
suspicions.

· Nothing but experience will teach the public to
distrust all headlines, to suspect all anonymity. The
experience can be positive as well as negative. A
statement issued by a responsible person, one known
to the public and enjoying a position which falsehood
would imperil, is usually found to be true. The habit
of looking for such statements and neglecting others
is what the public can cultivate. Even the sellers of
patent medicines attempt to give the air of
responsibility to their advertisements. It is not Mr.
Jones of Schenectady who has used their powders for
years, it is Mr. Adolph M. Jones of 2453 Schenectady
Turnpike, Schenectady, New York, who so testifies.
Jones may have received a dollar for the use of his
name and photograph, but on the point of
verifiability, the advertiser is safe. He has supplied a
definite person to whom inquiries may be addressed.
His advertisement is no longer anonymous.

The foregoing analysis of the ways to meet the
evils of publicity suggests that the proper technique of
publicity implies an ethic of its own which is
conformable to the highest ethical standards of the
community. The most practical considerations
compel the publicity man to this ethical standard. He
wants his publicity to be believed in, acted upon, to

be effective in the highest degree. He wants a temporary connection with a corporation or an industry to become permanent. Both he and the individual or group for whom he issues publicity want to continue in the enjoyment of public confidence.

The comparatively few men who have carried on the profession of publicity—a profession as new as the art is old—agree on the conditions of success. Publicity must be truthful. It is not an abstract qualification. It does not mean the truth, the whole truth, but it does mean nothing but the truth. It means selections from the truth, the truth made interesting, the truth arranged to fulfill a definite purpose. But it does not mean juggling with the truth so that one makes a lie. The juggler tossing dazzlingly colored Indian clubs in the air may make four appear to be five or six.[7] The publicist may arrange his facts in order to dazzle and to give a favorable impression, but they must remain facts. He cannot publish 16 statements of which 15 are true in order to insinuate the truth of the 16th, which is actually false. It is his duty to his employer to make out the best case; his duty to the public is to make the case out of the truth.

This is a purely technical necessity. It coincides with moral ideas and is connected with them because

---

[7] The Indian club (or "meel") is a bowling-pin shaped wooden club available in various weights, some as heavy as 50 pounds each. They are normally juggled as part of an exercise routine.

inaccuracies, errors, and falsehoods are eventually
exposed and break down exactly what the publicist is
trying to build up—relations with the public. If there
were no moral prejudice against lying, if the truth
were valued only because it made business easier to
conduct, the handler of publicity would still be
irrevocably bound to tell the truth. His own business
is jeopardized the moment he is caught willfully
uttering a lie. The law which punishes the uttering of
counterfeit money is on the statute books; the law
against uttering counterfeit publicity, however, is not
codified, but it operates nonetheless.

The technique of publicity indicates that, for
maximum effectiveness, a statement must have
responsibility and authority. That is effectiveness
measured in time, as well as in intensity. Duration is
as important in publicity as it is in physics, and if the
science of persuasion ever finds its Einstein, he will
show how the element of time affects every item in its
technique. A statement, irresponsible and without
authority, may exert maximum effect under specified
conditions at a given moment. It is influenced by
time, because, in time, the effect will wear off, and the
contrary statement may come to destroy it. Given
only a little time, the publicist may strive for quick
effects, operating at the level of the barker outside the
circus tent, the flaring poster, or the exaggerated
claim. With more time, he cannot indulge himself in

these tricks, because time is on the side of the public. Time for comparison, for quiet thinking, for hearing the other side, for verification, and, supremely, for accepting the object of publicity, testing it, and discarding it if the claims made for it are not met.

The minor techniques of publicity—calling attention, keeping interest, arousing desires, moving people to action—coincide with the simple laws of human behaviors, and with the findings of psychology. The major laws coincide with sound public action, and with the standard of ethics of civilized nations. It, nevertheless, remains for the public to apply those standards. Since professional publicity is new, and the subtle manipulations of human minds have gone unnoticed for centuries, the public does not know where to begin. The suggestion is here made that they begin with the technical side of publicity since, at each step in checking sound technique, they will check sound morals.

If a newspaper were to print "This is publicity for So-and-So" at the top of an article, many people would not read it, although they cheerfully read So-and-So's advertisement, which is also publicity. They listen to a speaker over the radio although they know he is a paid campaigner. They listen to a quartet, although the announcement is deliberately made that the quartet is singing for this coffee or that chewing gum, because the singing pleases. The public, in short,

is becoming acquainted with the ways of publicity and
learning to discriminate a little. It can annihilate all
the publicity which is anti-social in effect by learning
more of the technique governing all publicity. From
the publicist's point of view, it is desirable that the
public should say, "This is publicity, but I will pay
attention to it, keeping in mind that it is an *ex parte*
statement, but giving it a fair chance because all the
other statements issued by this publicist, or this
company, have been fair, honest and interesting."
And, to the publicist, it is also desirable if the public
notes that "This other is also publicity, but is
pretending to be something else. It is hiding the
identity of the interested party. It is interesting, but I
will pay no attention to it because it is tainted with
deceit." However, if the public were to say, "This is
publicity and, although I know it is, although every
statement is vouched for by authorities I respect, I
will reject it"—then publicity would be driven
underground again and be compelled to disguise itself.
The rejection of honest publicity would simply mean
the creation of a new type of irresponsibility. For the
effort to persuade people will go on so long as some
men have interests to prosper and other men have
power to aid them.

At the present time, publicity performs two
services to the public. The first, giving information, is
mixed. Since publicity is not yet subject to the

discrimination of a public aware of its methods, some of the information given is misleading. It is, with the minutest exception, partisan, but a portion of it is frankly and fairly partisan, and a portion is concealed and unfair.

The second service is that publicity and the threat of publicity act as a deterrent to anti-social practice. Hardly a corporation active in the United States today is immune from investigation. Its books may be hauled out and examined at any moment as the result of a rumor, of a hostile critic in Congress, or of public suspicion. Candidates for office, political parties, large industries, holders of public office, lobbies, and leagues for influencing legislation or opinion all are perpetually under the threat of publicity. The public may reflect with some cynicism that few are caught and fewer are sentenced; the public, even with its notoriously short memory, must recall times when few were even chased.

In the pre-convention investigation of presidential candidates' expenses in 1928, nothing was as effective as the frank pride taken in their contributions by some of the supporters of Democratic candidate Alfred Smith and of Republican candidate Herbert Hoover. Especially in Smith's campaign, the proportionately large contributions were announced in the pro-Smith press with positive triumph, as proof that Smith had friends who would, as one of them said, "Give their last cent." A public weary of back-room nominations suddenly finds itself in full possession of the facts and knows that, as a result of previous investigations, committee men have been chary of accepting funds which might suggest improper agreements. Just as a public man may not appear in certain places to which a private citizen can go, lest his presence give countenance to a doubtful event, so an institution which is public both in its business and in its subjection to the eye of publicity cannot do even legal acts if they seem discreditable to the public.

It is for the public to set bounds to this open survey of private affairs. So long as they wish institutions to live under the threat, they can make them do so. It would be at least as effective if the public turned to the other angle of publicity, learning its methods, and learning to be on guard against abuses. What is needed is judgment, and if the people of a democracy have neither the time nor the energy to exercise their judgment, they can at least deputize others to judge for them.

Chapter 23.
The Advisor in Public Relations

THROUGHOUT THIS BOOK, PUBLICITY has been
considered not primarily as the work of special
individuals, but as a function in human activities
which may be fulfilled in hundreds of different ways.
Every great corporation in America maintains a
department of publicity which probably includes
functionaries ranging from the humble press agent to
the grandiose "public relations counsel." Yet, in most
cases, their effective publicity is accomplished not so
much by these experts as by one of their officers who
has a peculiar command of public attention. The
example of Judge Elbert Gary, president of U.S. Steel,
has been cited. For a variety of reasons, men of his
caliber concentrate in themselves the interest of the
public, and receive from the public a definite
stimulus, so that they not only speak to America of
the intentions of their companies, but can and do
speak to their companies of the needs and desires of
the American people. The title given the functionary
is of no consequence; the function itself is incalculably
important.

Yet there is the special profession of publicity
which attempts to use science in the application of
stimuli designed to make the public respond in a
desired manner. In recent years, this profession has

taken over new powers and new authority. So far professional publicity has been considered as part of general publicity, but it has its special features. Among the most prominent is the dual relation suggested above: the publicity man stands between his employer and the public, with responsibilities to both. What is the effect of public opinion upon him and his employer?

Primarily the publicity man interprets the public to the private corporation. A railroad cannot order a plebiscite on every change of schedule or type of car. Railroads and other institutions have, indeed, asked the public for criticism, but they must ultimately depend on an expert individual to tell institutions what the public thinks and feels, and what the public is likely to feel in a given case. The man who does this well is invaluable. For example, if producers of plays could find a sufficient number of men who would anticipate the public verdict, the condition of the theatre would be completely changed. Actually, the experience of "sure-fire hits" which were disastrous failures, and of totally impossible plays which ran for years, proves that the men in the business have only the vaguest idea of what the public really wants. They know that a certain number of musical comedies, gaudily dressed, will succeed each year, but they have no way of telling whether the particular combination of music, dancing, and comedy into which they are putting their money will meet the public favor.

A corporation with an investment running into hundreds of millions cannot take the chances of a theatrical producer. Certain policies may be adopted for technical reasons and others because they give promise of large and immediate returns. Some policies may not affect the public at all. Wherever the public is touched, however, corporations are coming more and more to ask for expert guidance. For example, the Bell System recently found itself compelled to put in the European hand set instrument. People who had found them convenient abroad brought them back and, in spite of the clause in the contract forbidding the use of attachments, substituted these for the instruments provided by the company. The business of importing these instruments was begun. The company found its service impeded by these foreign sets and found also that, by supplying a similar set which conformed to the technical necessities of the service, it could add to its income. Subscribers with imported sets were irritated by the company's attitude and the entire business was confusing and annoying. Yet, the demand for the new instrument was strong, and the fact that the public wanted them could have been acted upon by the company long in advance. Actually, after some delay, the company announced that it would in the near future supply a superior hand set and this acted to deter subscribers from investing their money in privately made instruments. The Bell System, on this occasion, was led by the public, and the period of adjustment was difficult because a manifest public desire was not made clear to the officials in time.

By his interpretation of public feeling, the expert modifies corporate policy. The individual in whom this function is represented is properly called an advisor in public relations. Part of his work is that of the press agent, but the greater part is in representing the public side when any policy is in question. A great American corporation recently asked its legal advisor whether it could do business with Soviet Russia. Financial advice and the advice of experts in shipping had already been taken. The legal authority said that the company could do business with Soviet Russia. Sometime later he expressed, as a private individual, his opinion that no Americans should do business with that country. He was asked why he had not made this point to his client and his reply was that he was a legal and not an ethical advisor to the company.

The advisor in public relations is an ethical advisor. He not only has to know what the public will think of a given policy, but has to suggest to his employers the moral implications of such a policy. He has to see not the financial, not the technical, and not the legal effect—only the social effect. In that sense, he is concerned with the progress of man and the improvement of civilization.

The advisor in public relations arrives at this position of extraordinary authority by slow degrees. The fulcrum on which his lever rests is his connection with the public. At the beginning, a press agent may have been sought out because an institution was in urgent need for a competent and friendly contact with the press. In one case, it may have had to face a hostile public. In another, it may have needed support from the public in order to finance a developing industry or to create a favorable atmosphere for legislation permitting it to grow. It may have been threatened by investigations from the government or by laws which would strangle its development. The early press agent stepped in because the public had been either mishandled or neglected. He was a stop-gap, making up for absence of such a public policy as an advisor in public relations would have created. The press agent's activities were therefore limited. He gave to the newspapers information concerning the activities of his employer, he denied or disproved hostile reports, and, when inspired, he prepared events which could be used for publicity. If he had imagination, however, he found that all these busy activities were insufficient. A man might endow a college and receive the temporary applause of the public, but his business might still suffer from general indifference or hostility. The publicity man took the place of the press agent. He gave himself a new title because he was doing a new job. He was explaining in a favorable way the policies of his employer, and preparing the ground for the reception of new ideas. He did not omit the activities of the press agent, instead, he attached them to more significant things. Through him, the spirit of an institution was made manifest, and something approaching a genuine public feeling was created. One can easily see how this function began to have a modifying effect upon policy. The president of a manufacturing company might call in a publicity man and say "we are going to raise the price of our product by 10 percent, and you have got to put it over." The publicity man would reply that the thing was impossible unless it was accompanied by a corresponding raise in the wages of employees. If his word was taken, he would have made a beginning in affecting policy—not directly policy toward the public, but indirectly. He might say, "Do this. I can get fine publicity out of it," or "Don't do that because I can never put it over on the public."

This technical side of the publicity man's work coincides with his work as an ethical advisor. Eventually, corporations called the advisor in not merely to tell management what would be effective or pleasing to the public but what ought to be done in the interest of social good. In this sense, the advisor in public relations fulfills a social function and, in so far as he is upright and intelligent, performs a public service.

The claims made in this book for the press agent, publicity man, and advisor in public relations are intended to be modest ones. Others have placed these professional men in the position of a fifth estate more potent than the press because of their capacity to subdue the press to their own interests. If there is any doubt of the extent to which the profession of publicity can serve the public the answer to it is to be found in the violent opposition to publicity of those who either do not understand it or suffer from it. If the maker of publicity is, as his critics say, a menace to the public, and a subverter of opinion, this means only that his power is, at the moment, used for evil purposes. If he is that bad, the power he has would be equally great when dominated by honest and socially desirable motives. To appreciate the power of the wielder of publicity it is not necessary to listen to him boasting of his triumphs. The complaints of his enemies are a sufficient tribute. They speak only of his power because, until recently, power has been the publicity man's chief weapon. He has only begun to use justice.

IVY LEDBETTER LEE
WITH BURTON ST. JOHN III, PH.D.

Commentaries

Lee's Legacy on Responsibility: Never So Relevant

TONI MUZI FALCONI

For Ivy Lee, advertising is a part of publicity. For anyone who has lived and worked in public relations over the last 50 years, such a statement would seem inaccurate and/or grossly exaggerated. Public relations was far more relevant and powerful than advertising and marketing in most organizations well until the 1950s, when mass consumption and television exploded in the marketing craze, with PR quickly moving to a secondary role and advertising leading the way of the marketing mix, mostly given the respective sizes of the two budgets. With this new century's digital revolution and the consequent rise of social media, as well as the recent emergence of PESO (the Payed, Earned, Shared, Owned media model)[1] the supremacy of advertising over public relations has once again come into question. This is evident, for example, when Edelman (considered a global leader of public relations agencies) heralded, in 2015, the consolidated marketing communication description,

---

[1] Iliff, R. (2014, December 5). "Why PR is embracing the PESO model." *Mashable*. Retrieved from: http://mashable.com/2014/12/05/public-relations-industry/#7Or4NgE5.OqD

claiming a thought leadership role for public relations when it came to advocating for a client.[2]

Still, there is a striking resonance between some contemporary public relations thinkers and professionals and Ivy Lee concerning his concept of professional responsibility as well as that of how he describes the publicist as a creator of groups.

On the first aspect, Lee writes on page 294 that "The publicist with a feeling of responsibility...is responsible, on the one hand, to his client employer or to the cause for which he works; on the other hand, he has a responsibility to the public, to treat it fairly, and not to degrade it..." What is significant here is the consonance between the responsibility of the publicist to his client as well as to his publics and the 2013 Melbourne Mandate by the Global Alliance for Public Relations and Communication Management that for the first time affirmed diverse levels of the public relations professional's responsibility: to the client, to the profession, to the different publics, to the public interest, and to the future generations.[3]

---

[2] Edelman, R. (2014, September 21). "The rise of communications marketing." *Edelman*. Speech delivered at Arthur Page Society Hall of Fame Induction. Retrieved from: http://www.edelman.com/insights/intellectual-property/the-rise-of-communications-marketing/

[3] "The Melbourne Mandate" (2012, November). *ProCom*. Retrieved from: http://procom.fi/viestintaala/ohjeet-ja-periaatteet/melbourne-mandate/

On the second aspect—groups—Lee writes on page 271 that "It is the business of publicity to help in the creation of groups: the group that buys a new kind of safety razor, the group that goes to the first night of a spectacular movie, the group that waits outside the theatre to see the first group go in, [and] the group that votes for joining the League of Nations or for abstaining...." The big issue here is whether the public relations person helps in the creation of groups, as Lee appears to indicate, or more importantly (and maybe even more likely) in their very identification. That is, public relations appears to help groups create themselves when group members think they hold a specific or generic stake in the organization and interact with it by listening to their group expectations—necessarily involving interacting, dialoguing with and engaging with other groups members—so as to then accelerate, delay, or modify the achievement of the organization's objectives. There are some indirect notes in his writing that suggest this might be what he actually meant concerning the facilitative power of public relations because he also writes on page 294 that "...It seems incredible that on the substructure of a feeble reason, standing on the quick sands of emotion, man has been able to establish governments, churches, banks and ideals which have lasted for centuries..."

Finally, Ivy Lee understands, almost 100 years earlier than a significant percentage of his some five million contemporary colleagues today,[4] the utmost value of reputation. On page 345 of this book, he said:

> ...The publicist may arrange his facts in order to dazzle and to give a favorable impression—but they must remain facts.... It is his duty to his employer to make out the best case; his duty to the public is to make the case out of the truth.... If there were no moral prejudice against lying, if the truth were valued only because it made business easier to conduct, the handler of publicity would still be irrevocably bound to tell the truth. His own business is jeopardized the moment he is caught willfully uttering a lie.

This amounts to a stupefyingly contemporary statement that belongs to any serious professional in this day and age. Accordingly, Lee's legacy stands out because of this constant and repeated concern in establishing professional credibility for himself and his role.

As such, his observations about responsible interactions with groups are desperately necessary today, a time of rising concerns about fake news and malicious propaganda.

---

[4] Falconi, T. M. (2006, November 6). "How big is public relations (and why does it matter)?" *Institute for PR*. Retrieved from: http://www.instituteforpr.org/how-big-is-pr/

TONI MUZI FALCONI, teacher, polemist, and writer, has extensive global experience in public relations. In his now 55-year-long career he has worked in and for small, mid-sized and large organizations. He has created, developed, and sold consultancies, taught in universities in various countries, and written books and essays. Mostly he has enjoyed and continues to enjoy tense, controversial, and rewarding relationships with his fellow colleagues around the world, continuing to argue on behalf of a critical approach to the essential role of public relations in society at large.

Some Thoughts on "the Being and the Doing" of Ivy Lee

MEG LAMME

Scholars have long been interested in Ivy
Ledbetter Lee, often positioning him as a kind of foil
to his younger early 20th-century contemporary,
Edward L. Bernays, both of whom have been wrongly
called "the father of public relations." Wrongly
because first, we do not know enough yet to label
anyone as the progenitor of the industry but also and
more to the point, it's quite possible that there will
never be one single person, "father" or "mother," to
whom historians can point in any century given the
pervasiveness of public relations over time. As Lee
himself wrote on page 41 in this volume, "The
essential thing is the knowledge that publicity is not
merely the work of those professional men who have
specific titles. Publicity is the work—any work from
writing a song to signing a labor agreement—of any
man who attempts to influence the public."

Lee is often found among the pages of the
history chapters of introductory public relations
textbooks, greeting new students in sepia-toned
photos, sometimes standing, sometimes seated behind
a desk, always looking at once scholarly and

gentlemanly, calm and authoritative. Such images help to capture a decidedly corporate, privileged, and seemingly enduring vision of the field that belie some very real contradictions within Lee's work. He advocated good policy as driving good public relations, of walking the walk—"the *being* and the *doing*," not the saying.[1] He believed that the evil of propaganda lay in hidden sources, in not knowing the origins of an idea or an initiative. But he also believed real truth could only be found in mathematics; everything else, he said, was subject to interpretation, no matter how it was phrased, no matter where it was said or written or by whom. He was a man of faith, driven by service for good as well as by "human doubts and ego."[2] He was and is a conundrum and it is surprising how well we regard him in public relations considering what we know and, perhaps, what we do not yet know.

Public relations boasts a relatively small but excellent collection of secondary sources about Lee, including the only biography to date, Ray Hiebert's 1966 *Courtier to the Crowd*.[3] But short of poring

---

[1] Lee, I.L. (1925). *Publicity, Some of the Things It Is and Is Not.* New York: Industries Publishing Company, p. 64.

[2] Hiebert, R.E. (1966). *Courtier to the Crowd: The Story of Ivy Lee and the Development of Public Relations*, Ames, IA: Iowa State University Press, p. 14.

[3] Hiebert wrote this book based on his extensive immersion in and indexing of the Lee papers at Princeton. Other secondary sources

through his extensive manuscript collection at the Seeley G. Mudd Manuscript Library at Princeton University, academics, students, and industry professionals alike have had little to rely on to learn about Ivy Lee in his own words, notwithstanding his 1915 *Human Nature and Railroads* (based on a collection of speeches delivered between June 26, 1913, and January 17, 1915) and his 1925 book, *Publicity, Some of*

---

include: Hallahan, K. (2002). Ivy Lee and the Rockefellers' response to the 1913–1914 Colorado coal strike. *Journal of Public Relations Research 14*, pp. 265–313; Hainsworth, B.E. (1987). "Retrospective: Ivy Lee and the German Dye Trust," *Public Relations Review 13*, pp. 35-44; Harrison, S. & Moloney, K. (2004). "Comparing two public relations pioneers: American Ivy Lee and British John Elliot," *Public Relations Review 30*, pp. 205–215; Russell, K.M. &. Bishop, C.O. (2009). "Understanding Ivy Lee's declaration of principles: U.S. newspaper and magazine coverage of publicity and press agentry, 1865–1904," *Public Relations Review 35*, pp. 91–101; St. John III. B. (2006). "The case for ethical propaganda within a democracy: Ivy Lee's successful 1913–1914 railroad rate campaign," *Public Relations Review 32*, pp. 221–228. Also, see Cutlip S.M. (1994). *The Unseen Power. Public Relations: A History*, Hillsdale, New Jersey: Lawrence Erlbaum Associates, 37–72, pp. 114–158; Ewen S. (1996) *PR! A Social History of Spin*. New York: Basic Books, pp. 74–81; Lamme, M.O. (2014), *Public Relations and Religion in American History: Evangelism, Temperance, and Business*. New York: Routledge, pp. 92–114; Olasky, M. (1987). *Corporate Public Relations: A New Historical Perspective*, Hillsdale, New Jersey: Lawrence Erlbaum Associates, pp. 45–53; Raucher, A.R. (1968). *Public Relations and Business, 1900–1929*, Baltimore: Johns Hopkins Press, pp. 17–31; Zoch, L.M., Supa, D.W. & VanTuyll, D.R. (2014). "The Portrait of Public Relations in the Era of Ivy Lee Through the Lens of the *New York Times*," *Public Relations Review* 40, pp. 723–732.

the Things It Is and Is Not (a collection of three
speeches from 1916, 1924, and 1925).[4]

Lee was not as prolific as Bernays, who later
commissioned a bibliographer to catalogue his
published works.[5] Nevertheless, as the content for
these two books indicates, Lee was a prolific speaker,
advocating for clients' interests to community groups,
to executive groups, and to trade and professional
associations, to name a few. Additionally, he had an
active and increasingly successful string of publicity
firms, and he was quite well connected to some of the
most influential Americans of his time, most notably
John D. Rockefeller and his son, John D. Rockefeller,
Jr.; Pennsylvania Railroad executive John Thayer, who
died during the sinking of the Titanic; President
Woodrow Wilson, a teacher and mentor from Lee's
two years at Princeton; Arthur Brisbane, Hearst
newspaper editor; and, during his upbringing in
Cedartown, Georgia, Joel Chandler Harris, author and

---

[4] Lee, I. L. (1925) According to Lee's preface note in this book, Parts
I and II were based on his addresses to the American Association
of Teachers of Journalism, Chicago, December 20, 1924, and the
Advertising Club of New York, January 20, 1925, and the Q&As
following each one. Part III is based on his address to the Annual
Convention of the American Electric Railway Association, Atlantic
City, October 10, 1916.

[5] See Larson, K.A. (1978). *Public Relations, the Edward L. Bernayses and
the American Scene: A Bibliography.* Westwood, MA: F. W. Faxon
Company. Hiebert includes a selected bibliography of Lee in
Appendix C of *Courtier to the Crowd.*

journalist, and Henry Grady, editor of *The Atlanta Constitution* and spokesman for the post-Reconstruction New South. Lee was also greatly influenced by his father, Reverend James Wideman Lee, an influential, well-traveled, and well-connected Methodist minister serving congregations in Atlanta and St. Louis.

This new volume, then, is a welcome addition to the public relations history body of knowledge, providing new insight into what Lee thought, what he knew, and what he wanted others to know about public relations: "human beings exert influence on others, change their minds, and redirect their activities" (p. 40). Here, he sat down with the help of his staff to craft a codification of his work based on his 25-plus years of experience that encompassed the U.S. and abroad. He launched his career through political press agentry and soon shifted to corporate.[6] By 1908, he was fully employed by the Pennsylvania Railroad, took leave from there to work for the New York brokerage firm Harris, Winthrop, and Company to set up their London offices, worked for the Rockefellers, and then returned to agency life with Lee, Harris, and Lee (1916–1919), during which time he served as the assistant to the National Red Cross

---

[6] Lee worked as a reporter in New York for a few years before joining political press agent George Parker to create Parker & Lee from 1904–1908.

chair when in Europe during World War I and as volunteer assistant to the chair of the Red Cross War Council when stateside; in combining both roles, he said, he oversaw "publicity and propaganda of Red Cross throughout the world."[7] After the war, he launched Ivy L. Lee and Associates (1919–1933), and then Ivy Lee and T. J. Ross (1933–1960).

In the months leading up to the war, it was Arthur Brisbane, then editor of the New York *Evening Journal,* who recommended that the Rockefellers retain Lee in the aftermath of the Ludlow Massacre, the labor strike at the Colorado Fuel and Iron Company that sparked during the fall of 1913 and then erupted in violence the following April, resulting in more than 50 deaths, including women and children. John D. Rockefeller, Jr. held 40 percent ownership in the mine, making him the largest mine owner in the state, and Lee began working to recoup the family's reputation and that of the company's, while roundly criticized by pro-labor interests and the press.[8] Later, Upton Sinclair famously noted that the

---

[7] "Ivy Ledbetter Lee, A. B.," *Class of Eighteen Ninety Eight Twenty Fifth Year Book, 1898–1923,* compiled by Roswell Francis Easton, Class Secretary, Princeton: Princeton University Press, p. 177. This work, published in 1923, is available in the Princeton University Archives. Lee reported serving the Red Cross between May 10, 1917, and March 1, 1919.

[8] See Hiebert (1966), pp. 97–108; Hallahan (2002). For press reaction to the strike and to Lee, see Burt, E. (2011). "Shocking atrocities in

miners had dubbed Lee "Poison Ivy."[9] Two other
effects of Ludlow, however, are of particular note:
first, no less than *Time* magazine and the *New York
Times* concluded that Ludlow had been a boon to
Lee's career, drawing in corporate clients to his firm;
the other is that there are no records of these years,
1913–1915, in the Lee manuscript collection. That is,
the same time period that Lee drew upon to write and
publish *Human Nature and Railroads* offers no clue as
to Lee's thoughts or actions in relation to Ludlow, the
Rockefellers, or Penn Railroad, for whom Lee
continued to work during Ludlow.[10]

In the mid-1920s, Lee, a member of the Chamber
of Commerce of New York, sought to change the
Chamber's anti-communist stance on Russia. Lee's
solution was to increase engagement, to "stimulate

Colorado: Newspapers' responses to the Ludlow Massacre."
American Journalism 28, pp. 61–83.

[9] Sinclair, U. (1919/1970). *The Brass Check: A Study of American
Journalism*. New York: Arno/New York Times, p. 311.

[10] "Lee & Co.," *Time* (1933, August 7), p. 25; "Ivy Lee Dies of Brain
Ailment," *The New York Times* (1934, November 10), p. 15.
According to the Lee Finding Aid at Princeton, "Unfortunately,
correspondence from 1913 through 1915 is missing, the period when
Lee made some of the most important decisions of his life."
Subseries 5A: Correspondence, 1896–1934, Ivy Ledbetter Lee
Papers, 1881–2003 (bulk 1915–1946): Finding Aid, Princeton
University Library, Department of Rare Books and Special
Collections, Seeley G. Mudd Manuscript Library, Public Policy
Papers.

understanding rather than promote ignorance."[11] He set out his arguments in letters to Chamber members in early 1926, but when the *New York Times* found that two of Lee's clients, Standard Oil and Vacuum Oil, had just made a lucrative deal with Russia—oil for cash to the Soviet government—it exposed Lee's letters in March of that year, and Lee came under attack for promoting foreign interests against those of the U.S.[12] Such criticism did not put him off, however. Lee pursued his own study of the USSR, communism, and global relations, privately publishing a book in 1927, *USSR: A World Enigma* (Macmillan published it in 1928 as *Present-Day Russia*).[13]

Well on its way to completion in 1928, then, this current volume would have been published well after Walter Lippmann's 1922 *Public Opinion* and 1925 *The Phantom Public*, Edward L. Bernays's 1923 *Crystallizing Public Opinion*, and Harold D. Lasswell's 1927 *Propaganda Technique in the World War*. Had it been published around 1928 or 1929, Lee's book would have appeared in the wake of the public backlash against his stance on Russia and alongside Bernays' 1928

---

[11] Hiebert (1966), p. 272.

[12] Ibid., p. 273.

[13] Ibid., p. 274.

Propaganda and Lippmann's 1929 *Preface to Morals,*
some reasons, perhaps, for delaying publication.[14]
Other reasons for Lee's delay or suspension of
the book's publication, however, could have included
Black Friday, the stock market crash of 1929, and the
revelation just weeks before that "propaganda and
lobbying work" that had been conducted in 1926 and
1928 in collusion with the shipbuilding industry in
regard to the Geneva naval disarmament conference
had netted publicist William B. Shearer $25,000 and a
payment of $6,000 to Ivy Lee.[15] This time period also
would have been aligned with the point at which
James Wideman Lee II (Lee's son) took up residence
in Germany as a retainer to I.G. Farben, the German
Dye Trust, to bridge German and American business
interests.[16] The Farben/Nazi connection was one Lee
would later deny knowing about despite having made
many trips there himself and despite having been
retained by Farben in June 1933, three months after

---

[14] Because Lee died in November 1934, it's possible his intention was
just to delay publication, not to shelve the project altogether.

[15] Allen, R.S. (1929, October 10). Mr. Shearer likes a big navy. *The
Nation*, p. 378.

[16] House of Representatives, Subcommittee of the Special
Committee on Un-American Activities, New York City, N.Y.,
Wednesday, July 11, 1934. For analyses of his testimony and that of
others, see Hiebert (1966); Hainsworth, (1987); and Tyrone Steven
Bomba, "Howling with the Wolves: Ivy Lee and the Germans,"
MA thesis, California State University, Fullerton, 1982.

the *Machtergreifung* (the Nazi seizure of power). Lee said he had met with Hitler and Goebbels in the process, but had cut ties with Farben within the year, having tried unsuccessfully to advise Farben to cut ties with the Reich.[17] It was Lee's work with Farben that prompted the House Subcommittee of the Special Committee on Un-American Activities to call him to testify in May of 1934. Due to ill health, Lee was allowed to testify in closed session, but while he was out of the country that summer, the committee released his testimony.

The next day, Lee's testimony ran in the center of the front page of the *Times*, where it was reported that he had not only advised the Nazis, but had been well paid for it, as had his son. Lee said he had been working for Farben's American operations for five years when Farben's corporate headquarters in Berlin retained him for $25,000 a year under a verbal contract while Lee's son made $33,000 a year representing the Lee firm in Germany.[18] Lee's counsel to Farben, according to the *Times* story, conveyed via his son, concerned topics ranging from propaganda to disarmament, advising the Reich to engage with the foreign press there, ensuring Lee's suggestions would

---

[17] Hainsworth (1987), p. 38–40.

[18] "Ivy Lee, as Adviser to Nazis, Paid $25,000 by Dye Trust," *New York Times* (1934, July 12), p. A1

be attributed to a German source before releasing news of those initiatives in the U.S., and monitoring the American press for its coverage of Germany and then conveying those results to Germany. Additionally, Lee insisted in his testimony, his messages to the German government were consistent and adamant: no anti-Semitism and no Nazi propaganda in the U.S.[19]

This episode was arguably the nadir of Lee's career. Unwittingly or not, Lee had served as the hidden propagandist in concert with the Reich; he was the unknown source, that root of propaganda evil that he had warned against. It is true that he extricated himself upon realizing the scale of his error—but it should be noted that he nevertheless received a final payment from Farben in April 1934.[20] And then he moved on.

In October 1934, Lee urged his firm's partners to recalibrate their mission toward initiative and innovation: to shift away from order-taking and focus instead on earning the clients' trust and money by immersing in each client's business and anticipating its needs and interests. He envisioned a step toward "a

---

[19] Ibid.

[20] House Subcommittee of the Special Committee on Un-American Activities. Lee testified that his last payment from Farben came on April 3, 1934 in the amount of $14,450.

new conception" of the firm's work as "a brain trust."[21] It is not clear whether Lee's experiences of that past year had in some way prompted this shift, nor is it clear as to what might have become of this new direction for the firm—and the impact on public relations. Lee died at age 57 that November, leaving us to determine answers to these questions and others.

For these reasons and more, this volume can help us glean more about the history of U.S. public relations in the twentieth century from an eyewitness immersed in the understanding of public relations and the wielding of its power, but also about the eyewitness himself.

MEG LAMME, PH.D., APR, is a professor of public relations at the University of Alabama, Tuscaloosa, and a Plank Center Scholar. Building on 15 years of public relations experience in the corporate, nonprofit, and government sectors, her contributions in the academy include teaching public relations, conducting research in the history of the field, and mentoring public relations students in reaching their goals in research and in industry. Lamme is the author or co-author of more than 35 academic publications, including: *Public Relations and*

---

[21] "Ivy Lee and T. J. Ross Partner's Dinner, The Cloud Club, New York, Thursday, October 4, 1934," Ivy Ledbetter Lee Papers, Box 27, Folder 13. See also Lamme (2014), 112–113.

Religion in American History: Evangelism, Temperance, and Business (New York: Routledge, 2014), winner of the American Journalism Historians Association's 2015 Book Award and finalist in AEJMC's 2015 Tankard Book Award, and co-editor of *Pathways to Public Relations: Histories of Practice and Profession* (London: Routledge, 2014), also a finalist for AEJMC's 2015 Tankard Book Award.

Responsible Publicity as a Public Service

KAREN MILLER RUSSELL

LONG REGARDED AS THE FIRST significant pioneer in the history of U.S. corporate public relations, Ivy Lee has figured prominently in the literature, relevant to both the history and theories of the field. *Mr. Lee's Publicity Book: A Citizen's Guide to Public Relations* provides an inside view of his philosophy and approach to the practice, adding to our knowledge of the strategies and tactics employed by one of the field's most important founders—for instance, Lee's move to release a statement to the press prior to the head of the Pennsylvania Railroad's testimony before Congress, thus completely undermining the committee's subsequent decision not to allow him to make a statement—but more broadly to discussion of the development of public relations during and after World War I. Many aspects of the manuscript deserve scholarly attention, but three stand out: Lee's sophisticated understanding of the processes of persuasion and public opinion; his thoughts on the ethics of "responsible publicity"; and, closely related, his analysis of the social role of corporate publicity.

Lee's opening gambit, the lengthy vignette about persuasive influences on Mr. Jones, is deceptively simple in tone and structure. Received wisdom would suggest that, working in the post-World War I era, Lee should have believed in a "magic bullet" or direct effects model of media influence. Scholars point to people like George Creel, head of the U.S. propaganda efforts during World War I, who seem to have learned from their experiences that people were relatively easy to influence, as evidence that the post-war spread of what came to be called public relations was based on a direct-effects model. Creel, for instance, titled his war memoir, *How We Advertised America: The First Telling of the Amazing Story of the Committee on Public Information that Carried the Gospel of Americanism to Every Corner of the Globe* (1920). And Lee definitely did believe that publicity could be influential, noting in this manuscript the effectiveness of images, especially moving pictures, music, oratory, and the printed word, particularly the slogan, which is "a sentence or phrase or a word which will take root and flourish in the public mind" (p. 191).

However, Lee also demonstrated that he was well aware that the process of persuasion was multilayered, complex. He provided examples of the ways Jones knowledge, attitudes, opinions, and behaviors were influenced not just by the publicist but also by word of mouth communication, the press, and personal experience, all concepts still under investigation today by both scholars and practitioners of public relations. In addition, in Part IV, Lee offered a nuanced understanding of "groups," aligning with what scholars might today call "publics," noting that it was the business of publicity to help in the creation of groups, not just to communicate with extant audiences. Drawing on important thinkers of the day, he differentiated crowds from groups and individuals, citing throughout the book a number of still familiar experts, including Walter Lippmann on stereotypes, Sigmund Freud (but interestingly, not Freud's nephew Edward Bernays) on psychology, and Gustave Le Bon on the irrationality of crowds. In short, Lee had quite obviously read and thought deeply on the social and psychological mechanisms of persuasion.

He also thought long and hard on the ethics of publicity, both corporate and political. As in his 1925 book, *Publicity: Some of the Things It Is and Is Not*, Lee began this manuscript by trying to define publicity in part by separating it from advertising and from propaganda. In both places he argued that advertising was simply one part of the larger publicity umbrella, but he found the line between propaganda and publicity harder to draw. In this book he considered whether the difference between them is truth, or verifiability, or even the relationship of the communication to censorship, concluding that truth alone is not the defining factor, if only because the difficulty of producing and maintaining a lie over time makes it a poor tactic. "Responsible publicity is the enemy of rumor," he says on page 108. He also maintained, and he differentiated between responsible publicity and the type manufactured by P.T. Barnum, defining ballyhoo as creating curiosity and judging it to be essentially harmless because people should know that such publicity is not the literal truth. Lee concluded that truly irresponsible publicity was marked by a number of characteristics, including secrecy; reaching audiences that cannot discriminate; the use of money or power to corrupt basic institutions; lack of opportunity for verification; communication that offers no proof; and the use of money to drown out opposing views. In the end, though, he argued that secrecy was the biggest problem with propaganda; as he wrote in 1925, "The essential evil of propaganda is failure to disclose the source of information."[1]

By contrast, responsible publicity consisted of actions in addition to words, providing facts, and—as he stated as early as his 1905 declaration of principles—being open about the source of

---

[1] Lee, I. L. (1925). *Publicity: Some of the Things It Is and Is Not*. New York: Industries Publishing. See page 23.

communication.[2] Lee did not define publicity as "public information" as proposed by Bernays and perpetuated by Cutlip and Grunig.[3] On page 294 of this volume, he baldly states that the publicist "has to consider both the elements of reason and passion," with the publicist responsible to both the client and the public, and said that facts and statistics should be made more palatable when "dramatized and...soaked in human interest."

He was also adamant that responsible publicity was not solely for the benefit of the public. Continuously informing the public, not just when something went wrong, was a way for organizations to avoid being on the defensive during troubled times. Although communication could be two-way, all publicity is "one-sided," Lee acknowledged on page 327. The solution he offered was the responsibility of individual communicators to be open and fair and the need for audience members to be enlightened consumers—even if this meant that publicists had to be the ones educating the public. This solution is problematic, though, especially given Lee's stated

---

[2] Morse, S. (1906, September). "An awakening in Wall Street," *The American Magazine* 62: pp. 457–463.

[3] For more see Hoy, P., Raaz, O., & Wehmeier, S. (2007). "From facts to stories or from stories to facts? Analyzing public relations history in public relations textbooks." *Public Relations Review* 33: pp. 191–200.

beliefs in this book that the "the average voter is not qualified to judge the major issues of politics" (p. 262) and that "The public has to provide its own suspicions" (p. 344). "The solution is not to be found in running away from publicity, in condemning it, or trying to forbid it by law," he wrote here, adding that "Nor is it to be found in an abdication of all intelligence, in supinely accepting whatever publicity and propaganda put forth" (p. 39). Suggesting that regulation wouldn't work, he argued instead for the fullest publicity for everyone. Lee admitted that money was a problem in that it made some voices much louder than others in the marketplace of ideas, a charge levied against Lee by muckrakers like Ray Stannard Baker, but Lee stated that spending a lot of money was not in itself a sign of hostile intent; only anonymous, irresponsible communication was hostile to the public.[4] Despite these contradictions, Lee relied primarily on open sponsorship of communication to solve ethical dilemmas.

In the end, Lee argued that publicity men were driven to high ethical standards by practical considerations. Their communications must be truthful, for inaccuracies and lies are eventually exposed, even if facts are selected, made interesting, and arranged for a purpose. Publicists were not just

---

[4] Baker, R. S. (1906, March). "Railroads on trial, part V." *McClure's Magazine*. Pp. 535–49.

press agents pushing out news and staging events, but ethical advisors whose position as liaison between organization and public meant they had to drive a client toward the highest community standards, thus serving as "a deterrent to anti-social practice" he said on page 349.

Lee therefore concluded that publicity fulfilled an important social function and constituted a public service. In the Mr. Jones vignette in this work, rejection of all publicity led to isolation, and Jones "had to do the work of a 100,000 experts before he could make the simplest decision," Lee suggested (p. 39). Under these circumstances and noting that publicity "is something that goes on all the time" (p. 52), he saw the only viable solution as educating people about the ways people try to "influence public opinion and move it in a desired direction" (p. 41), which he attempted to do himself in writing this book. Only by exposing the methods of publicity and propaganda would people "cease to be victims" (p. 40).

Lee's approach adds a third position on public relations ethics to those exemplified by John Hill and Arthur W. Page, each of whom began his PR career in 1927, the year before this manuscript was under development.[5] For Hill, founder of the still successful

---

[5] Russell, K.M. (2009). "Character and the practice of public relations: Arthur W. Page and John W. Hill." In Heath, R. L.,

agency Hill & Knowlton, the primary ethical decision
was in client choice: he thought that it was important
to influence client policy, but believed that once a
practitioner agreed to represent a client, any ethical
strategy was appropriate. Working for AT&T (whose
communications Lee praised in this manuscript), Page
saw the Information Department as the conscience of
the corporation. Lee agreed with Page, but added that
the most important element of ethics was the open
admission of the source. "A signed lie is worth more
than an anonymous truth," he stated on page 341 of
this volume. With this idea as his guiding principle, it
made perfect sense for Lee to agree to work for Nazi
Germany's I. G. Farben corporation. Cutlip has
documented that Lee was not the least secretive
about accepting the account in the early 1930s, having
first consulted with the U.S. State Department and
then meeting with the American ambassador and
press corps in Berlin.[3] From Lee's perspective, he had
done nothing wrong, and he was more than willing to
testify before Congress about his work for the
chemical company, but his death in 1934 left a cloud
of suspicion over his name. In this book he writes, "If

Toth, E. L. & Waymer, D. (Eds). *Rhetorical and Critical Approaches
to Public Relations*. New York, NY: Routledge.

[3] Cutlip, S. M. (1994). *Public Relations: The Unseen Power*. Hillsdale,
New Jersey: Lawrence Erlbaum.

the publicity man cannot stand publicity, he will be destroyed" (p. 336) and, ironically, this has been the truth about his own reputation, simply because he was unable to defend himself.

Mr. Lee's Publicity Book: A Citizen's Guide to Public Relations clarifies Ivy Lee's opinions on key issues that are still under debate: the processes of persuasion, the ethics of sponsored, strategic communication, and the social role of public relations in a democratic society. This previously forgotten manuscript represents a treasure trove of thinking about the purpose, strategies and tactics, and social contribution of early twentieth century U.S. public relations, and scholars and practitioners are fortunate to have access to it today.

KAREN MILLER RUSSELL, PH.D., and Jim Kennedy Professor of New Media, is associate professor at the University of Georgia, where she has taught since 1993. She completed her doctorate in Mass Communication at the University of Wisconsin-Madison in 1993, winning the Nafziger-White award from the Association for Education in Journalism and Mass Communication for best dissertation in mass communication, and her dissertation placed in the top four at the Business History Conference, both in 1995. She is the author of the 1999 book *The Voice of Business: Hill and Knowlton and Postwar Public Relations*

(University of North Carolina Press), winner of the National Communication Association's PR Division PRide Award for Top Book of the Year in 1999. She was awarded the 2001 Pathfinder Award from the Institute for Public Relations in recognition of original scholarly research that has made a significant contribution to the body of knowledge and practice of public relations. She was named a Josiah Meigs Distinguished Teaching Professor by the University of Georgia in 2017.

The Writings of Ivy Lee—
At Last!

FRASER P. SEITEL

It is ironic that the individual proclaimed as a *"father"* of the communications art of public relations had not one, by today's standards, full-length published book to show for his labors.

Indeed, the writings of Ivy Ledbetter Lee, the straight-laced, stiff-collared former newspaperman who helped create the practice of modern public relations more than 100 years ago, were virtually non-existent. Until now, when a long-forgotten manuscript has been reborn in the form of *Ivy Lee's Publicity Book: A Citizen's Guide to Public Relations.*

More than any other work, this book provides a window into Ivy Lee's thinking, concerns and commitment as he considered the new field of management communication that he helped create.

And a wide window it is.

Lee's manuscript ranges far and wide into the intricacies of the nascent profession he foresees.

- He acknowledges the importance of publicity as a means of persuasion; a societal force to be neither exaggerated nor feared.

- He insists on every citizen's responsibility to examine critically what he or she reads or hears and search for the facts—or lack thereof— within.
- He warns against the practice of conveying falsehoods to further an argument or earn a profit. "In commerce," he writes on page 103, "the difficulty of lying becomes enormous."
- Alternatively, on page 113, he counsels, "tell the truth." And he is particularly critical of disciples of his wisdom engaging in bogus stunts or dishonest news accounts to further their aims. Today we call such people purveyors of fake news.
- Lee's manuscript is dominated by publicity prescriptions and a nuts and bolts discussion of how the new publicity methods and values differ from the traditional notions of advertising. All of these observations are fascinating and, surprisingly, most are still relevant today; a miraculous achievement when one considers Ivy Lee penned this manuscript almost a century ago.

But the real enduring value of Lee's work may lie in two simple sentences that he tucks, humbly, in the midst of his lengthy manuscript. The subject is another of contemporary value to 21st century practitioners of public relations: ethics.

Remember that over the years, critics of Ivy Lee—and indeed, of the practice of public relations—have castigated him for fronting for Adolph Hitler. They've questioned whether Lee even considered "ethics in the conduct of his own business affairs. Lee, himself, was unmercifully pilloried on this issue by a Congressional committee, which chastised him for his retention by a German company tied to Hitler's Nazis.

So the question has arisen: What did Ivy Lee believe were his ethical responsibilities, if any, in the conduct of his activities? Here, for the first time, Ivy Lee leaves no doubt where he stood on "ethics" in public relations. He writes, on page 354:

> The advisor in public relations is an ethical advisor. He not only has to know what the public will think of a given policy, but has to suggest to his employers the moral implications of such a policy. He has to see not the financial, not the technical, and not the legal effect—only the social effect. In that sense, he is concerned with the progress of man and the improvement of civilization.

That one passage, in which Ivy Lee confirms once and for all that the practice of public relations should be underpinned by acting ethically—by doing the right thing—is proof alone of the enormous contribution of this particular manuscript to the lasting literature of the practice of public relations.

FRASER P. SEITEL has been a communications consultant, commentator, author, and teacher for four decades. He was a communications manager with The Chase Manhattan Bank for more than two decades. *PR Week* named Seitel one of the "100 Most Distinguished Public Relations Professionals of the 20th Century." After leaving Chase, Seitel became a communications consultant and has provided management and communications counsel to hundreds of financial institutions, corporations, trade associations, non-profits, and individuals. Seitel has served as an adjunct professor in public relations at the New York University School of Continuing and Professional Studies since 2005. The 13th edition of his book, *The Practice of Public Relations,* used in 200 colleges and universities, was published by Pearson in 2016.

Homiletics of Ivy Lee, A Preacher's Son

TOM WATSON

From an historian's perspective, this unpublished book is an opportunity to reconsider Ivy Ledbetter Lee's attitudes, perspectives and the context of his times. As it is a book prepared under his supervision, with colleagues apparently writing whole or part chapters, it does not give the insight into his motives and beliefs that would come from personal letters, diaries or similar personal material. However, it is a valuable addition to understanding of the early development of public relations in the United States in the mid to late 1920s. That it was not published, and Lee still had six years to live [he died in 1934], may also indicate that the author, a man who had a strong sense of his own importance, was not satisfied with the manuscript and let the project lapse. Nonetheless, even unpublished writings offer valuable insights.

In this commentary, two aspects of the book are reviewed. The first is the initial section on the nature of publicity and Lee's argument on the pervasiveness of publicity (the "Mr. Jones" scenario) and the second is the critique of Great War propaganda in the

United States and the role of George Creel's
Committee of Public Information. Both
commentaries show elements of Lee's character: one
is a barely disguised contempt for fellow citizens,
while the other is a form of revenge on George Creel.
In the latter case, Lee may have thought better of his
critique of Creel and so did not go into hard print.

Lee's life was first brought to us in 1966 in Ray
Eldon Hiebert's biography, *Courtier to the Crowd,*[1]
which was probably the first historical study of public
relations in the United States. Hiebert reveals that
this tall, erect figure was the son of a Methodist
circuit preacher from Georgia who later moved to St.
Louis. Reverend James Lee had a lasting impact on his
eldest child. "Most of his father's sermons were about
thrift, love, diligence, and moral duties," said Hiebert[2]
His father appears to have been very personable and
an effective networker whose "many techniques for
maintaining personal relations with people were later
adopted by his son Ivy in a new profession."[3] The
influence of his preacher father was profound and is
evidenced in this book. Many sections are written in a

---

[1] Hiebert, R.E. (1966) *Courtier to the Crowd: The Story of Ivy Lee and the Development of Public Relations.* Ames, IA: Iowa State University Press

[2] Ibid., p. 18.

[3] Ibid., p. 19.

didactic style with the argumentation of a Sunday sermon and all the sophistry that accompanies these.

In the opening section of the book, *The Dilemma of Mr. Jones*, Lee makes a case that Mr. Jones, an office worker who is possibly a manager and who commutes by train to work, cannot escape the influence of information and publicity.

> He is a Republican, who once only voted Democrat, and no longer considered himself a slave to any party, or to influence of any kind. To himself, Jones appeared as the perfect embodiment of Robert Burns' ideal—'the man of independent mind.' He rather looked down on people who whose minds were continually being made up for them (p. 25).

So Lee sets the scene of a man who thinks he is immune to influence by other people's opinions and to publicity and advertising by organizations and corporations. This is a well-known homiletic (or preaching) device—the preacher puts forward a scenario that may seem to be apparent to all, and then methodically dissects it to show that the opposite is the case. Lee's treatment of Jones' attitudes shows the benefit of all those years listening to his father's sermons in the churches of Atlanta and St. Louis.

Poor Jones and his opinions on trains, Chinese food, his office, lunchtime eating, shaving habits, clothing, walking, bedding, etc. are sneeringly reviewed, but leavened with the occasional "Jones' beliefs were almost all of the result of his own thinking" to imply the man was deluded about his independence of mind (p. 30). This critique of the average middle class male in a major U.S. city rambles on for ten typescript pages and is increasingly tedious. For a reader in the late 1920s, much more accustomed to church-going than now, Lee's preacher's style of writing and argumentation would have been like sitting through an interminable sermon on a sunny day. Lee concludes that citizens should not be "running away from publicity" (p. 39) but embracing it in a critical examination and an informed judgment of all its works. Stupid, deluded Jones was ignorant of the methods and purposes of publicity. Lee goes on to set out his philosophy of publicity—"the art of influencing men's minds...which is the sum of all the arts used to influence public opinion and move it in a desired direction," (p. 41) although he tends to overlook the "desired" element and who desires the movement of opinion.

Lee, throughout his career, was influenced by fears of the crowd and the outcomes of untrammeled democracy that were posited by writers like Walter Lippmann, Gustave Le Bon and Gabriel Tarde.[4] He also lived in a time when the results of the Russian Revolution of 1917 were creating fear of violent

---

[4] Ewen, S. (1996), *PR! A Social History of Spin*. New York: Basic Books.

change in Europe and North America, and where corporate America's behavior was constantly criticized by muckraker journalists, Congress, and civil society. His analysis of Jones also reflects a fear that even educated crowds were not able to analyze the world around them, and thus respond. They were sheep who were being led by others, without realizing it.

There are extensive discussions of propaganda. Lee constantly seeks to create a virtuous gap between his concepts of publicity and propaganda. It is notable that while "propaganda" was still being used in British governmental parlance in the 1920s as equivalent to publicity and the dissemination of information,[5] it had a much more negative connotation across the Atlantic. Lee refers to the "evil associations with the word propaganda, due to the excesses of the war" but adds that "it can prevent wars and cement friendship between peoples" (p. 56). In sections within Chapter 3's "The Range of Publicity" and the whole of Part II, Lee discusses propaganda definitions and its applications in the Great War by combatants on both sides, and links it to crowd psychology.

Lee asserts that the Committee on Public Information, headed by George Creel, was just as much a propaganda operation as the Germans—he

---

[5] Anthony, S. (2012). *Public Relations and the Making of Modern Britain.* Manchester, UK: Manchester University Press.

claims, on page 79, "In short, the Committee was a
propagandist." Before discussing Lee's analysis of the
Committee, which had a profound influence on the
post-war rapid expansion of the publicity industry in
the U.S. and was considered to be a laboratory of
promotional communication methods, it is relevant to
discuss Lee's relationship with Creel. This dated back
to 1914 when Lee was advising John D. Rockefeller Sr.
and his son John Jr. over violent conflicts between
their corporation and miners and local communities
during the notorious Colorado mine strikes, especially
the Ludlow Massacre. Hiebert writes that Creel, then
a journalist, "attacked Lee's methods in the Colorado
strike" but came to Washington in 1917 to use "the
same techniques which Lee had used in that strike"[6]
in the national interest. It is debatable whether Creel
would have offered that interpretation as, in a *Harper's
Magazine* article of 1914, he discredited Lee's methods
as giving an "entirely false view of the situation" and
said Lee was attempting to be a "poisoner of public
opinion"; Stuart Ewen notes that "the sobriquet
'Poison Ivy' would hound Lee for years."[7]

Lee critiques the work of the Committee with
faint praise by claiming that its work was undertaken
in full public view but was utterly propagandist in

---

[6] Hiebert, p. 253.

[7] Ewen, p. 83.

nature. Later, he refers to Creel's account of submarine attacks against U.S. shipping in July 1917—claims that were later revealed to be false—as a "hoax."

Lee writes on page 102 of this book that Creel was "not trying to keep alive a lie. He was trying to make people believe an item of publicity which had [Lee's emphasis] *merely been questioned.*" The public response to the story after three years of wartime propaganda, he says, was to criticize the Committee. He then asks a rhetorical question on that same page: "If an unproved and anonymous denial caused so much trouble, what would have an authoritative nailing of a lie have done?" The implication being that had the Committee checked the story in the first place, it would not have had the opprobrium which Creel felt had created an unfair reputational impact. However, the Committee had damaged its credibility by not withdrawing the story. Lee, in some ways, was getting his revenge on Creel for his 1914 criticism by pointing to Creel's failure to manage an untrue story.

Overall, the manuscript is a rather assertion-heavy text to read. If its aim was at the lay reader, who was served by a wide range of excellent and popular magazines, it seems to be mis-targeted. The didactic style and the homiletic structure of chapters and sections demand deep concentration. Perhaps Ivy Lee, considered by many as the "father of public relations"[8] recognized that this method of publicity was not going to be influencing men's minds and "move [them] in a desired direction" (p. 41) and dropped the project.

TOM WATSON, PH.D., is Emeritus Professor in the Faculty of Media & Communication at Bournemouth University in England. He is the founder of the annual International History of Public Relations Conference and edited the seven-book series "National Perspectives on the Development of Public Relations: Other Voices" published by Palgrave Macmillan between 2014 and 2017.

---

[8] Tye, L. (1998). *The Father of Spin—Edward L. Bernays and the Birth of Public Relations*. New York: Henry Holt, p. 229.